The Courtesan's Memory, Voice, and Late Ming Drama

The Courtesan's Memory, Voice, and Late Ming Drama

Peng Xu

University of Michigan Press
Ann Arbor

Published in the United States of America by the
University of Michigan Press
First published September 2025

A CIP catalog record for this book is available from the British Library.

Library of Congress Cataloging-in-Publication Data

Names: Xu, Peng, 1977– author. | Michigan Publishing (University of Michigan), publisher.
Title: The courtesan's memory, voice, and Late Ming drama / Peng Xu.
Description: Ann Arbor [Michigan] : University of Michigan Press, 2025. | "New Chuanqi Plays from the Era, 1570–1600" in Appendix (pages 193–195). | Includes bibliographical references (pages 197–211) and index. | Text in English; some text and citations also in Chinese script.
Identifiers: LCCN 2025011008 (print) | LCCN 2025011009 (ebook) | ISBN 9780472077229 (hardcover) | ISBN 9780472057221 (paperback) | ISBN 9780472222018 (ebook)
Subjects: LCSH: Chinese drama—Ming dynasty, 1368–1644—History and criticism. | Chinese drama—Ming dynasty, 1368–1644—Social aspects. | Theater—China—History and criticism. | Theater and society—China. | Courtesans—Social aspects—China. | Dramatists, Chinese—History. | Dramatists, Chinese—Social aspects. | Sex role in the theater—China—History.
Classification: LCC PN2871 .X8365 2025 (print) | LCC PN2871 (ebook) | DDC 792.951/0903—dc23/eng/20250527
LC record available at https://lccn.loc.gov/2025011008
LC ebook record available at https://lccn.loc.gov/2025011009

DOI: https://doi.org/10.3998/mpub.14366479

Cover image: Gu vase with courtesans rehearsing the *Story of the Western Wing*, Shunzhi reign (ca. 1645–1655). © The Butler Collection

Authorized Representative: Easy Access System Europe, Mustamäe tee 50, 10621 Tallinn, Estonia, gpsr.requests@easproject.com

Dedicated to my dear mother FAN Rufang,
who loves singing Chinese opera,
and to my dear father XU Jiansheng,
who has loved to hear us sing.

Contents

Digital materials related to this title can be found at the following citable URL: https://doi.org/10.3998/mpub.14366479

Illustrations

Tables

Acknowledgments

It would be inappropriate to consider this book a revision of my dissertation, though it certainly owes a great deal to research seminars I took at the University of Chicago at that time. Numerous references to the sixteenth-century novel *The Plum in the Golden Vase* in this book are tributes to the training I received from Professor David T. Roy. Anthony C. Yu, Reginald Jackson, Yuming He, Wu Hung, Judith T. Zeitlin, Jason McGrath, Kristin Harris, and David Bevington were all excellent intellectual influences, to various degrees and in different ways.

Reginald Jackson, though, deserves a category to himself. My venture into the field of performance studies did not take place in my dissertation writing years (2010–13)—my dissertation focuses solely on the sonic dimension of late Ming theater. In a long phone conversation in winter 2014, Professor Jackson mentioned to me five groundbreaking publications in performance studies. I was then an assistant professor of Chinese at the Virginia Military Institute. VMI's friendly atmosphere created the mental space and precious time for my intellectual growth and expansion into performance studies, an almost untouched field by sinologists at the time. Every other Sunday I would drive seventy miles on a meandering mountain road to the libraries of the University of Virginia at Charlottesville and became a voracious reader of books in performance studies and music history. Those trips, especially on foggy or rainy days, exhausted me physically, but delighted me deeply because I was able to recalibrate my post-dissertation brain and embark on a new quest to consider gendered performance and its relation to late Ming drama. It is Professor Jackson's unfailing encouragement that spurred my intellectual rebirth after my Chicago years.

My work moved to a higher level when I was a postdoctoral fellow at the Center for Chinese Studies at the University of California at Berkeley (2016–17), and I wish to thank Ling Hon Lam and others for giving me the opportunity to spend time in that wonderful place. Ling Hon Lam, Weihong Bao, and Yu Luo have also been my treasured friends during the fellowship year and since. Other Berkeley professors who have been great intellectual resources to me include Andrew Jones and Wenhsin Yeh.

Crucial portions of this book were written when I was an assistant professor of Chinese theater at the University of Hawai'i at Mānoa between 2020 and 2023. I wish to thank Professor Emeritus Lo Chin-t'ang, a towering figure in the field of Yuan Ming drama studies, the first PhD student of Dr. Hu Shih. Ninety-seven years old, he has willingly given devoted guidance to young scholars like me. While Professor Jackson urged me to engage my theoretical work in English scholarship of performance studies and gender studies, Professor Lo compelled me to think beyond the paradigm of American academia and to desire to dialogue with the "mainstream" understandings about Chinese drama in the vast Chinese-language scholarship. By the end of 2021, I had accomplished the central task on my list—to become aware of various scholarship styles and approaches and to make my own aesthetic choices in writing styles.

I benefited greatly from the Rainbow Singing Club, created by Professor Lo in the 1980s. It is the most civilized of the *kunqu* communities I have participated in and was home to multiple pleasant music gatherings during my term at UHM. Daniel Chan, a former member of the Rainbow Singing Club of *kunqu*, has been a reliable source of wisdom and insights. I should also single out Mr. and Mrs. Tang (Chongshih and Grace), *kunqu*-loving scientists of UHM, who provided tremendous emotional support. Shanon Brown, Cindy Ning, Jonathan Pitt, Ming-bao Yue, and others at UHM's Center for Chinese Studies, manifest the great strengths of the institution which opened the door to many intellectual pursuits. Besides the scholarly circles, Honolulu's Chinese communities were a source of heartwarming friendship. Mr. Vernon Ching brought his friends to the debut of *Madame Cassia*, my English *kunqu* production, and provided lodging for my guest artists from New York as well as delicious cakes for a humble reception in a classroom downstairs in the theater building of UHM (they were eaten up by an enthusiastic audience who followed us there from the theater and lingered there for two hours). I also have fond memories of being invited to Honolulu Opera events that Drs. Clifford Lau and Adrienne Lau sponsored.

I benefited too from the Fulbright American Scholar Award in 2021, which was made possible by a Faculty Research Assignment Leave, kindly granted by Dean Peter Arnade. My Fulbright host institute was the Kyujanggak Institute of Seoul National University, where Professors Sang Hwan Seong, Ryu Jun-Pil, Wonjung Min, Hyunjeong Lee (University of Seoul), Hyun Suk Park (University of California at Los Angeles), Suyoung Son (Cornell University), and the rest of the fellows and staff provided me with an ideal professional environment. An irreplaceable resource of inspiration has been ShanghaiTech University's senior leadership team and my colleagues at the Institute of Humanities, such as Peter Raccuglia and Ming Xie (University of Toronto), where the last fine-tuning of this work was done.

Part of chapter 3 was published in *T'oung pao* and the *Harvard Journal of Asiatic Studies*, under the sterling editorship of Pierre-Etienne Will and David Howell, respectively. Permission to use this material is gratefully acknowledged. The first draft of chapter 4 was presented at both the Center for Chinese Studies at the University of California at Berkeley and the sixty-first annual meeting of the American Society of Theatre Research in Atlanta, where Joseph Roach and other panelists shared their profound insights. A small portion of the introduction was presented to a large audience at Ohio State University's East Asian Studies Center in April 2019. OSU colleagues, especially Professor Patricia Sieber and her graduate students, expressed keen interest in and enthusiasm for my work-in-progress, which helped me feel more confident in my project at a crucial stage.

Although it would be impossible for me to mention by name every librarian and editor who has assisted me, I cannot afford to leave out Jianye He, Dongyun Ni, Feng Kun, and Victoria Scott. My well-loved Peking University professor, Zhang Ming, used his personal connections in the National Library in Beijing to procure rare images; others who also helped greatly with this respect of the book include Professor Chia-yi Lin (National Tsing-hua University, Taipei), Professor Luo Shuhua and his PhD student Wang Yifei (Fudan University), as well as my ShanghaiTech colleague Gu Zhenglue. I thank Professor Norikazu Hirabayashi's (Waseda University) timely help with Japanese *hiragana*. Professor Wu Dan (Sun Yat-sen University) generously shared her archive of photographed pages from *Examination and Correction of "The Western Wing" in Its Northern Version* when other means to approach this important music score were impossible in Honolulu. I also wish to express a debt of gratitude to the editorial and production team of the University of Michigan Press for their encouragement and patience. For their inspired and enthusiastic work in getting my manuscript to better clarity, I thank the two anonymous readers.

I am grateful to members of an unofficial WeChat writing group consisting of female faculty members living in America and China. I will continue to be a devoted member and witness more scholarly outputs from this phenomenally encouraging group.

At last, I would like to acknowledge the effect of the many moves that punctuate my journey to becoming a zealous advocate for interdisciplinary research—I moved across five American states within seven years after graduation from Chicago. Thanks to all the moves (occasionally, setbacks), I have a better understanding of how one could live an errant existence, similar to experiences that the nameless women entertainers of the sixteenth and seventeenth centuries in my book may have endured. I hope that my book is a legitimate space in which the marginalized speak of their marginalization.

Introduction

Brothels as a Creative Space

Sometime between 1567 and 1570, an eccentric cultural celebrity who frequented Nanjing's high-end brothels wrote a *zaju* 雜劇 (northern drama) entitled *Ms. Red Silk* (*Hongxian nü* 紅線女).[1] Shortly thereafter, the same author completed his landmark *chuanqi* 傳奇 (southern drama) *Washing Gauze* (*Huansha ji* 浣紗記), which receives a close reading in chapter 4 of this book. This playwright, Liang Chenyu 梁辰魚 (1519–1591), was popular with the city's male elites and courtesans alike for his great productivity in literature, virtuosity in the vocal arts, and capacity for imbibing alcohol. His stellar presence in dramatic history, however, has long overshadowed his debt to the Nanjing courtesans, whose influence on his creative work may well have been profound. This hierarchy, embraced by standard historiography, is, however, reversed in a preface to *Ms. Red Silk* written by a Nanjing courtesan Ma Xianglan 馬湘蘭 (1548–1605), then twenty-five years old, where the literatus playwright is mentioned in passing as "a Mr. Liang from Kunshan" 崑山梁氏.[2] Ma Xianglan's edition of *Ms. Red Silk* was lost.

1. This play has two Ming woodblock editions and two modern typeset editions based on them: (1) Meng Chengshun 孟稱舜 (1594–1684), comp., *Leijiang ji* 酹江集, facsimile in *Guben xiqu congkan*, series No. 4; (2) Shen Tai 沈泰, comp., *Sheng Ming zaju* 盛明雜劇, facsimile (Hefei: Huangshan shushe, 1993); (3) Wu Shuyin 吳書蔭, ed., *Liang Chenyu ji* 梁辰魚集 (Shanghai: Shanghai guji chubanshe, 1998), 423–40; (4) Li Guotao 黎國韜 and Zhou Peiwen 周佩文, *Liang Chenyu yanjiu* 梁辰魚研究 (Guangzhou: Zhongshan daxue chubanshe, 2007), appendix 5, 266–300.

2. Typically, however, Ma's involvement in performing is emphasized less in her

But thanks to a 1628 anthology of women's writings, her preface has been passed down to us. This preface offers the strongest evidence I have found of the multiple roles of one courtesan in the creation of a new play, and thus highlights a rare case in which female agency and authority were not entirely erased. It begins with a long passage that sets the stage for her encounter with the new play within the context of her seeking a solution for her own moral dilemma and inner conflicts:[3]

> I deeply believe that, however drastic the distinctions between the immortal and the mortal, they share in common an innate quality bestowed by heaven; and that women in the inner chambers love deeply, which becomes rooted in their nature. [Such women's virtues as they are portrayed in] the classical song of "The Islet in the River" can never be surpassed, whereas amorous rendezvous [abound]—how despicable! Alas, my name has been registered [in the brothel], and just like white sand imbrued with dirt, I lament that it can never be clean again. My body resembles a roadside willow tree, and I hate it that my black hair grows in vain. I would envy the lucky wife named Meng Guang who served her husband with a tray respectfully [held up to her eyebrows]. I would gaze into the sky [daydreaming of] Prince Charming riding a phoenix. Many times I was going to jump off a building to my death, yet [wondered] whom my aged mother could rely on [after my death]. For a long time, I was determined to be a convert holding the Buddhist alms bowl, and yet it is hard to meet a real Patriarch Bodhi who would teach me. For these reasons I have set my heart on the art of painting, my jadeite pure heart thus expressed through the secluded orchards and bamboos [in my painting]; I have also indulged in those classics and histories, my lofty spirit thus verified in the stories of chaste, heroic women and their husbands. I chanced upon the poetry and lyrics about Ms. Red Silk composed by Mr. Liang from Kunshan.
>
> 竊惟仙凡界徑固殊,稟乎天資;而閨壺情深,實均原于人性。河洲之詠,莫可尚矣;濮上之期,何其鄙哉!嬌也藉染污泥,悼白沙無由終潔;軀鄰歧柳,恨

biographical sketches written by her male contemporaries than are her achievements in other arts—she was a renowned painter in the genre of "orchard and bamboo," a calligrapher, and a poet.

3. Ma Xianglan (a.k.a Ma Yuejiao 馬月嬌), "Hongxian chuanqi xiaoyin" 紅線傳奇小引, in Zhao Shijie 趙世杰, *Gujin nüshi* 古今女史, *juan* 9, 11a–b. Digital library, "Ming Qing Women's Writings." Digital access: https://digital.library.mcgill.ca/mingqing/search/results-work.php

> 青絲徒爾增攀。涎垂舉案之孟光，目斷驂鸞之蕭史。欲墜樓者屢矣，而高年之母孰依？思傳缽者久焉，而悟空之師難遇。用是托諸丹素，見冰心於幽蘭叢竹之間；嗜彼簡編，徵雅志於烈女夫君之際。偶值崑山梁氏所輯《紅線》詩詞。

The prose then takes an abrupt turn to explain that Ma Xianglan has herself generously sponsored the printing of the play. Her sponsorship was driven entirely by the parallel she had found between the heroine, Ms. Red Silk, and herself. Ms. Red Silk represented her inner self: they shared the ultimate dream of living in an immortal land free of sexual activity, even though Ma Xianglan's Confucian duty of filial piety necessitated her supporting her mother by working in a brothel. They also shared the same temperament as female knights-errant—Ms. Red Silk by saving her man, and Ma Xianglan by lavishing money on Ms. Red Silk's creator Liang Chenyu, who was one of Ma Xianglan's lovers and who taught vocal music in the brothels. She writes:

> Within a few ticking sounds of the jade water clock, Ms. Red Silk mystically flew over thousands of miles; snatching the golden box by means of stratagems, she scared the enemy into disarray. Speaking of her complete detachment from the mundane world, how can the maidservant of the Yang family, Hongfu [the title role in a popular play of 1545], be compared to her? Her fragrance eternally lingers on the immortal island, which must surely humble Ms. Diaochan of the Han dynasty [the heroine of another popular play of 1522]. How remarkable Ms. Red Silk's achievements are! And truly her valor is mighty. I, thereupon, commissioned excellent engravers to carve woodblocks and print it out.
>
> 漏滴玉壺，瞬息神飛萬里；計收金盒，倉皇膽落三軍。況茲脫跡塵寰，奚翅楊家之侍拂；永爾流芳瑤島，更卑漢室之貂蟬。功云奇也，勇非大敷！迺屬良工，爰俾繡梓。

Ma Xianglan's preface makes no explicit mention of her being involved in editing or revising Liang's words for the staging of *Ms. Red Silk* before the play was engraved on woodblocks. Such a preface is nevertheless extremely rare, and certainly suggests that virtuoso courtesans exerted great influence on the dramatic literature of the day by conjoining brothels with the stage. They participated in theater activities with great passion, actively seeking profitable and suitable new plays, and thus turned their living space into a locale for theatrical and literary creativity. The end of the essay reveals the commercial value of the imprints that Ma Xianglan had bankrolled, which were to be used as textual aids for the clients of her house, where a troupe consisting of courtesans had been trained as theater women:

> Our dancing sleeves, broad and long, can offer you as much as five nights of delectation; our singing voices, delicate and sweet, are just right for accompanying ten days of banqueting. Gentlemen with profound tastes and insights, how can they not be deeply affected while viewing this play? With their affectionate memories rekindled, they shall then better understand my inner self.
>
> 郎當舞袖，儘可供五夜之歡；婉轉歌喉，尚可佐十日之飲。玄覽君子，能無觸目激衷，感往事以諒余衷者哉！

If we bring our imagination more vigorously into play, it may have been Ma Xianglan's own dwelling that served both as the creative milieu of Liang's script and as the first venue for staging *Ms. Red Silk*. Historically, Ma Xianglan owned a compound in the Nanjing pleasure quarters near the Qinhuai River, where she trained her own courtesan troupe specializing in staging *zaju* drama in the "authentic" Yuan-dynasty style. (The courtesan's role in transmitting such a style, called "strings," or *xiansuo* 弦索, is described in chapter 1.) Evidence suggests that a garden located at the center of the walled brothel area in the urban center of Nanjing may have served as the "public" venue for full-fledged performances of courtesan residents. Pan Zhiheng's 潘之恆 (1556–1622) commemorative essay "The Long Bridge" (*Changbanqiao ji* 長板橋記) is to my knowledge the only direct account of this theater space within the Nanjing pleasure quarters: "A flower-patterned lock opened the gate into the spacious courtyard, where a rug made a stage when the moon rose. Winding railings zigzagged along a ravine, kingfisher feathers [from women's hairpins] stirring in gentle breezes. To the east [of the garden] was Ma Xianglan's garden estate." 葳蕤開瑣鑰於廣庭，氍毹月上；曲折轉闌干於邃谷，翡翠風輕。其前則馬湘蘭有園.[4]

Recovering and translating noncanonical dramatic texts written by female authors has been one of the main outcomes of the feminist approach

4. Pan Zhiheng, "The Long Bridge," in *Luanxiao xiaopin* 鸞嘯小品, original in Shanghai Library, *juan* 6, 27a–28b. The piece must have been published first in the 1610s, but for some reason Pan chose to revise it for another printing project in the last two years of his life (1621–1622). Several years later his son compiled his posthumous collection (1626) and included the version that we have in our hands today.

Fig. 1. A view of the "Old Compound," the first-rate pleasure quarters of Nanjing, at the lower left corner of the woodblock illustration from a 1623 city guide *Odes of Nanjing with Illustrations* (*Jinling tuyong*). (Courtesy of Nanjing Library.)

to Chinese women's playwritings.[5] But the slippery nature of women's participation in theater makes such endeavors a daunting task. If we adopt the traditional notion of "authorship," and if we visit the archive of late Ming drama only for written records of female agency and authorship, then the evidence in these written records strongly supports the general absence of women authors that is posited in the standard historiography of Ming drama. For instance, a 2016 monograph on women playwrights in early modern China credits nine catalogued plays to seven Ming women (two of them courtesans), among which six plays, unfortunately, were lost.[6] Ma Xianglan was one of the two courtesan-authors; her *chuanqi* play, *Life After Life: The Jade Hairpin* (*Sansheng zhuan Yuzan ji* 三生傳玉簪記), featuring a courtesan heroine, has survived in a contemporaneous drama anthology (discussed in detail in chapter 2). In contrast, the archive of Ming drama boasts more than four hundred playwrights and in excess of 1,500 plays, according to two modern catalogues.[7]

In the genre of *chuanqi* or southern-style romantic comedies that dominated plays both performed in the theater and printed on the page in the late Ming, a 1613 catalogue records that the long sixteenth century saw the birth of 183 new *chuanqi* works written by eighty-eight playwrights, the great majority of whom were men of letters.[8] It is true that by the early 1600s composing *chuanqi* plays had been in vogue among men of letters for some

5. Wu Zao's 吳藻 (1799–1862) "The Fake Image" (*Qiao ying* 喬影), in *The Red Brush: Writing Women of Imperial China*, trans. Wilt Idema, ed. Beata Grant (Cambridge, MA: Harvard University Asia Center, 2004), 685–702; for an alternative translation, see Sophie Volpp, "Drinking Wine and Reading 'Encountering Sorrow'" in *Under Confucian Eyes: Writings on Gender in Chinese History*, ed. Susan Mann (Berkeley: University of California Press, 2001), 239–50. Excerpted scenes from Ma Xianglan's *Sansheng zhuan Yuzanji* 三生傳玉簪記 are preserved in Hu Wenhuan's anthology *Qunyin leixuan* 群音類選. Hua Wei 華瑋, "Ma Xianglan yu Mingdai houqi de qutan" 馬湘蘭與明代後期的曲壇, *Xiqu xuebao* 戲曲學報 2 (2007): 55–82.

6. Liu Junhua 劉軍華, *Ming Qing nüxing zuojia xiqu chuangzuo yanjiu* 明清女性作家戲曲創作研究 (Beijing: Kexue chubanshe, 2015), 169. Among the three existing women's plays, Liu credits *The Swallow Letter* (*Yanzi jian* 燕子箋) to Ruan Lizhen 阮麗珍, but her coauthorship of the play with her father, Ruan Dacheng 阮大鋮 (1587–1646), requires more evidence.

7. Catalogues of Ming drama include Fu Xihua 傅惜華, *Mingdai chuanqi quanmu* 明代傳奇全目 (Beijing: Renmin wenxue chubanshe, 1959); Zhuang Yifu 莊一拂, *Gudian xiqu cunmu huikao* 古典戲曲存目彙考 (Shanghai: Shanghai Guji chubanshe, 1982); Guo Yingde, *Ming Qing chuanqi zonglu* 明清傳奇總目 (Shijiazhuang: Hebei jiaoyu chubanshe, 1997).

8. Wu Shuyin 吳書蔭, *Qupin jiaozhu* 曲品校注 (Beijing: Zhonghua shuju, 1990).

time. Although this book investigates the role of female artists in the drama history of the late Ming dynasty, ranging from the 1550s to 1640s, readers will find the three decades—from the 1570s to 1600s—receive an intensive historical treatment. It may not be coincidental that the 1570s were a watershed period in both the performance history and the print history of Yuan dramas, for it not only witnessed the courtesan's Yuan repertoire shrinking in size, with Yuan libretti in far less demand at entertainments than popular songs, but also saw drama manuscripts still in the possession of the privileged few, with Yuan drama compendiums yet to become widely available on the market. As will become clear in the ensuing chapters, from the 1570s to the 1600s, courtesan actresses launched into the public view and thus restarted the broken female genealogy from the Yuan dynasty. In music history, these three decades witnessed the increasing flexibility of the courtesan's rendition of the traditional *xiansuo* music; while in literary history, this period manifested the strongest female impact on the century-long blooming of dramatic literature. Brothel musical staging served as a productive space in which cultural products such as new plays and their printed scripts were manufactured. The appendix provides a limited list of extant plays written between 1570 and 1600 in chronological order (based on my own dating), featuring a constellation of esteemed literatus-playwrights.

The question, then, is not how to dig up a female counter-canon for studies of female agency and authorship, but how to critically engage with and creatively rethink the absence of documentation. The first and foremost reason for my writing this book is the lack of a recognized history of women and theatrical performance in China in the late Ming period. There is no watershed in history that marks the launching of female theatricals in Chinese theater, unlike the year 1660 in British history, when professional women performers received Charles II's royal sanction to appear on the English stage. However, several new conceptions in recent cultural studies in the setting of early modern Europe are pivotal to my argumentation. First, there has been a shift in focus away from the traditional notion of authorship—as consisting of putting ideas on paper—and toward the notion of the actress as the "author" not only of texts but also of her own memory, vocal production, acting, dance, and public image.[9] The narrower definition of author-

9. For the idea of actresses as authors in eighteenth-century Europe, see Judith Pascoe, *Romantic Theatricality: Gender, Poetry, and Spectatorship* (Ithaca: Cornell University Press, 1997); Cheryl Wanko, *Roles of Authority: Thespian Biography and Celebrity in Eighteenth-Century Britain* (Lubbock: Texas Tech University Press, 2003); Nora Nachumi, *Acting Like a Lady: British Women Novelists and the Late Eighteenth Century Stage* (New York: AMS Press, 2008); Emily Hodgson Anderson, *Eighteenth-Century*

ship confines our research to salutary archival and anthologizing work, with the result that the essential body of early modern Chinese drama can be supplemented only with sporadic female elements.[10] The new, broader concept, proposed and considered by performance studies scholars, links different aspects of cultural studies (material culture, print culture, sound culture, visual culture, etc.) to the paradigms of theater and performance. By applying this new notion of authorship to the case of late Ming courtesans, we shall see that their vocal, kinetic, and literary renditions of theater and their productive power lie in their participation in the writing discourse as a driving force.

Second, the notion of "embodied knowledge" helps us rethink the division between classical and vernacular knowledge, and between those who work with their minds—playwrights—and those who work with their bodies—courtesan-actresses.[11] A useful distinction is the one Diana Taylor proposes: the distinction between the *repertoire* of embodied practice (i.e., spoken language, dance, sports, ritual) vis-à-vis the *archive* of supposedly enduring materials (i.e., texts, documents, buildings, bones).[12] Despite the evaporating nature of bodily and spoken language (i.e., the repertoire), traces of it can still be found in material form. In my prolonged archival research, I gathered information on courtesan performances from a wide range of written and visual sources: rare drama editions, novels, poetry, musical notations, drama miscellanies, city guides, courtesan biographies, diaries, woodblock illustrations, and porcelain paintings. Studying such a diverse group of sources opens up new ways of understanding the history of Chinese drama written by the performing bodies of real women.

Third, the notion of "writing" per se can be expanded to mean "anything that encodes information in order to stimulate the memory to store or retrieve information."[13] *Memory* is one of the two key notions that appear

Authorship and the Play of Fiction: Novels and the Theater, Haywood to Austen (New York: Routledge, 2009); Laura Engel, *Fashioning Celebrity: Eighteenth-Century British Actresses and Strategies for Image Making* (Columbus: Ohio State University Press, 2011).

10. See, for example, Hua Wei, ed., *Ming Qing funü xiqu ji* 明清婦女戲曲集 (Taipei: Academia Sinica, 2003; repr., 2005).

11. Joseph Roach, *Cities of the Dead: Circum-Atlantic Performance* (New York: Columbia University Press, 1996), 26.

12. Diana Taylor, *The Archive and the Repertoire: Performing Cultural Memory in the Americas* (Durham: Duke University Press, 2003), xvi–46.

13. Mary Carruthers, *The Book of Memory: A Study of Memory in Medieval Culture* (Cambridge: Cambridge University Press, 1990), 32.

in the title of my book, precisely because it was the courtesan's memory and mental representation of musical and acting styles as the artistic legacy of the bygone Yuan dynasty that gave birth to music scores and song anthologies of *xiansuo* and to the new composition of northern plays to enact them. In chapter 1, for example, I argue that a famous anthology of Yuan drama released in 1615 and 1616 was an effort to use the memorial utility of the printed word to replace the courtesan's dwindling memorial archive. There had been continuing complaints among literati with conservative mindsets lamenting the weakening of the memorial basis of the medieval musical culture in the pleasure quarters. Here I follow Mary Carruthers's adjusted usage of the term "memorial" to connote a more medieval idea that is related not to death but to "the voices of what is past" gaining a new life in the present in memory.[14] The courtesan's memorial archive was thus relevant to various cultural practices and procedures—the making of books, compositional structures and principles, the layout of music imprints, and pedagogical instructions.

Fourth, the second key notion in my title is *voice* as both "voice" in general—a metaphor for the set of distinctive features of a literary work in terms of spoken utterance—and in particular, a sign of agency, as defined by Carolyn Abbate in her studies of female stars' voices in European opera. To Abbate, a female opera star's voice empowers her to "stand before us having wrested the composing voice away from the librettist and composer who wrote the score."[15] Taking a cue from Abbate's proposal, the dance historian Sally Banes reflects on its counterpart in ballerina performance: "The plot may verbally describe a female character as weak or passive, while the physical prowess of the dancer performing the role may saturate it with agency. Thus, even dances with misogynist narratives or patriarchal themes tend to depict women as active and vital."[16] Digressing from this notion of voice that focuses on its physical prowess, the Chinese courtesan's voice discussed in this book not only had a powerful hold on an audience but also shaped literary creativity for theater. Her memory habits and vocal preferences, as I argue in chapter 2, constitute the gendered foundation of the plays created

14. Carruthers, *The Book of Memory*, 111, 260.

15. Carolyn Abbate, "Opera; or, the Envoicing of Women," in *Musicology and Difference: Gender and Sexuality in Music Scholarship*, ed. Ruth A. Solie (Berkeley: University of California Press, 1993), 254. The same theme appears repeatedly in her brilliant book, *Unsung Voices: Opera and Musical Narrative in the Nineteenth Century* (Princeton: Princeton University Press, 1991).

16. Sally Banes, *Dancing Women: Female Bodies on Stage* (London: Routledge, 1998), 9.

in this period. Her voice participated in the writing discourse and is linked to literary aesthetics, characterization of feminine beauty and space, dramaturgical designs, and eroticism, all of which worked to suit the courtesan's artistic feats, helped catapult her to stardom, and thus enabled her to leave a strong mark on the literary landscape. "Voice" in the book title can thus be understood as both the courtesan's singing voice and her authorial voice behind the dramatic work, a general critical concept related to the "author."

Last, to revise the male-dominated theater/drama history, my interrogation shifts focus away from the reconstruction of a singular literary past, created by literati heroes, and toward a discussion of the brothel as the theatrical space. My hypothesis is that literary creativity is not inhabited by a single group of individuals, such as the literati, but is, rather, *spatially* located. By the spatiality of literary creativity, I do not refer to the physical geography of the pleasure quarters but to the shared material and mental conditions of performance in which the broader modus operandi of a courtesan-actress can be observed. It was the brothel as a theatrical space that made possible these courtesans' ascendency in the theater world as operatic stars, from which the creative synergy of drama sprang.

The most outstanding feature of the brothel performance was its mixture of actors of both genders. Besides courtesans, brothel theaters engaged professional teachers, male amateurs, and hangers-on specializing in theatrical performance (*qingke* 清客 or *chuanke* 串客 in Chinese). Lu Eting, the foremost scholar of *kunqu* history, has conducted extensive historical studies on this topic.[17] Although these male actors are not the protagonists of my book, I would add to Lu's thorough studies the observation that brothel staging was arranged according to a casting system in which courtesan stars were supported by male guest performers, who could also serve as tutors for courtesans. For the poet Shen Defu 沈德符 (1578–1642), for example, this diverse group of men belonged to an umbrella category he called "Dandies of the Qinhuai River" (*Qinhuai ye'er* 秦淮冶兒), about whom he wrote a set of sixteen poems in 1627.[18] His fourth poem delineates the multiple roles such men could play in the brothel entertainments—they were teachers of vocal and dance arts, and meanwhile could be cast in various supporting roles in courtesan performances:

---

17. Lu Eting, *Qingdai xiqu jia congkao* 清代戲劇家叢攷 (Shanghai: Xuelin chubanshe, 1996), particularly two essays, "Su Kunsheng yu kunqiang" 蘇崑生與昆腔 and "Shi *chuan*" 釋串.

18. Shen Defu, "Songs Dedicated to the Dandies in the Qinhuai River Area" 秦淮冶兒曲, in *Qingquantang ji* 清權堂集, 22 juan in vol. 1377 of *Xuxiu Siku quanshu* 續修四庫全書, *juan* 5, 8a–9b.

Toiling in the pleasure quarters to teach music, they never complain.
On dances they demand swift turns; on singing they require high notes.
[At one moment] they paint their faces to play the comic role;
[At another] they play onstage scholar-officials in dignifying caps with hairpins, walking with an elegant gait.

平康傳譜敢辭勤
舞要迴風歌遏雲
粉墨自塗蒼鶻面
冠簪雅步又參軍

Female Performance versus "Literati *Chuanqi*"

To understand what mixed-gender troupes meant to the late Ming audience, we need to place them within the historical context of female performance in China. William Dolby points out that the gender imbalance of Ming performers was an evolving, dynamic process. "We hear much more of male performers," he declares, which is because "towards the end of the dynasty the age-old moral prejudices . . . against actresses and mixed troupes were strongly favouring all-male troupes."[19] Two recent studies in Chinese, however, provide insights into the significance of private troupes of both sexes at the time.[20] There is no question that all-female troupes did exist and thrive, if not dominate, in private theater as embellishments to the household master's personal life, whereas all-male troupes were allowed to expand into the public arena and circulate from one rich household to another as they sold their performances.[21] Anecdotes abound about how all-female private troupes were reserved for the delectation of the household master, his family, and his close-knit circle of friends. Only occasionally do we see him voluntarily bringing his trained theater women to public events to show off their finesse, his taste, and the otherwise exclusive delights of watching them perform. In one anecdote, a master's refusal to put on a show for local officials is reported to have incurred resentment and subsequent

19. William Dolby, *A History of Chinese Drama* (New York: Barnes and Noble, 1976), 109.

20. Liu Shuiyun 劉水雲, *Ming Qing jiayue yanjiu* 明清家樂研究 (Shanghai: Shanghai guji chubanshe, 2005); Zhang Faying 張發穎, *Zhongguo jiayue xiban* 中國家樂戲班 (Beijing: Xueyuan chubanshe, 2002), 73–256.

21. Wang Ning 王寧 and Ren Xiaowen 任孝溫, *Kunqu yu Ming Qing yueji* 崑曲與明清樂妓 (Shenyang: Chunfeng wenyi chubanshe, 2005).

disastrous retaliation.[22] Similar anecdotes share in common a depiction of the stubborn mind of the master who is all too aware of his right to keep the women unseen by unwanted guests. The gender inequity in the theater during the Ming, therefore, was not so much about which gender was performing as about who remained in the public vision and who was removed from it. By modern standards, theater women in the Ming belong to the social categories of courtesans, concubines, household maids, and actresses in private troupes—women whose presence in the public view was heavily conditioned and limited.

That the Ming witnessed the turning point in women's retreat from the public view into the private sphere becomes even clearer when we compare the Ming to the bygone Yuan dynasty (1279–1368). Mixed troupes stood as a corollary to Mongol rule in the Yuan, and women allegedly dominated in these troupes, playing both female and male roles. According to a Yuan literatus's comprehensive account, *The Green Bower* (*Qinglou ji* 青樓集), women enthralled the public with their exuberant acting and singing.[23] The main arena within which these itinerant Yuan actresses thrived was the urban commercial theater, generally known as *goulan* 勾欄, or "the balustrade," which people paid pennies to enter. The balustrade-like theater space, similar to playhouses in Shakespearean London, never came into being in Tang Xianzu's 湯顯祖 (1553–1610) Nanjing and other cities in China. Along with the disappearance of commercial playhouses during the Ming, female stardom dimmed up until the era of its comeback, on a much smaller scale, in the pleasure quarters located in various urban centers.

After itinerant female performers' withdrawal from the public stage of Ming performance culture after the Yuan dynasty collapsed, there was a brief hiatus in the male desire to view women's gender-specific performing arts onstage. This gap was then filled by courtesan-performers as serious artists, led by virtuoso courtesans such as Ma Xianglan, producing a new taste in staged feminine beauty different from that created by the female impersonators who are also a significant strand within Chinese theater history. The rising male dominance of itinerant troupes (playing both male and female roles) and the gradual withdrawal of professional actresses from them con-

22. Ye Shaoyuan 葉紹袁 (1589–1648), *Ye Tianliao nianpu bieji* 葉天寥年譜別記, the fifth month of the thirteenth year in the Wanli reign (1640), in A Ying 阿英, ed., *Ye Tianliao sizhong* 葉天寥四種 (Shanghai: Shanghai beiye shanfang, 1936), 87. For more examples of exclusively selected audience for private female theatrical performances, see Liu Shuiyun, *Ming Qing jiayue yanjiu*, 211–14.

23. Xia Tingzhi 夏庭芝, *Qinglou ji*, in *Zhongguo gudian xiqu lunzhu jicheng* 中國古典戲曲論著集成 (Beijing: Zhongguo xiju chubanshe, 1959, rpt. 1980), 2:3–84.

stitute an important backdrop to the ascendancy of courtesans as theater artists. This ascent was a response to the increased public craving to see the singing and dancing bodies of theater women after the two-centuries-long absence of women performers in the public arena.

There is an entrenched conception that needs to be rectified—namely, that the late Ming courtesans' theatrical performances were mainly for their patrons' private delectation in luxury settings. After the shutdown of the main commercial venues in the early Ming, the residual public venues were temples and marketplaces, and other open spaces used for temporary stages during public events and festivals, most likely with free admission, and these sites were reserved mostly for male actors.[24] It was through these free public venues, however, that the heroines of this book were launched into the theater scene of the late Ming. The starting date of this piece of history is 1570, when the first well-documented courtesan singing festival that I know of was sponsored by local elites, causing a public sensation (see chapter 3). This festival was likely a point in history when, after two hundred years of silence, the singing diva's voice again bathed the audience on a public stage, albeit temporarily.

The lack of a female counter-canon in the performance repertoire of traditional Chinese theater goes hand in hand with the historical dominance of female impersonators. The Manchu rulers of the Qing dynasty (1644–1911) imposed prohibitions on women's participation in public performances as professional performers.[25] At the Qing court, female entertainers were replaced by trained palace eunuchs.[26] The top-down decision to remove women entirely from the theater in the early Qing nurtured the great tradition of males acting the roles of heroines, which reached its apogee in the

24. Wang Anqi 王安祈, *Mingdai chuanqi zhi juchang jiqi yishu* 明代傳奇之劇場及其藝術 (Taipei: Xuesheng shuju, 1986), 121–75.

25. Dolby, *A History of Chinese Drama*, 124. Supporting evidence that scholars often quote include Kangxi emperor's three edicts of 1671, 1706, and 1714, and Qianlong emperor's 1769 edict, which expelled female entertainers from Beijing. See Wang Liqi 王利器, ed., *Yuan Ming Qing sandai jinhui xiaoshuo xiqu shiliao* 元明清三代禁燬小說戲曲史料 (Shanghai: Shanghai guji chubanshe, 1981), 20, 23, 29. But Zhang Faying feels that these female entertainers did not perform in theater and that there might have been female theater practitioners in the Kangxi and Qianlong reign. See Zhang Faying 張發穎, *Zhongguo xibanshi* 中國戲班史 (Beijing: Xueyuan chubanshe, 2003), 447.

26. Dolby, *A History of Chinese Drama*, 144. The only primary source I know of that supports Dolby's statement is *Da Qing wuchao huidian Kangxi huidian* 大清五朝會典康熙會典, in which we do observe decreasing numbers of female court musicians and increasing numbers of eunuch performers throughout the Kangxi reign.

connoisseurship of boy-actresses in the long nineteenth century, the subject of Andrea Goldman's monograph *Opera and the City*.[27]

In the first half of the twentieth century, female impersonators soared in popularity in China and also achieved fabulous international successes, as epitomized by Mei Lanfang's 梅蘭芳 (1894–1961) tour of America in the early 1930s.[28] The performance culture surrounding these stars is considered, and finely argued by Joshua Goldstein, to be integral to the Chinese experience of modernity. Another manifestation of the Chinese taste for this particular tradition of female representation is the early twentieth-century invention of a hybrid form that encapsulated both indigenous and foreign elements, namely, civilization drama (*wenmingxi* 文明戲). It started out with all-male casts in which men played female characters, and early Chinese feature films inherited this approach partly because of the sharing of personnel.[29] Around the same time, in metropolitan cities, theater women entered public view, and some enjoyed fleeting box-office success and burgeoning stage careers, thus ending the centuries-long monopoly of male performers on the public stage.[30]

The post-1930s era witnessed the rise of gender-appropriate casting and the new representation of women: the seductress dressed in modern cheongsam typical of the Japanese occupation of China (1937–1945), as part of the colonial policies to "intoxicate" the male audience with more realistic female sexuality,[31] or the robust revolutionary woman onstage during the early Communist regime (1950s–1970s) because of the government's rejection of female impersonation as "dross from decayed feudal society." The "ideal woman" portrayed by the female impersonators in the golden days of the early twentieth century, however, continues to be seen as the epitome of eternal feminine beauty created by unbeatable artistry.

---

27. Andrea S. Goldman, *Opera and the City: The Politics of Culture in Beijing, 1770–1900* (Stanford: Stanford University Press, 2012), 9–11, 17–60.

28. Joshua Goldstein, "Nationalization Through Iconification," in *Drama Kings: Players and Public in the Recreation of Peking Opera, 1870–1937* (Berkeley: University of California Press, 2007).

29. Liu Siyuan, *Performing Hybridity in Colonial-Modern China* (New York: Palgrave Macmillan, 2013).

30. For a sociology of women stage artists' lives in two metropolitan cities in northern China in the early twentieth century, see Weikun Cheng, "The Challenge of the Actresses: Female Performers and Cultural Alternatives in Early Twentieth Century Beijing and Tianjin," *Modern China* 22, no. 2 (1996): 197–233.

31. See, for example, Tong Zhiling's memoir which depicts her ascendency in popularity in Shanghai through acting in notoriously erotic plays during this period. Zhu Jipeng 朱繼彭, *Tong Zhiling* 童芷苓 (Shanghai: Huadong shifan daxue chubanshe, 1995), 57–68, 74–81.

Such recent memories that fondly recall preeminent female impersonators on the operatic stage, however, apparently prevented theater historians from noticing the fleeting but important flourishing of theater women in brothels. In scholarship, this influential idea made itself known on two levels: first, dramatic theory and criticism that failed to take into account female performance became received wisdom in Ming theater history; and second, female performance in its relation to dramatic literature never gained autonomy as a subject of study, despite the vast Chinese scholarship on Ming drama to which this book remains indebted.[32] Alongside the thriving of feminist scholarship in the China field—especially in early modern China studies—comes a great opportunity to write in a new direction for theater historiography.

My title, *The Courtesan's Memory, Voice, and Late Ming Drama*, foregrounds the courtesan's arts as an autonomous domain rather than an auxiliary one overshadowed by the elite's artistic pursuits. This emphasis differentiates my study from the rest of the burgeoning subfield of Chinese courtesan studies, which focuses on the courtesan's relationship with men, highlighting her arts—painting, poetry, singing, and so on—as ways of communicating with her patrons, and her vernacular songs, in particular, as being appropriated by the literati printing enterprise.[33] My second intervention takes place within the academic history of *chuanqi* drama, especially vis-à-vis the emphatic term "literati-*chuanqi* drama" (*wenren chuanqi* 文人傳奇) coined in modern scholarship. To prefix the term *chuanqi* with the qualifier "literati" implies that women (and lower-class men as well) played little part in the literary phenomenon of *chuanqi*, and that literati alone were responsible for the full flowering of the *chuanqi* dramatic genre. It also neglects an important dimension of the process of writing a play at the time—namely, the fact that playwriting was a performative art in its own right, in terms of both the playwright's social relations and the physical enactments of the plays themselves.

The origins of the term "literati-*chuanqi* drama" can be traced back to the 1930s, when two pioneering histories of *chuanqi* drama were published in Shanghai, one by the Chinese scholar Lu Qian 盧前 (1905–1951), the other by the Japanese scholar Aoki Masaru 青木正兒 (1887–1964; original Japanese edition published in 1930).[34] Both scholars argue that *chuanqi* was literary

32. One exception is Zhang Faying's discussions of the organization and operation of private troupes in the Ming from a sociological perspective, although his study relies heavily on anecdotes.

33. For example, Ōki Yasushi and Paolo Santangelo, *Shan'ge, the 'Mountain Songs': Love Songs in Ming China* (Leiden: Brill, 2011).

34. Aoki Masaru, *Shina kinsei gikyokushi* 支那近世戲曲史 (Tokyo: Kobundo sho-

theater and deserved canonical status in Chinese literature. Among their supporting evidence, what has earned general scholarly agreement is Aoki's famous observation about two camps of late Ming literatus-playwrights debating each other on whether to write drama texts for staging purposes (*changshang zhi qu* 場上之曲) or to be published as "desktop" reading matter (*antou zhi qu* 案頭之曲). It then became firmly entrenched that, as a new trend after the midpoint of the sixteenth century, literatus-playwrights opted to write "closet drama" for gentlemen's leisure. Briefly, Aoki's widely accepted hypothesis reinforced the old paradigm of great minds producing great works, and the assumption that the literati class formed the major creative milieu within Ming dramatic history.

This idea is reiterated by Andrew Plaks in his influential 1987 monograph on the rise of the Ming novel as a foundation on which to put forward the concept of "literati novel." Plaks acutely points out the two literary forms' coincidental rise to popularity in the late sixteenth century and the aesthetic similarities between them, including their texts' great length, the rhetoric mix of lyric and spoken passages, and their literatus-authors' "intellectual seriousness" and philosophical inquiries.[35] In English scholarship, the sixteenth century is therefore widely conceived as the literati's time to produce "serious fiction" alongside serious drama; it is also believed that it is the highly intelligent, aesthetically elegant characteristics of these genres that boosted them to great popularity in late Ming society. It is an apparent paradox, therefore, that a play's elite positioning and intellectual sophistication would have contributed to its wide popularity.[36]

---

ten, 1930), Chinese translation entitled *Zhongguo jinshi xiqushi* 中國近世戲曲史, trans. Wang Gulu 王古魯 (Shanghai: Shangwu yinshuguan, 1936; reprint, Zhonghua shuju, 2010), 147–61. Lu Qian, *Ming Qing xiqushi* 明清戲曲史 (Shanghai: Shangwu yinshuguan, 1935).

35. Andrew Plaks, *The Four Masterworks of the Ming Novel* (Princeton: Princeton University Press, 1987), 41–43.

36. Yuming He's 2008 article responds to this paradox by scrutinizing the musical designs of a play that both connected it to the stage and posed difficulties to those who attempted to fully render it in music. Yuming He, "Difficulties of Performance: The Musical Career of Xu Wei's *The Mad Drummer*," *Harvard Journal of Asiatic Studies* 68, no. 2 (2008): 77–114. The play is one of the four works written in a hybrid dramatic genre called "the South's northern drama" (*nan zaju* 南雜劇), collectively known as *Four Cries of the Gibbon* (*Sisheng yuan* 四聲猿), dated to circa 1558 by Xu Shuofang 徐朔方. See Xu, *Wan Ming qujia nianpu* 晚明曲家年譜 (Hangzhou: Zhejiang guji chubanshe, 1993), 2:53–54, 96–99. For the enduring popularity of the four plays in sixteenth-century Jiangnan, see Wilt L. Idema, "Female Talent and Female Virtue: Xu Wei's *Nü zhuangyuan* and Meng Chengshun's *Zhenwenji*," in Hua Wei and Wang Ail-

The notion that creativity resided in the best brains of society is not untypical of the cultural studies conception of "diffusion"—a model that "operated like a French filter coffee machine" in which "ideas trickled down from an intellectual elite to the general public," to borrow Robert Darnton's metaphor of French book historians' methodology.[37] This analytical model of cultural studies led inevitably to an appreciation of the role of the intellectual elite in shaping the way commoners feel and think. Adapting this line of inquiry to the context of Chinese scholarship on drama, Guo Yingde is a pioneer of the idea of literati-*chuanqi* drama. Among his monographs is one published in 1991 that bears the term in its title.[38] In a 2004 book, he further ascribes all the genre specificities of *chuanqi* drama to the aspirations and mentalities of the literatus-playwright. The elite's appropriation and renovation of the popular (*minjian* 民間), he argues, concentrated on transforming and reconfiguring the old, if not vulgar, mode of narrative into something new—a mode that is "narrative, allegorical, illusionistic, remarkable, and carefully constructed" 敘事性、寓言性、虛構性、傳奇性和結構性.[39] Moreover, "to probe the possibilities of a new literary genre was to establish the literati's values and status as historical subjects" 對新型文體的探求，以確立自身作為歷史主體的價值和地位. In other words, the literati's creativity sprang from their absolute, self-assured certainty about their own ideas and values.

This book challenges exactly this assumption about men's dominance in the history of classical Chinese drama, an assumption that has been shared in the field for too long. It pursues a historical argument that late Ming courtesans were proactive in theater and that their impact manifested in a greater number of fields, albeit concealed or even erased, than any other social group. Concomitantly, this book also intervenes in the oversimplified understanding about *kunqu*'s strong ties to elite literary culture. Literary historians such as Aoki Masaru have used it to demarcate a new era in the history of southern drama—on his timeline, plays are divided into those writ-

ing 王瑷玲 eds., *Ming Qing xiqu guoji yantaohui lunwen ji* 明清戲曲國際研討會論文集 (Taipei: Academia Sinica, 1998), 2:549–71.

37. Quoted in M. Paterson, *The Senses of Touch: Haptics, Affects, and Technologies* (Oxford: Berg, 2007), 34.

38. Guo Yingde, *Ming Qing wenren chuanqi yanjiu* 明清文人傳奇研究 (Taipei: Wenxin chubanshe, 1991); Guo Yingde, *Ming Qing chuanqi shi* 明清傳奇史 (Nanjing: Jiangsu guji chubanshe, 1999); Guo Yingde, *Ming Qing chuanqi xiqu wenti yanjiu* 明清傳奇戲曲文體研究 (Beijing: Shangwu yinshuguan, 2004).

39. Guo Yingde, *Ming Qing chuanqi xiqu wenti yanjiu*, 8.

ten before, during, or after the era of *kunqu* (or *kunqu*-southern-drama);[40] and music historians have focused on its musical novelty devised by the great genius Wei Liangfu 魏良輔 (fl. sixteenth century), who led a top-down musical reform championed by literati cohorts.[41] But for historians of gendered performance, I discuss the courtesan's *kunqu* training that focused less on memorizing libretti than on music literacy, and describe how the diva's voice in the *xiansuo* performance transcended the generic boundaries of music and remained a powerful force in the field of *kunqu*-southern-drama (see chapters 2 and 3).

The four chapters of the book each demonstrates one crucial change in literary history prompted by the courtesan's artistic choices. Chapter 1 centers on the emergence of the idea of writing for brothel girls—either writing musically "authentic" northern *zaju* drama or incorporating familiar northern tunes and skits into southern *chuanqi* plays. At the same time, the booming late Ming print culture produced new archives of Yuan dramatic texts, replaced the courtesan's dwindling memorial archive, and concomitantly erased the courtesan from the cultural memory of the genesis of knowledge production and transmission. Chapter 2 compares the old mnemonic method that courtesans inherited from rigorous medieval music pedagogy with the "modern" southern method pivoted on improvisation. It argues that the female kinesthetic learner's pro-*kunqu* preference, vis-à-vis the male playwright's literary choices, constitute the context and agent of the rise of the *kunqu* theater. Chapter 3 elaborates on the concept of musical eroticism and its changing connotations alongside the evolution of taste in the demimonde from the mid- to the late sixteenth century. Nostalgia for the vigorous vocal tradition of the old-style choral singing led to a new musical ideal for a female soloist. Last, through close reading of two great *kunqu* plays produced during the 1570–1600 era, chapter 4 suggests that brothel staging created a synthetic experience in which theater and life often mingled, with the heroine's image superimposed onto that of the courtesan-actress.

40. Aoki Masaru, *Shina kinsei gikyokushi*; Zhou Yibai 周貽白, *Zhongguo xijushi changbian* 中國戲劇史長編 (1960; repr., Shanghai: Shanghai shudian, 2004); Guo Yingde, *Ming Qing chuanqi shi*.

41. I disagree with the vision of a creative genius singlehandedly bringing musical novelty to *kunqu*. For my argument about brothels as the social foundation of Wei Liangfu's music reform, see Peng Xu, "The Music Teacher: The Professionalization of Singing and the Development of Erotic Vocal Style During Late Ming China," *Harvard Journal of Asiatic Studies* 75, no. 2 (2015): 259–97.

An Early Qing Dramatization of the Late Ming Courtesans as "Authors"

To illuminate the raison d'être of this book, let us now consider one most characteristic instance that suggests how female agency in the theater was overshadowed and erased. My example comes, inevitably, from Kong Shangren's 孔尚任 (1648–1718) historical drama of 1699, *The Peach Blossom Fan* (*Taohua shan* 桃花扇). In history, the courtesan's stellar performance stunned audiences until the last few years of the Ming dynasty, leaving numerous traces in dramatic works whose authors were nostalgic about her performance. The *Peach Blossom Fan* is imbued with faithful representation of late Ming performance culture and distressed at its dissipation during the dynastic transition that began in 1644. Scenes are dated with a precise year by the playwright, and the central dramatic action is premised on a temporal sequence, creating the sense of a chronicle. To some extent, the *Peach Blossom Fan* can be read as a collection of musical performances that are quintessentially late Ming in terms of their aesthetic indulgence in pleasure-seeking and their reflection of the social memory of Ming loyalists.

My example is a dramatized event in which a courtesan-authored performance is improvised, watched, commented on, and forgotten. One day in the first month of 1645, the heroine Li Xiangjun 李香君, a courtesan separated from her lover during the turmoil of dynastic transition in 1644, is summoned to serve at a banquet concert (scene 24). Two men in the onstage audience in the play turn out to be none other than courtiers of the Southern Ming (1644–1662)—a remnant of the Han Chinese court that briefly established rule over the southern land after the Ming collapsed—who have persecuted her lover in scene 12. Due to their notorious liaisons with a corrupt Ming eunuch who has been executed, they are doomed to be condemned in history, and yet somehow rise in power in the nascent southern regime.

Li Xiangjun demonstrates her knowledge of *chuanqi* theater by referring in her aria to a historical drama completed between 1567 and 1593, *Singing Phoenixes* (*Mingfeng ji* 鳴鳳記, attributed to Wang Shizhen 王世貞, 1526–1590, *jinshi* 1547), in which, by theatrical convention, the corrupt eunuch and his cohort are cast as clowns/villains with powdered faces. Li Xiangjun imagines the two men she is about to meet to be actors with their faces powdered, performing the roles of the eunuch and his flatterer and acting "in an ugly, obsequious manner" in *Singing Phoenixes* 醜腔惡態，演出真鳴鳳.[42] Then

42. Kong Shangren, *Taohua shan*, ed. Wang Jisi 王季思 et al. (Beijing: Renmin wenxue chubanshe, 1997), 161. The English translation is adapted from Chen Shih-

she continues in the same aria to cast herself in another play in the male lead role, by naming herself a "female Mi Heng" 女禰衡. Mi Heng (173–198) was a historical literatus who was disgraced by the tyrant Cao Cao and forced to serve as a drummer at a banquet, and who then cursed Cao Cao during the drumming. Among the many dramatizations of the Mi Heng story—which the character Li Xiangjun might have been assumed to be familiar with—is a popular play called *The Mad Drummer* (*Kuang gushi* 狂鼓史), written in the late 1550s by the eccentric dramatist Xu Wei 徐渭 (1521–1593). Xu Wei gives his protagonist thirteen songs cursing Cao Cao, interspersed with dialogues between his "audiences" onstage and female entertainers' songs. Resembling Mi Heng in Xu Wei's play, Li Xiangjun, though assigned only three songs in her own cursing scene, seizes her powerful moment of improvisation to vent her opinions and rage 正好吐俺胸中之气.

In the dramatic presentation of the improvisation, Li Xiangjun and the two villains (her audience onstage) share what Roland Barthes has called a "writerly" moment, or, in Susan Leigh Foster's words, an engagement "in developing the form of the event."[43] The three arias are well adapted to the three preexisting tunes that late Ming courtesans were most familiar with, and that escalate in emotional intensity. The first song recounts her personal sufferings—the destruction of her "family" following her lover's escape; the second accuses the courtiers of negligence in their duties to the state; and the third reveals their blemished political careers in the Ming dynasty by calling them "the upstart foster sons of the eunuch." With increased understanding of her point after each aria she sings, the two villains respond with growing anger. Finally, they order that she be cast out into the snow. She sings her last three lines of improvisation in the snow, pushing the scene to its climax:

> My limbs are transparent as ice, and my heart is chaste as snow.
> With my will of iron, I have no fear of freezing.
> Until I die, I shall never staunch the longings in my breast.
>
> 冰肌雪腸原自同
> 鐵心石腹何愁凍
> 吐不盡杜鵑血滿胸

Hsiang and Harold Acton, trans., *The Peach Blossom Fan by K'ung Shang-jen* (Berkeley: University of California Press, 1976), 180–84.

43. Roland Barthes, *S/Z: An Essay*, trans. Richard Miller (New York: Hill and Wang, 1970), 3–4; Susan Leigh Foster, "Improvising History," in *Theorizing Practice: Redefining Theatre History*, ed. W. B. Worthen and Peter Holland (New York: Palgrave Macmillan, 2003), 196.

These lines are interspersed with the two men's dialogue about how to punish her, as well as with the dramatic action of pushing and stamping on her until she is at last dragged off the stage.

It is decided that Li Xiangjun will be "sent to the Inner Court to perform the most arduous roles" 送入內庭，揀著極苦的腳色，叫他去當. In scene 25, "The Cast Selected," this most arduous role for a courtesan-performer turns out to be that of a clown.[44] This plan to persecute Li Xiangjun fails, however, because by convention a courtesan-clown did not have to put on a powdered face; as a result, the emperor in the audience is able to see Li Xiangjun's natural beauty and eventually has her cast back into the lead female role. To the emperor, a beauty should act the female lead, and it is wrong to have a heroine act the clown 太屈他了.[45]

But the real irony lies in the fact that the rehearsal at the Inner Court, in which Li Xiangjun is forced to participate, is for a *chuanqi* play called *The Swallow Letter* (*Yanzi jian* 燕子箋), newly completed by none other than one of the two villains in 1645, whose literary achievement has earned the play niche status in the literary museum of *chuanqi* drama. The confrontation is, then, not just between the courtesan and her rivals, but also between the (heroine's) female authorship—disrupted, despised, and then dissipated—and the (villains') glorified, canonized, "serious" male authorship. Earlier cataloguing and archival work has proved that there were women who wrote for the theater at the two high tides of women's literature in early modern China.[46] In his *Peach Blossom Fan*, however, Kong Shangren reminds us of what has been left out—namely, the courtesans' creations that had no written components. In his description, Li Xiangjun's performance encompasses many aspects of the historical expressive culture of the day—music composition, singing, verbal and nonverbal acting—though none of them is recorded in writing. This mini "play within a play" thus epitomizes the ephemerality of a female authorial voice.

Kong's historical drama has preserved from facile erasure Li Xiangjun's "writerly" position within the mini "play within a play." It stands out among the series of dramatizations of courtesans' performances in the *Peach Blossom Fan* because, as a scripted performance, it is reproducible, and it there-

44. Kong Shangren, *Taohua shan*, 163; English translation by Chen Shih-Hsiang and Harold Acton, 184.

45. Kong Shangren, *Taohua shan*, 169; English translation, 190.

46. Liu Junhua 劉軍華, *Ming Qing nüxing zuojia xiqu chuangzuo yanjiu*. For the first massive bibliography of women's works, see Hu Wenkai 胡文楷, *Lidai funü zhuzuo kao* 歷代婦女著作考 (Shanghai: Shanghai guji chubanshe, [1957, 1985] 2008). For the periodization and translated works, see Idema and Grant, *The Red Brush*, part 3 and part 4, esp. 347–58, 567–77.

fore "documents" (thus an *archive*) a script that is not predetermined but improvised (thus a *repertoire*) by a female author. The complex nature of the "female authorial voice"—at once visible and invisible, at once ephemeral and lasting—is thus encapsulated in the tiny sample that Kong Shangren offers.

Notably, even the improvisation in *The Mad Drummer* is sung by Mi Heng's ghost in hell, not by the living man. Thus the "writerly" moments of a ghost or a woman, such as the ones elaborated by Kong Shangren and Xu Wei, are easily omitted from history but are restored in imaginative literature. Just as Mi Heng's ghost's singing has been eternalized in the living repertoire of *kunqu* opera, so Li Xiangjun's mini scene has been publicly recognized and admired by viewers of the *Peach Blossom Fan* of different times, in variegated stagings of the play and in diegetic musical renditions in film adaptations.[47]

47. The most striking film presentation of this scene appears in a 1963 feature film *Peach Blossom Fan*, starring Wang Danfeng 王丹鳳 (1924–2018) whose singing of the three improvised arias was dubbed in a *kunqu*/Peking-opera actress Yu Junfang's 虞俊芳 (1935–1997) voice.

CHAPTER 1

The Courtesan's Memorial Archive of Northern Drama

To stage his *zaju* 雜劇 (northern drama) *Soaring the Sky* (*Lingyun ji* 凌雲記), the Cantonese poet Han Shanggui 韓上桂 (1572–1644), sojourning in Nanjing in summer 1609, commissioned a courtesan named Fu Shou 傅寿, style name Nimble Beauty 靈修, to play the female lead. With the help of his poetry-club friend Pan Zhiheng 潘之恆 (1556–1622), a patron of the Fu family and an avid connoisseur of music and the courtesan's arts, he successfully engaged Nimble Beauty to play the heroine Zhuo Wenjun 卓文君, with her brother as the hero Sima Xiangru 司馬相如. Both Han and Pan left detailed accounts of the production that give us a rare opportunity to glimpse Nimble Beauty's performance and its reception. The play was presented in her dwelling, located within the Old Compound (*jiuyuan* 舊院, also known as *quzhong* 曲中), Nanjing's top-notch pleasure quarters (see fig. 1 in the introduction). It took her just one night to read the play—either in its entirety or the female lead's part only—and seven days to rehearse and then perform eight scenes (selected from the twenty scenes of the play) for the audience that Pan organized for the show.[1] She would study one act for

1. 一夕而竟，十日而成音. I think the word 十 (ten) is a typo for 七 (seven). Pan Zhiheng, "Fu Lingxiu zhuan" 傅靈修傳, in *Genshi* 亙史, *Yanbu Jinling* 艷部金陵, *juan* 20, reprint in *Siku quanshu cunmu congshu* 四庫全書存目叢書 (Jinan: Qilu shushe, 1997), hereafter CMCS, *zibu*, vol. 193; Pan Zhiheng, *Luanxiao xiaopin*, 鸞嘯小品, 1628 edition in the Shanghai Library, *juan* 8, 16a; also in Wang Xiaoyi 汪效漪, ed., *Pan Zhiheng quhua* 潘之恆曲話 (Beijing: Zhongguo xiju chubanshe, 1988), 126. 習七日而成八齣. 數十人 . . . 集飲七日. See Han Shanggui, "Pan Jingsheng xiansheng *Luanxiao xiaopin* xu" [Preface to *Luanxiao xiaopin*], in *Luanxiao xiaopin*, 2a–b.

one day, and the next day the new act would be staged in her courtyard.[2] For the seven-day performance Han spent extravagantly, and Pan put together several dozen elite audiences, who bestowed "pearl or emerald jewelry" upon the troupe after each performance.[3]

The worth of Nimble Beauty's performance lay in its rarity in the eyes of this cohort of men of letters. Their seemingly ostentatious generosity was not merely an exhibition of literati romanticism or *fengliu* behavior. Rather, they watched each of the performances with reverence, moved by nostalgia for the musical style in which she specialized—namely, the "authentic" *xiansuo* 弦索 (lit., "string-instrument") style of northern drama passed down from the glorious Yuan (1279–1368) music tradition. Both Pan and Han, and perhaps some of the other male audience members as well, were leading advocates of this declining vocal style. By 1609 courtesans were known to instead favor fashionable literary and musical styles, resulting in their dwindling memory of the "authentic" *xiansuo* style and also in a telescoped northern drama repertoire in brothel performances. Nimble Beauty, however, had inherited the *xiansuo* style from her father, in the traditional approach of "notes and tones learned by heart" 口傳音調.[4] Her father had been a renowned *zaju* actor, registered in a "Hao Kecheng's boy company" 郝可成班 in Nanjing that thrived in the late 1550s.[5] That he and his two beautiful children—both of whom starred in the lead roles in *Soaring the Sky*—excelled in the *xiansuo* style despite its loss of popular appeal must have soothed a nostalgic corner of many northern-drama connoisseurs' hearts.[6]

A different account of this theatrical event, offered by Huang Zongxi 黃宗羲 (1610–1695)—Han's junior by almost thirty years, who lived next door to Han in Beijing in the 1630s and was too young to understand Han's zeal for the music per se—suggests that Han's romantic feelings for Nimble Beauty were the driving force behind his dramatic creation. In Huang's

2. 日習一折，再折則為陳於庭. In Pan Zhiheng, "Chuyan" 初艷, see Wang, *Pan Zhiheng quhua*, 32; Pan Zhiheng, *Luanxiao xiaopin*, *juan* 2, 19b; *Genshi*, *zaju* 雜部, *juan* 4.

3. Pan Zhiheng, "Fu Lingxiu zhuan," in *Genshi waiji* 亙史外紀, *juan* 20, reprint in CMCS, vol. 193; also in *Luanxiao xiaopin*, *juan* 8, 15a–16b. Wang Xiaoyi, ed., *Pan Zhiheng quhua*, 126. 每齣一奏，侑以珠或翠. See Han Shanggui, "Pan Jingsheng xiansheng *Luanxiao xiaopin* xu."

4. 金陵之工吳音，自傳靈修以登場聲揚. Pan Zhiheng, *Genshi waiji*, *juan* 20; Wang Xiaoyi, ed., *Pan Zhiheng quhua*, 120. 南北音兼美. Pan Zhiheng, *Luanxiao xiaopin*, *juan* 2, 23a; Wang Xiaoyi, ed., *Pan Zhiheng quhua*, 51.

5. Pan Zhiheng, "Chuyan"; "Fu Lingxiu zhuan"; "Yueji" 樂技, in *Luanxiao xiaopin*, *juan* 2, 23a; also see Wang, *Pan Zhiheng quhua*, 32, 51, 126.

6. 至老猶不失度. "Yueji." Wang, *Pan Zhiheng quhua*, 32.

imagination, Han completed the play *for* "the actress Nimble Beauty" while stopping over in the Old Compound.[7]

The story ended sadly. Shortly after Pan Zhiheng left for his hometown in the winter of 1609, Nimble Beauty married and disappeared from public view. When Pan returned to Nanjing a few months later, he was deeply disappointed, lamenting the "death of northern tunes" 余獨惜北音絕矣 and even fretting about Han's not having "married her right away (after the show of *Soaring the Sky*)" 景升每書來，輒責余 . . . 不即載靈修去.[8] Elsewhere Pan reiterates: "Ever since the [troupe of] *Soaring the Sky* was disbanded, the five parts of the *'The Western Wing' in Its Northern Version* thereupon were no longer passed down" 自從淩雲記解散, 而北西廂五劇亦遂不傳.[9] Likewise, Shen Defu 沈德符 (1578–1642), in his encyclopedic accounts of all things in fashion, *Private Gleanings of the Wanli Era* (*Wanli yehuobian*, pref. 1619), pessimistically averred that the profession's loss of Nimble Beauty to domestic life emblematized the complete erasure of Yuan music drama from the living repertoire.[10]

There is no doubt that Han wrote exclusively for an "authentic" voice of northern drama and for its realization in brothel performances. What insights, then, does the 1609 performance of *Soaring the Sky* provide into the lost "authentic" voice of the courtesan in her northern drama repertoire? How do we assess her share of the authorial role in creating *Soaring the Sky*, in tandem with the male poet Han Shanggui? First, I address the question of whether the courtesan had a distinct performance tradition. To trace musical renditions unique to the courtesan's tradition, I compare the play's tune arrangements and other musical features with their counterparts in sixteenth-century song anthologies and mid-seventeenth-century song formulas. Second, switching from this microscopic vision to a panoramic view,

7. See Huang Zongxi, *Sijiu lu* 思舊錄, in *Huang Zongxi quanji* 黃宗羲全集 (Hangzhou: Zhejiang guji chubanshe, 1985), 353. Huang also recounts that Han rewarded Nimble Beauty one hundred taels of silver for her acting in each act. Han took his second exam in Nanjing in 1607, yet failed, and so it is possible that he did stay in or frequent the pleasure quarters until he left Nanjing after the show, but not necessarily with Nimble Beauty.

8. Han Shanggui, "Pan Jingsheng xiansheng *Luanxiao xiaopin* xu" 潘景升先生鸞嘯小品序, 3a, in Pan Zhiheng, *Luanxiao xiaopin*.

9. Wang Xiaoyi, ed., *Pan Zhiheng quhua*, 130; Pan Zhiheng, *Luanxiao xiaopin*, *juan* 3, 15a.

10. Shen Defu, *Guqu zayan* 顧曲雜言, *juan* 25 of his *Wanli yehuobian* 萬曆野獲編 (Beijing: Zhonghua shuju, 1959), 2:647; also in Yu Weimin 俞為民 and Sun Rongrong 孫蓉蓉, eds., *Lidai quhua huibian: Mingdai bian* 歷代曲話彙編明代編 (Hefei: Huangshan chubanshe 2009), 1:69.

I situate the play within a particular chain of dramatic works spun from the idea of writing musically "authentic" northern dramas for brothel girls, who were then to provide full-fledged staging for the new plays in the pleasure quarters, as Nimble Beauty did for Han.

To reinforce my emphasis on the female authorial voice in these male-authored northern dramas, I juxtapose the conventional archive of Yuan drama—full-text Yuan dramas in print—with the courtesan's own "memorial archive," and suggest that the latter's impact on subsequent playwriting goes far beyond what earlier historians have imagined. Most importantly, these two kinds of archives should be seen as two autonomic but intertwining discourses. A concept crucial to my argument is Diana Taylor's emphasis on embodied memory/practice/knowledge (i.e., spoken language, dance, singing, and acting) that "exceeds the archive's ability to capture it."[11] She challenges the presumption that performance is ephemeral whereas an archive is faithful and permanent. Instead of seeing performance as being doomed to disappear without a trace (before the advent of modern technologies), I propose revisiting the "last sunset" moment of Yuan drama in the late Ming with a new focus on the role of the courtesan-performer in transmitting this embodied knowledge.

The key term "memorial archive" is borrowed from Mary Carruthers's pathbreaking monograph *The Book of Memory*.[12] To Carruthers, the minds of the medieval European reciters who learned, stored, and transmitted knowledge were seen in their own time as more reliable repositories than were transcriptions. Similar to the European reciters, the Chinese courtesans learned, inherited, and transmitted Yuan lyrics through live performances, thereby retaining a modality of late medieval musical culture. I would go one step further and suggest that in the genealogy of Yuan drama, courtesans played a crucial, albeit forgotten, role in changing the face of literary history—their repertoire was a parallel aesthetic to the conventional archive, their memorial archives the very crucible for innovations in playwriting. To take the 1609 performance of *Soaring the Sky* as an example, the various narratives I used to weave the story that opens this chapter were written exclusively from the perspective of the play's literatus-patrons, for whom the event was a nostalgic chance to bask in the sunset beams of the "authentic" performance of Yuan drama. If our source materials are grounded only in literati accounts, the voice of the courtesan Nimble Beauty remains unheard.

11. Diana Taylor, *The Archive and the Repertoire: Performing Cultural Memory in the Americas* (Durham: Duke University Press, 2003), 20–21.

12. Mary Carruthers, *The Book of Memory: A Study of Memory in Medieval Culture* (Cambridge: Cambridge University Press, 1990), especially chapters 1, 3, and 5.

But a study centering on the notion of the courtesan's "memorial archive," as reflected in the 1609 northern-style musicking in the Nanjing brothel, can take us to the core of the problematics of the courtesan-actress's own performance tradition that nourished and changed the literary practice of northern drama.

Writing New Northern Dramas, Currying the Courtesan's Favor

Playwrights have long been attracted to the dramatic subject of a rich young widow eloping with a talented, ambitious, but destitute scholar: examples include the Ming prince Zhu Quan's 朱權 (1378–1448) *Zhuo Wenjun Elopes with Xiangru* (*Zhuo Wenjun siben Xiangru* 卓文君私奔相如),[13] Sun You's 孫柚 (1540–ca. 1613) *The Zither and Lust* (*Qinxin ji* 琴心記, ca. 1586),[14] Chen Yuchan's 陳玉蟾 *The Phoenix Lovers* (*Feng qiu huang* 鳳求凰, 1573–1620),[15] Yuan Yuling's[16] 袁于令 (1592–1674) *The Sushuang Feather Cloak* (*Sushuang qiu* 鷫鸘裘), and beyond.[17] All these contemporaneous works are in the

13. Wang Jilie 王季烈, comp., *Guben Yuan Ming zaju* 孤本元明雜劇 (Changsha: Shangwu yinshuguan, 1941), case 2, ce 10. Modern typeset annotated edition: Zhou Yibai 周貽白, *Mingren zaju xuan* 明人雜劇選 (Beijing: Renmin wenxue chubanshe, 1958), 116–39.

14. Cheng Huaping dates this play to the 1540s. See Cheng, *Ming Qing chuanqi biannian shigao* 明清傳奇編年史稿 (Jinan: Qi Lu shushe, 2008), 35. Xu Shuofang speculates that the play was completed in 1569 or slightly earlier. See Xu, *Wan Ming qujia nianpu* 晚明曲家年譜 (Hangzhou: Zhejiang guji chubanshe, 1993), 1:256. My suggestion of 1586 as the year of the completion is grounded on my premise of the synchronizing relationship between Sun You's aesthetic garden and his literary creation. See Peng Xu, "Editing *Pipa ji* for the Late Ming Popular Theater: The Identity of the 'Singing Hermit' and His Editorial Work," *Late Imperial China* 41, no. 1 (2020): 188–89, especially note 85.

15. Included in *Yuxiazhai chuanqi shizhong* 玉夏齋傳奇十種, late Ming edition, facsimile in *Guben xiqu congkan*, series 2.

16. On Yuan Yuling, see Deng Changfeng 鄧長風, *Ming Qing xiqujia kaolüe* 明清戲曲家考略 (Shanghai: Shanghai guji chubanshe, 1994), 99–104.

17. *The Zither and Lust* was included in Mao Jin's 毛晉 (1599–1659) compendium *The Sixty Plays* (*Liushi zhong qu* 六十種曲) with widespread favor ever since its first release in the Chongzhen reign (1628–1644). Among the lost late Ming dramas are Chen Zhenyi's 陳貞貽 *Danglu ji* 當壚記, Chen Jizhi's 陳濟之 *Tiqiao ji* 題橋記, and Yang Rousheng's 楊柔勝 *Lüqi ji* 綠綺記. For a fuller list of *zaju* or *chuanqi* dramas on the same subject, see Zhou Yibai, *Zhongguo xijushi changbian* 中國戲劇史長編 (Shanghai: Shanghai shudian, 2004), 614. To the list we can add a contemporary stage production—Guo Qihong's 郭啟宏 *kunqu* play *Sima Xiangru* 司馬相如 (debuted Shanghai, 1995).

genre of southern drama, or *chuanqi* 傳奇, within which, by 1609, *The Zither and Lust* had for several decades possessed the position of honor in the late Ming repertoire. Popular as *chuanqi* was, however, the generic conventions of southern drama dictated that it could not sustain the phenomenon of the diva. Not only do *chuanqi*'s aria assignments to major and minor figures alternate more than is the case in northern drama, but meanwhile the load of singing is distributed more equally among characters onstage. In this sense, in *chuanqi* the hero and other minor singing voices could more easily steal the thunder of the diva, whereas in northern drama the audience would focus on the diva's acrobatic vocal performance.

The organizer of the seven-day program of the northern drama *Soaring the Sky* would have faced no difficulties in putting together eight scenes in which the diva shone through almost every consecutive evening. Equipped with the details provided by Pan and Han in different sources, and by the manuscript of *Soaring the Sky* preserved by Han's descendants of Republican China (the handwritten copy of a lost late Ming illustrated woodblock edition), we can reconstruct the seven-day eight-scene program as shown in table 1.[18] Most notable is Nimble Beauty's debut night in summer 1609, consisting of two scenes in which she sang a total of eighteen arias. Not a single minor role sang that night. It was a performance designed to focus on the spectacular capabilities of the prima donna, with an adequate proportion given to the male lead—nine arias, just half the number of the diva's assignment. On the last two nights of the serialized play, following four less strenuous evenings for her voice, audiences must again have sat spellbound through one solo after another delivered by Nimble Beauty. In these last two shows she sang twenty-eight arias versus just three sung by other roles—a proportion reminiscent of the all-arias-by-female-lead category (*danben* 旦本) of Yuan *zaju* drama. Only from a northern drama such as *Soaring the Sky*, as opposed to a southern drama such as *The Zither and Lust*, could eight scenes be conveniently excerpted and packaged together into a program celebrating the courtesan-diva's dazzling virtuosity.

Table 1 gives us a rough sense of the capacity of a talented brothel singer's memory, which is the only medium for the glory of any literary composition in the northern dramatic genre. The highest number of arias that Nimble Beauty learned by heart after a one-day rehearsal was fifteen, a demanding

18. Facsimile reprint in Luo Kanglie 羅忼烈, *Ming guben chuanqi* Lingyun ji 明孤本傳奇凌雲記 (Hongkong: Shuye gongsi, 1975), 1–169. When the female lead appears in a few other scenes such as the last scene of happy reunion, there are many minor roles onstage, which I believe did not fit in the scale and purpose of the 1609 performance.

Table 1. Nimble Beauty's Seven-Day Performance Schedule (Eight Scenes in Total)

	Day 1	Day 2	Day 3	Day 4	Day 5	Day 6	Day 7
Staging	sc. 3, 8	sc. 9	sc. 10	sc. 11	sc. 12	sc. 16	sc. 18
Female lead's assigned arias	18	3	6	5.5	11	15	13
Male lead's assigned arias	9	12	9	5.5	7	2	0
Minor Characters or group singing	0	1	1	3	0	0	1
Total number of songs at one show	27	16	16	14	18	17	14

Note: The scenes (sc.) staged are as follows—
Scene 3, "Wenjun Newly Widowed" (*Wenjun xingua* 文君新寡), 13 arias for the female lead.
Scene 8, "Fragrant Garden, Blocked Paths" (*Fangyuan luge* 芳園路隔), 5 arias for the female lead.
Scene 9, "The Phoenix Lovers Flee" (*Fenghuang yufei* 鳳凰于飛).
Scene 10, "Galloping Off, Returning to Chengdu" (*Chi huan Chengdu* 馳還成都).
Scene 11, "Opening a Tavern, Selling Liquor" (*Danglu gujiu* 當壚沽酒).
Scene 12, "Inscribing the Bridge, Bidding Farewell" (*Songbie tiqiao* 送別題橋).
Scene 16, "Expressing Her Sorrows with the *Song of White Hair*" (*Baitou xieyuan* 白頭寫怨).
Scene 18, "Hearing About the Rioter" (*Wenluan shizhi* 聞亂誓志).

task indeed. Her fast memorization was possible in part thanks to the playwright Han's compositional skills.

In the *xiansuo* style, the melodies were predetermined by tune patterns, and therefore memory of the lyrics was the major technical virtuosity required of the singer. The new *kunqu* style operated on a different logic that redefined the meaning of "virtuosity," to which we will return in the next chapter. For the *zaju* playwright Han, matching his literary creativity as closely as possible with the melodies that were already in Nimble Beauty's memorial archive was key to facilitating her quick mastery of the lyrics. Playwrights who were anxious about losing the authenticity of Yuan musical expressions, such as Han, thus had to make their new libretti match the courtesan-performer's existing repertoire, which resulted in their loosened attitude toward the written rules of Yuan drama. Whenever they found a discrepancy between the courtesan's memorial archive and the textual tradition—whether the more authoritative written formulas or respectful Yuan drama copies—they complied with the courtesan's memorial archive.

The idea that *Soaring the Sky* set out to satisfy the craze among literati for the "authentic" *xiansuo*-style performance and thereby substituted the courtesan's tradition in place of the written version when necessary, however, seems to have been a source of embarrassment to highbrow critics such as Qi

Biaojia 祁彪佳 (1602–1645; *jinshi* 1642). Qi bestowed accolades on *Soaring the Sky*'s rigidity in following the strict prosodic rules of northern drama song-formularies: "Not a single aria is transferred to a different mode-suite; not a single mode-suite is mixed with others. Since the beginning of the Ming dynasty, this is the only case where one sees [such fidelity to old formulas]" 詞不易宮,宮不易調,入明以來,僅見於此.[19] Though in most of his writings Qi was a reliable source, a close reading of the prosodic dimension of *Soaring the Sky* reveals many bold innovations that breach the rules, as will become clear in the following analysis. Moreover, Han's digression from the rules was unquestionably a conscious choice rather than a manifestation of ignorance of the rules. This is clear because the intense intellectual interest in northern song formularies in the late Ming has provided us with at least six extant late Ming woodblock editions and one manuscript of Zhu Quan's *Formulary for Correct Sounds in an Era of Great Harmony* (*Taihe zhengyin pu* 太和正音譜).[20]

The chances of knowledge occlusion are further reduced by the fact that Han lived in a circle of friends who participated in the printing project of a 1602 edition of Zhu Quan's formulary under a new title, *The Northern Elegance* (*Beiya* 北雅), compiled by Han's fellow townsman Zhang Xuan 張萱 (1558–1641; top candidate in the Canton provincial examination of 1582).[21] Zhang and Han, together with Deng Yunxiao 鄧雲霄 (1566–1632; *jinshi* 1598), were recognized as the three foremost Cantonese literati versed in northern drama. They exchanged poems and wrote prefaces advocating one another's new plays. Their mutual friend Pan Zhiheng wrote a biography for Zhang's concubine Deng Baoqin 登寶琴 (1580–1602), style name Double Virtue (Shuangcheng 雙成), whose hand-copied text with editorial work based on her practical knowledge as a *xiansuo* performer

19. Qi Biaojia, *Yuanshantang qupin*. Digital version, Chinese Text Project, http://ctext.org/wiki.pl?if=en&chapter=716601, under the rubric of "The Good Plays" (*nengpin* 能品), 426–27. Also in *Zhongguo gudian xiqu lunzhu jicheng*, 6:62.

20. Zhu Quan, *Taihe zhengyin pu*, in *Lidai quhua huibian: Mingdai bian*, ed. Yu and Sun, 1:27–190. For a brief print history of the book, see Li Jian 李健, "*Taihe zhengyin pu* xiancun banben xulu" 太和正音譜現存版本敘錄, in *Xiqu yu suwenxue yanjiu* 戲曲與俗文學研究 9 (2020): 136–73 (Beijing: Shehui kexue wenxian chubanshe, 2020). The most notable editions include the 1528 edition [comp. Kang Hai 康海 (1475–1540)], 1594 edition [comp. He Fang 何鈁 (1525–1603)], 1602 edition [comp. Zhang Xuan], 1619 edition [comp. Cheng Mingshan 程明善 (1590–1656)], and the 1628–1644 edition [comp. Fan Wenruo 范文若 (1587–1634; *jinshi* 1619)].

21. For a bibliographical description of Zhang Xuan's work, see Mo Boji 莫伯驥 (1878–1958), "Liushu gu" 六書故, in *Wushiwan juan lou qunshu bawen* 五十萬卷樓群書跋文 (Beijing: Zhonghua shuju, 2019), unpaginated, manuscript completed in 1947.

was the very basis on which Zhang expanded and further edited into *The Northern Elegance*.[22] Zhang's preface to *The Northern Elegance* appears in both the two extant editions of the book and as an attachment to Pan's biography of Double Virtue. There is no reason to doubt the claim Zhang makes in the preface that the printing project, initiated after Double Virtue's untimely death in 1602, was designed to publicly commemorate her intellectual achievements as a music editor despite her humble origins. "Let music connoisseurs of later generations know," he proclaims, "that there was a courtesan (*fu jiaoshu*) living in the House of Black Jade who served her master with more than her sexual allure" 令後世賞音亦知黛玉軒有副校書者非獨以色事人.[23] An early nineteenth-century gazetteer that copied this preface verbatim interprets Double Virtue's identity frankly as that of a "singsong girl" 歌兒.[24] One might think of the House of Black Jade, built by Zhang for Double Virtue, as an ideal sanctuary for courtesans in possession of the virtuosity and knowledge of northern drama—a dream home that Pan and Han might have dreamed of providing for their Nimble Beauty. Pan entitled Double Virtue's biography *The Story of the House of Black Jade* (*Daiyu xuan ji* 黛玉軒記).

With *The Northern Elegance* on his desk, Han would have had all the tools he needed to rigorously follow the standard formulas passed down from Zhu Quan. Yet he chose to produce "imperfections" that defied Qi's praise. Han's innovations aligned with a lower level within the hierarchy, that is, with contemporary popular-song anthologies that preserved traces of the living tradition of brothel performances, including *New Songs of a Surpassing Age* (*Shengshi xinsheng* 盛世新聲; pref. 1517), *Select Flowers from the Forest of Song* (*Cilin zhaiyan* 詞林摘艷; pref. 1525), *Songs in a Harmonious Era* (*Yongxi yuefu* 雍熙樂府; pref. 1566), and *A String of Lyric Pearls*

22. Pan, "Daiyu xuan ji" 黛玉軒記, in *Genshi waiji*, *juan* 4, 1a–4b, CMCS, vol. 193, 537–39. Double Virtue is the name of the Queen Mother of the West's maidservant in Daoist lore. Here Zhang gave this style name to his concubine because of the love token in their dramatic love story—there was a legal case involving a precious *qin* zither Zhang bequeathed to her, whose name happened to mean "a precious *qin* zither." Double Virtue's name Baoqin also means "a precious *qin* zither." In their happy marriage, therefore, the two "precious *qin* zithers" became one.

23. Zhang Xuan, "Beiya tici" 北雅題詞, *Beiya*, 3a. The original is in the National Library, Beijing; another copy of the same edition is preserved in Naikaku Bunko, Tokyo.

24. "Fanyu Xianzhi benzhuan" 番禺縣誌本傳 in Han Shanggui, *Duoyun shanfang yigao* 朵雲山房遺稿, early nineteenth-century edition, *juanshou* 卷首, 5a. Facsimile e-book on google.com.

(*Yuefu qunzhu* 樂府群珠).[25] Examples of this kind of song abound in *Soaring the Sky*.

The two examples examined in the next few pages—(1) a tune pattern called *Little Peach Blossoms in Red* (*Xiao taohong* 小桃紅), relocated from its proper position to the beginning of a northern song suite of the Yue Mode (*Yuediao* 越調);[26] and (2) a southern tune pattern, *Cassia Twigs Scenting of Fragrance* (*Guizhi xiang* 桂枝香), misplaced in a northern song suite of the Xianlü Mode (*Xianlü gong* 仙呂宮)—suggest Han's unconventional use of tune sequencing by intermixing southern tunes with northern ones, an intermixing that nonetheless conformed to popular renditions of the time.

My first example, the fourteen arias in the Yue Mode, comes from scene 4 of *Soaring the Sky*. Conventionally, the tune pattern *Fighting Quails* (*Dou anchun* 鬥鵪鶉) should open the song sequence, a rule unanimously followed by existing Ming imprints of Yuan drama; and *Little Peach Blossoms in Red* is supposed to appear in the sixth or seventh position in the sequence. Yet Han switched their places in this song suite, a displacement which would raise many critics' eyebrows (though Qi Biaojia seems to have ignored it). However, to use *Little Peach Blossoms in Red* as the first northern song in a Yue Mode suite would not have surprised brothel performers who were familiar with a popular song suite entitled "A Summer Scene" (*Xiajing* 夏景) in the Yue Mode, which takes the form of a mixture of southern and northern arias (*nanbei hetao* 南北合套):[27]

1. southern song: *Xiu tingzhen* 繡停針
2. northern song: *Xiao taohong* (*Little Peach Blossoms in Red*)
3. northern song: *Hesheng daohe* 合笙道合
4. northern song: *Tiaoxiao ling* 調笑令
5. southern song: *Shan make* 山馬客

25. *Shengshi xinsheng*, fac. rpr. (Beijing: Wenxue guji kanxingshe, 1955); Zhang Lu 張祿, comp., *Cilin zhaiyan*, fac. rpr. in *Xuxiu siku quanshu* 續修四庫全書 (Shanghai: Shanghai guji chubanshe, 2002), vol. 1740, hereafter XXSKQS; *Yongxi yuefu*, fac. rpr. XXSKQS, vol. 1740; *Yuefu qunzhu*, modern edition edited by Lu Qian 盧前 (Shanghai: Shangwu yinshuguan, 1957). A variation of the below-quoted anonymous song sung by the fifth wife, for example, appears in the *Yongxi yuefu*, *ce* 20, p. 7a, II. 2–4, and the *Yuefu qunzhu*, p. 57, II. 8–9.

26. There is a southern tune pattern with the same title which appears in both the Zhenggong 正宮 Mode and the Yue Mode. The distinction between the southern and northern tune with the same title is clear: the southern tune has eleven or twelve lines, the northern tune eight lines. When the southern tune appears in the Zhenggong mode, it commonly is placed at the beginning.

27. *Cilin zhaiyan*, *juan* 10, *Gui ji* 癸集, page 甲乙-丙丑, in XXSKQS, 1740:296.

6. southern song: *Yi duojiao* 憶多嬌
7. northern song: *Tu si'er* 禿廝兒
8. northern song: *Sheng Yaowang* 聖藥王
9. northern song: *Jin jiaoye* 金蕉葉
10. southern song: *Baozi ling* 豹子令
11. southern song: *Meihua jiu* 梅花酒
12. southern coda: *Yuyin* 餘音

Faced with a choice between the textual and the oral traditions, between the banal and the novel, Han decided upon the latter. He must have known that brothel performers, for whom he was writing the play, were familiar with or even welcomed the freshness of this unusual tune organization. It is a hasty mistake to ascribe this special arrangement to Han's ignorance of northern song formularies. Any such "flaws" would have been quite easy to stamp out for erudite readers of northern song formularies such as Han and his literati friends.

My next example, the "misplacement" of a southern tune pattern entitled *Cassia Twigs Scenting of Fragrance* in a northern song suite, occurs in both scene 1 and scene 6 of *Soaring the Sky*. The repeated use of the same sequence reinforces my identification of it as a conscious choice of the playwright rather than a careless mistake. *Cassia Twigs Scenting of Fragrance* is unerringly a southern song since it never appears in any northern song formularies. However, we find this tune in a typical "mixture of southern and northern arias" in *Songs in a Harmonious Era*;[28] furthermore, for this southern-northern song suite, we find an earlier model in the early fourteenth-century southern drama (*nanxi* 南戲) *A Playboy from a Noble House Opts for the Wrong Career* (*Huanmen zidi cuolishen* 宦門子弟錯立身) included in *The Grand Canon of the Yongle Reign* (*Yongle dadian* 永樂大典, 1407). The comparison in table 2 shows a rough three-step expansion of the song suite from the southern drama to the sixteenth-century song anthology *Songs in a Harmonious Era*, and thence to *Soaring the Sky*.[29] Clearly, there is a mini-sequence familiar

28. *Yongxi yuefu*, *juan* 4, 65b, "Shanghua shi nan bei diao" 賞花時南北調, reprint in XXSKQS, 1740:454.

29. Qian Nanyang 錢南揚, *Yongle dadian xiwen sanzhong jiaozhu* 永樂大典戲文三種校注 (Beijing: Zhonghua shuju, 2009). For an English translation, see Wilt Idema and Stephen H. West, "A Playboy from a Noble House Opts for the Wrong Career," in *Chinese Theater 1100–1450: A Source Book* (Wiesbaden: Steiner, 1982), 235–78; alternatively, see William Dolby, "Grandee's Son Takes the Wrong Career," in *Eight Chinese Plays: From the Thirteenth Century to the Present* (New York: Columbia University Press, 1978), 30–52. For an analysis of the lack of "spectatorship" in this play's famous self-reflexive moments, see Ling Hon Lam, "What Is Wrong with the Wrong Career?

Table 2. The Use of *Cassia Twigs Scenting of Fragrance* in Three Similar Sequences Over Time

Songs in a Harmonious Era	Scene 5 of *A Playboy from a Noble House Opts for the Wrong Career*	Scene 1 of *Soaring the Sky*
(mid-16th century)	(early 14th century)	(1610)
		Northern song: *Dian jiangchun* 點絳唇
	Southern Song: *Zui luopo* 醉落魄	Northern song: *Hunjiang long* 混江龍
Northern song: *Shanghua shi* 賞花時	Northern song: *Shanghua shi*	Northern song: *You hulu* 油葫蘆
Southern song: *Paige* 排歌	Southern song: *Paige*	Northern song: *Tianxia le* 天下樂
*Northern song: *Nezha ling* 哪吒令	*Northern song: *Nezha ling*	*Northern song: *Nezha ling*
Southern song: *Paige*	Southern song: *Paige*	
*Northern song: *Quetazhi* 鵲踏枝	*Northern song: *Quetazhi*	*Northern song: *Quetazhi*
*Southern song: *Guizhi xiang* (*Cassia Twigs Scenting of Fragrance*)		*Southern song: *Guizhi xiang* (*Cassia Twigs Scenting of Fragrance*)
*Northern song: *Jisheng cao* 寄生草		*Northern song: *Jisheng cao*
Southern song: *Anleshen* 安樂神	Southern song: *Anleshen*	Northern song: *Jinzhan'er* 金盞兒
Northern song: *Liuyao xu* 六幺序	Northern song: *Liuyao xu*	Northern song: *Houting hua* 後庭花
Southern song: *Weisheng* 尾聲	Southern song: *Weisheng*	Northern song: *Qingge'er* 青歌兒
		Northern song: *Liuye'er* 柳葉兒
		Northern song: *Weisheng*

Note: Similar tune arrangements are marked with an asterisk [*].

to the courtesan of the day who performed the *xiansuo* style—*Nezha ling, Quetazhi, Guizhi xiang, Jisheng cao*—which evolved from a shorter model represented by the fourteenth-century southern drama.

When and how this mix of southern and northern took place in the brothel performances of the *xiansuo* style can never be answered by more than speculation. But one important factor that has often been ignored in modern scholarship is the *xiansuo* style's musical capacity to render both northern and southern plays; in addition, the historical agent—brothel performers of both sexes—remained quite stable, which guaranteed the continuity within their pedagogical traditions and repertories. Hypothetically, the northern and southern components had long been mixed by brothel *xiansuo* performers of high bandwidth. The earliest literary example is the early fourteenth-century drama listed in table 2, whose setting happened to be Jurchen Jin (1115–1234) brothels. Our best historical source for understanding the inclusiveness of the courtesan's *xiansuo* repertoire is Hu Wenhuan's 胡文煥 (fl. 1592–1617) *Categorized Selections from Essential Dramas* (*Qunyin leixuan* 群音類選), published no later than 1596, which categorizes theatrical and nontheatrical arias by musical genre.[30] The category of "northern style," or *beiqiang* 北腔, I contend, denotes the *xiansuo* style specialized in by brothel performers before the 1590s. The defining feature of *beiqiang* is the use of tune sequencing in the manner that courtesan-performers would have been familiar with. With its emphasis on performance rather than literary genres, Hu Wenhuan's *beiqiang* category offers us a precious glimpse into the sixteenth-century musical experiences of the *xiansuo* style.

The six volumes of that category consist of both northern and southern dramas. For example, we find in the *beiqiang* category a northern song suite excerpted from Liang Chenyu's 梁辰魚 (1519–1591) *chuanqi* play *Washing Gauze* (*Huansha ji* 浣紗記; ca. 1570), deemed by standard historiography to be the first drama ever written "exclusively" for *kunqu* music.[31] This example proves the boundary-breaking power of actors. To borrow Michel de Certeau's metaphor, people walk through the grids of city streets, making turns and detours, following their own "walking rhetoric."[32] The presumption

A Genealogy of Playgrounds," chap. 3 in his monograph, *The Spatiality of Emotion in Early Modern China* (New York: Columbia University Press, 2018), 91–146.

30. Hu Wenhuan, comp., *Qunyin leixuan*. See *Qunyin leixuan jiaojian* 群音類選校箋, ed. Li Zhiyuan 李志遠 (Beijing: Zhonghua shuju, 2018).

31. To a further analytical reading of the heroine as a prototype of late Ming courtesans we will return in chapter 4.

32. Michel de Certeau, *The Practice of Everyday Life*, trans. Steven Rendall (Berkeley: University of California Press, 1984), 85.

that actors walked only on routes mapped out by literary rules is a serious misconception.

The most vivid account of the courtesan's *xiansuo* renditions of both southern and northern plays is found in the late sixteenth-century novel *The Plum in the Golden Vase* (*Jin Ping Mei cihua* 金瓶梅詞話). Despite the Song-dynasty setting of its plot, prevailing scholarship has regarded this novel as a reliable source for studying late Ming daily musical activities due to its mimetic representation of the pleasures of late Ming life.[33] The novel's anonymous author often chose to record verbatim a northern or southern drama conducted in the *xiansuo* style, describing the circumstances in detail—although, curiously, all the full-fledged stagings of southern dramas provided by noncourtesan performers receive only a passing mention of their play titles. The contrast between the lavish versus the meager descriptions of plays in these two genres suggests that the novelist makes it a point, whenever possible, to reveal the reality of the courtesans' performing repertories.[34]

33. David Rolston, "Research Note: Introducing a Resource on Music and Oral Performing Literature in the Ming Novel *Jin Ping Mei cihua* Made Available in Celebration of the Completion of David Tod Roy's Translation," *CHINOPERL papers* 33, no. 1 (2014): 94–95; David T. Roy, "The Use of Songs as a Means of Self-Expression and Self-Characterization in the *Chin P'ing Mei*," *Chinese Literature: Essays, Articles, Reviews (CLEAR)* 20 (1998): 101–26; Shang Wei, "The Making of the Everyday World: *Jin Ping Mei cihua* and Encyclopedias for Daily Use," in *Dynastic Crisis and Cultural Innovation: From the Late Ming to the Late Qing and Beyond*, ed. David Der-wei Wang and Shang Wei (Cambridge, MA: Harvard University Press, 2005), 63–92. Quite influential is Shang Wei's view of the novel as an "encyclopedic cultural form" that "draws a great variety of texts to present Ximen Qing's daily existence and leisure activities" (79); but Roy's article emphasizes another dimension of the use of popular songs in the novel as a rhetorical technique, which satirically reveals "the inadequacy of such traditional stereotypes to convey the complexity and problematic quality of human reality" through contrasting the emotional content of the lyrics with that of the singer in a fictional setting (126). Other scholars who painstakingly sorted out source materials for studies of Chinese drama include Feng Yuanjun and Patrick Hanan. See Feng, "*Jin Ping Mei cihua* zhong de wenxue shiliao" 金瓶梅詞話中的文學史料, in *Guju shuohui* 古劇說匯 (Beijing: Zuojia chubanshe, 1956), 170–213; Hanan, "Sources of the *Chin P'ing Mei*," *Asia Major* 10, no 2 (1963): 23–67.

34. Possibly the entertainment world represented in *The Plum in the Golden Vase* is one near the 1570s. Xu Shuofang applied the same reasoning to the fact that no mention of the word *kunqu* is found in scenes of dramatic performance in the novel and concluded that the completion of the novel must have been at some point between 1547 and approximately 1570. Although I agree with his sensibility to the abrupt change in courtesan performances during the early Wanli reign, admittedly, his understanding of the *kunqu* history is mistaken: *Kunqu* was not established as the dominant mode of performance in brothels until after the 1570s, when Liang Chenyu's *Washing*

In the novel, nine northern song suites (plus two arias excerpted from northern dramas) are performed by courtesans or by boy actors who serve in the same brothels with them—conceivably they all share the same repertoire and compatible performance styles. These arias belong to seven *zaju* dramas, including four Yuan *zaju* plays (nos. 1–4) and three early Ming *zaju* plays (nos. 5–7):

1. *The Story of the Western Wing* (*Xixiang ji* 西廂記) in chapters 58, 68, and 74
2. *Marriage Destiny over Two Lifetimes* (*Liangshi yinyuan* 兩世因緣) in chapter 41
3. *The Disembodied Soul* (*Qiannü lihun* 倩女離魂) in chapter 54
4. *A Red Leaf Afloat in the Palace Moat* (*Yushui liu hongye* 御水流紅葉) in chapter 61
5. *Gold Boy and Emerald Girl* (*Jintong yunü* 金童玉女) in chapter 32
6. *Heroes of the Storm* (*Fengyun hui* 風雲會) in chapter 71
7. *People United in Marriage* (*Shijian pei'ou* 世間配偶) in chapter 72

Note that Nos. 1, 2, and 4 above have excerpts included in the *beiqiang* volumes of Hu's *Categorized Selections from Essential Dramas.* Parallel to the seven northern dramas, six southern plays—*The Decorated Pavilion* (*Cailou ji* 彩樓記, categorized as *beiqiang* in Hu's anthology), *The Lute* (*Pipa ji* 琵琶記), *The Heaven-Blessed Reunion of the Mother and Son* (*Zimu yuanjia* 子母冤家), *Zhang Cuilian* 張翠蓮, *Lin Zhaode* 林招得, and *The Precious Sword* (*Baojian ji* 寶劍記)—rendered in the *xiansuo*-style group singing, appear in chapters 20, 27, 46, 61, and 70, respectively. Except for *The Lute*, whose performers are the protagonist and his concubines, the other five plays are all performed by courtesans, boy singers, and, on one occasion, a blind female entertainer. The fictional description must have reflected a normative practice in the brothel repertories of the day, that is, having almost equal components of the southern and northern plays executed in the *xiansuo* style.

Han's mixing of southern and northern tunes, as is exemplified above, stands outside the compositional paradigm defined by elite formularies. More boldly, he also reshuffled the established Yuan suite structuring (*liantao* 聯套) and created new combinations of various musical modes. The best example is scene 16 of *Soaring the Sky*, as shown in table 3. There is a hidden

---

Gauze was written for brothel performances, as I will argue in chapter 4. See Xu Shuofang, "*Jin Ping Mei* chengshu xintan" 金瓶梅成書新探, *Zhonghua wenshi congshu* 中華文史論叢, no. 3 (1984): 159–98.

ingeniousness in the *Weisheng*, or coda, of this song suite: it differs drastically from that in the same mode in Zhu Quan's and other formularies of northern songs. It has six lines arranged in the following pattern: 6 words + 6 words + 8 words + 10 words + 7 words + 10 words. Although this Shang Mode coda has many varieties in the popular song anthology *Select Flowers from the Forest of Song*, consisting of three, or five, or six, or seven lines, the six-line pattern with a similar word structure outnumbers other variations.[35] In Zhu Quan's formulary, in contrast, the only example of a Shang Mode coda has eight lines, each with a different number of words:[36] 10 words + 5 words + 5 words + 3 words + 3 words + 8 words + 7 words + 10 words. Briefly, Han devised an unconventional ending aria that was informed by brothel performances rather than conforming to the specifications of authoritative formularies. He took a fascinating detour to fit his play squarely and conveniently into the courtesan-performer's mental formulary.

The evidence just supplied suffices to reinforce my reading of Han's general design toward a performance that was differently institutionalized from the textual tradition. Han emulated the tune sequencing in the northern drama *The Story of the Western Wing*, a staple in the courtesan's *xiansuo* repertoire since its completion in the fourteenth century. A little more context is necessary to understand the significance of this play in the courtesan's performance tradition. In the late Ming, this canonical work was commonly known as the *"The Western Wing" in Its Northern Version* (*Bei Xixiang* 北西廂, hereafter the Northern Version), in parallel with the Southern Version, or *Nan Xixiang* 南西廂 (hereafter the Southern Version). Wang Anqi and Ling Hon Lam rightly stress that the stage life of the Northern Version continued to thrive in the "vulgar" Yiyang 弋陽 musical genre, sharing attention with the Southern Version, which was an adaptation of the original Northern Version made by two lesser-known dramatists for *kunqu*'s predecessor between 1520 and 1540. The Southern Version flourished in elite theater, where it was favored by the upper class of society due to its musical rendition in the refined *kunqu* style.[37] The proposal of such an antithesis between

35. *Cilin zhaiyan*, in XXSKQS, *juan* 7, vol. 1740.

36. Zhu, *Taihe zhengyin pu*, 185. In addition, Li Yu's 李玉 (ca. 1610–after 1670) northern song formulary heavily influenced by *kunqu* practices as opposed to *xiansuo*, *Beici guangzheng pu* 北詞廣正譜, puts forward yet another different pattern that has four lines, facsimile reprint in Wang Qiugui 王秋桂, in *Shanben xiqu congkan* 善本戲曲叢刊 (Taipei: Xuesheng shuju, 1987), 81:496–97.

37. Ling Hon Lam, "The Matriarch's Private Ear: Performance, Reading, Censorship and the Fabrication of Interiority in 'The Story of the Stone,'" *Harvard Journal of Asiatic Studies* 65, no. 2 (2005): 367–70. Wang Anqi 王安祈, *Ming xiqu wulun* 明戲曲

Table 3. Unconventional Suite Structuring in Scene 16 of *Soaring the Sky*

Xianlü Mode Shang Mode 商調	*Shanghua shi* (2 arias) *Ji xianbin* 集賢賓 *Xiaoyao le* 逍遙樂 *Jinju xiang* 金菊香 *Wuye'er* 梧葉兒 *Cu hulu* 醋葫蘆 (4 arias)	Unconventional mixing of a traditional "wedge" (*xiezi* 楔子) section—the two *Shanghua shi* arias in the Xianlü Mode—with a Shang Mode song suite.
Huangzhong Mode 黃鍾	*Jiejie gao* 節節高	Conventional borrowing of the tune pattern *Jiejie gao* into a Xianlü Mode song suite.
Xianlü Mode	*Yuanhe ling* 元和令 *Shangma jiao* 上馬嬌 *Sheng hulu* 勝葫蘆 *Houting hua*	Unconventional insertion of a Xianlü Mode sequence within a Shang Mode song suite.
Shang Mode	*Fengluan yin* 鳳鑾吟 *Weisheng*	– *Unconventional. See explanations in the text.

these two versions, however, disregards the third type of performance of the Northern Version, namely, the *xiansuo* singing by brothel performers. The division of the Northern Version and the Southern Version is clear in Hu Wenhuan's *Categorized Selections from Essential Dramas*, which devotes almost its entire first volume of the category of "northern style" to selected scenes from the Northern Version and categorizes the Southern Version as the "Official Music," or *guanqiang* 官腔, an honorific term for *kunqu*.[38] It may not be coincidental that in the novel *The Plum in the Golden Vase*, full-fledged staging by itinerant troupes is always performed in accord with the Southern Version, whereas group *xiansuo* singing consists without exception of excerpts from the Northern Version, sung by brothel performers.

In the history of brothel performance, the Northern Version was an essential component, a sine qua non. In 1604, five years before the debut of Han's play, Ma Xianglan 馬湘蘭 (1548–1604), head of one of the largest

五論 (Taipei: Da'an chubanshe, 1990), 132–33. *Shanben xiqu congkan* provides strong textual evidence for this observation: excerpted scenes (*zhezi xi*) from the Northern Version were found in many Wanli-reign (1573–1620) song anthologies included in this collectanea of facsimiles, including *Yuefu jinghua* 樂府菁華, *Cilin yizhi* 詞林一枝, *Baneng zoujin* 八能奏錦, *Da Ming chun* 大明春, *Zhaijin qiyin* 摘錦奇音, *Yaotian yue* 堯天樂, *Yuefu wanxiang xin* 樂府萬象新, and *Yuefu yushu ying* 樂府玉樹英.

38. Hu, comp., *Qunyin leixuan*, "guanqiang," *juan* 6–26, 1–1051.

brothel houses in the Old Compound (it housed her three "daughters" and a troupe of no fewer than fifteen actresses), created a cultural sensation by traveling to Suzhou with her entire troupe to mount onstage the *"The Western Wing" in Its Northern Version* for her long-time lover Wang Zhideng's 王穉登 (1535–1612) seventieth birthday.[39] She died shortly after returning to Nanjing. According to Shen Defu, the year of Ma's death marked the demise of the living tradition of staging the Northern Version; five years later, Nimble Beauty's resignation from brothel life further denoted the end of the "authentic" *xiansuo* performance onstage in general.[40]

The highly significant position of the Northern Version in the courtesan's repertoire meant that Han would have aspired to recreate a similar triumph in brothel performances with his *Soaring the Sky*. Critic Qi Biaojia observed that Han "used the lyrics of *Soaring the Sky* to emulate those of the *Story of the Western Wing*" 以凌雲詞擬西廂.[41] Here *Story of the Western Wing* refers neither to the Southern Version performed in the *kunqu* style, nor to the variegated Northern Version performed in the "vulgar" Yiyang style or its subgenres, but to the Northern Version in the *xiansuo* style, signifying the time-honored brothel tradition passed down from the early Ming. The best strategy for Han, therefore, was to stick to the Northern Version's tune sequencing in his new composition. Table 4 shows the similarities between the Zhenggong Mode 正宮 song suite in scene 19 in *Soaring the Sky* and that in scene 3, act 4 of the Northern Version. Except for minor changes—the addition of aria no. 7 and the reduction of two refrains of the ending tune *Kids Playing* (*Shua hai'er* 耍孩兒)—Han used the Northern Version as his prototype. Furthermore, the usage of *Kids Playing* in the Northern Version differs significantly from published song formularies, whose examples are too numerous to list here;[42] Han opted without fail to follow the Northern Version rather than published formularies, which I would argue was a deliberate choice to ease the mind of his courtesan-performer Nimble Beauty.

Thus far, we have explored manifestations of Han's practical consciousness of a living, present oral tradition carried on in brothels vis-à-vis a textualist rendition designated in published formularies. It is a mistake to ignore

39. Feng Mengzhen 馮夢禎 (1548–1606; *jinshi* 1577), *Kuaixuetang riji* 快雪堂日記, *juan* 15, ed. Ding Xiaoming (Nanjing: Fenghuang chubanshe, 2010), 210; Shen Defu, *Guqu zayan*, 646 (in Yu and Sun, 69); Qian Qianyi 錢謙益 (1582–1664; *jinshi* 1610), *Liechao shiji xiaozhuan* 列朝詩集小傳 (Beijing: Zhonghua shuju, 1959), 765.

40. Shen, *Guqu zayan*, 646 (in Yu and Sun, 69).

41. Qi, *Yuanshantang qupin*, 426.

42. For example, one can find many variations of this tune in different musical modes in Li Yu's *Beici guangzheng pu*. In Zhu Quan's formulary, this tune only appears once in the *Banshe diao* Mode 般涉調.

Table 4. Comparison between the Song Suite of Scene 19 in *Soaring the Sky* and the Song Suite of Scene 3, Act 4 of the *Northern Version of the Story of the Western Wing*

	Scene 19, *Soaring the Sky*		Scene 3, Act 4, the *Northern Version of the Story of the Western Wing*
1	*Duanzhenghao* 端正好	1	*Duanzhenghao*
2	*Gun xiuqiu* 滚繡球	2	*Gun xiuqiu*
3	*Daodao ling* 叨叨令	3	*Daodao ling*
4	*Tuo bushan* 脱布衫	4	*Tuo bushan*
5	*Xiao Liangzhou* 小梁州	5	*Xiao Liangzhou*
6	*Yao* 幺	6	*Yao*
7	*Tianshui ling* 甜水令	–	
8	*Shang xiaolou* 上小樓	7	*Shang xiaolou*
9	*Yao*	8	*Yao*
10	*Manting fang* 滿庭芳	9	*Manting fang*
11	*Kuaihuosan* 快活三	10	*Kuaihuosan*
12	*Chao tianzi* 朝天子	11	*Chao tianzi*
13	*Sibian jing* 四邊靜	12	*Sibian jing*
14	*Shua hai'er*	13	*Shua hai'er*
–		14	*Wu sha* 五煞 (1st refrain of No. 13)
–		15	*Si sha* 四煞 (2nd refrain of No. 13)
15	*San sha* 三煞 (1st refrain of No. 14)	16	*San sha* (3rd refrain of No. 13)
16	*Er sha* 二煞 (2nd refrain of No. 14)	17	*Er sha* (4th refrain of No. 13)
17	*Yi sha* 一煞 (3rd refrain of No. 14)	18	*Yi sha* (5th refrain of No. 13)
18	*Weisheng*	19	*Weisheng*

the autonomy of the courtesans' *xiansuo* performance tradition and exclude it from the dichotomy of *kunqu* (high culture) versus Yiyang (low culture). One adverse result of the exclusion of the courtesan from our interpretive models of late Ming drama is an overemphasis on formularies (i.e., the high-brow written genre), thereby cutting off human performance from textual analysis. The examples discussed above nonetheless reveal a typical mentality of Yuan *zaju* drama connoisseurs of the Ming: writing for courtesans who were capable of the "authentic" *xiansuo* style, the last vestiges of Yuan performance separable from prescribed forms, was honorable.

During the early seventeenth-century crisis of the *xiansuo* performance, Han was far from the only dramatist who contributed to this courtesan-friendly subgenre. In this sense, *Soaring the Sky* can be seen as an early seventeenth-century effort to expand the *beiqiang* category in Hu Wenhuan's *Categorized Selections from Essential Dramas*, whose existing volumes contain only fourteen titles of the *xiansuo* style specialized in by brothel performers, with two volumes entirely missing. If one were to name some of the titles that must have been included in the lost volumes of Hu's *beiqiang* selections, the earliest model brothel production would have to be Liang Chenyu's *zaju* drama *Ms. Red Silk* (*Hongxian nü* 紅線女), completed sometime between 1567 and 1570, which has been discussed in the Introduction and to which we will return at several points in this book. A predecessor of *Soaring the Sky* by almost a half century, it was presented in a full-fledged ten-day season by the Nanjing courtesan Ma Xianglan's private troupe. The second play that fits the bill would be Mei Dingzuo's 梅鼎祚 (1549–1615) northern drama *The Barbarian Slave* (*Kunlun nu* 崑崙奴, 1584), which assigns to the title role, that of a heroic male character, all the sung parts.[43]

There seems to have been a second tide of new northern dramas for brothel performance at the turn of the sixteenth century, roughly from 1598 to 1605. Around 1605, Ling Mengchu 凌濛初 (1580–1644) completed *"Ms. Red Whisk" in Its Northern Version* (*Bei Hongfu* 北紅拂), in contrast to Zhang Fengyi's 張鳳翼 (1527–1613) southern play *Ms. Red Whisk* (*Hongfu ji* 紅拂記, ca. 1545). Assigning the title role to the heroine and giving all the arias to her instead of to the Barbarian Slave as in Mei Dingzuo's northern drama, Ling transformed the story into a stronger expression of the diva, and in this sense echoes Liang's *Ms. Red Silk*. The thematic innovation against Mei's *The Barbarian Slave*, Ling declares, was the driving force behind the literary creation: "No one can deny Miss Red Whisk's intelligence and wisdom on a par with wise men" 谁谓其智乃出丈夫下哉.[44] Like Han's *Soaring the Sky*, Ling's play showcases the diva's distinctive and dominant voice.

An allusion to this play being performed in the *xiansuo* style is embedded in Zou Diguang's 鄒迪光 (1550–1626; *jinshi* 1574) poem, written between 1604 and 1626, entitled "Gathering with Friends in the Hall of One Finger, Watching the *Stories of the Barbarian Slave and Miss Red Silk*, on the Sixteenth Night of the First Month" 正月十六夜集友人於一指堂觀演崑崙奴紅線故事.[45] Whether or not the play was presented by Zou's boy actors or a female

43. Yuan Hongdao 袁宏道 (1568–1610; *jinshi* 1592) quotes Xu Wei's 徐渭 (1521–1593) assessment of the style of *Kunlun nu*: "It follows the style of (Liang Chenyu's) southern play *Washing Gauze*" 謂其用南曲浣紗體也. See Yuan, "Gedaixiao xu" 歌代嘯序 in Yu and Sun, eds., *Lidai quhua huibian Mingdai bian*, 2:412. As I have emphasized, northern song suites from *Washing Gauze* belong to the *beiqiang* category.

44. Ling, "Hongfu zaju xiaoyin" 紅拂雜劇小引, in *Bei Hongfu*, Chongzhen edition, published by Ling Mengchu, original in Shanghai Library.

45. Zou Diguang, *Shiyuzhai ji* 石語齋集, facsimile reprint in CMCS, *jibu*, vol. 159, *juan* 9; Hou Rongchuan 侯榮川 and Lu Lin 陸林, eds., *Mei Dingzuo xiquji* 梅鼎祚戲曲集 (Hefei: Huangshan shushe, 2016), 46. The Hall of One Finger, located in

troupe is a matter of conjecture, but the poem mentions a plucked instrument with thirteen wild-goose-shaped bridges 十三鴈柱, a clear reference to the zither, or *zheng* 箏, that was one of the signature string instruments in a full-scale *xiansuo* performance. In *The Plum in the Golden Vase*, the protagonist's favorite maidservant happens also to specialize in this instrument, studying it under the instruction of a boy singer from a brothel.

Around the same time as Ling's *"Ms. Red Whisk" in Its Northern Version* (completed between 1598 and 1605), Han Shanggui's two Cantonese friends Zhang Xuan and Deng Yunxiao each wrote a nonextant drama composed exclusively for *xiansuo* performance.[46] After publishing *The Northern Elegance* in 1602, Zhang Xuan could not stop mourning the loss of his beloved concubine Double Virtue and hence began to write a northern drama entitled *The Spring Dream* (*Chunmeng ji* 春夢記) as a second project to commemorate her. The inspiration came from his voracious reading of roughly a hundred Yuan dramas in the Wanli emperor's royal library in 1598, the year in which many personal events had happened to him: bringing his newlywed concubine Double Virtue to his new prestigious position in Beijing; hiring a female teacher for her so that she could study *xiansuo* singing; and then her sickness caused by her travail of editing *The Northern Elegance*, which Zhang was convinced, in hindsight, had led to her untimely death four years later.[47] It is not surprising that growing out of his traumatic memories, the play was never brought to completion. In 1608 he found his disintegrating earlier manuscript and gave it up completely.[48]

Perhaps this was why, some years later, Zhang Xuan published his prominent friend Deng Yunxiao's play *The Bamboo Grove* (*Zhulin ji* 竹林記), which modern scholar Fu Xihua lists as anonymous in his *Complete Catalogue of*

Zou's garden estate in the Hui Mountain 惠山 in his hometown Wuxi, was his favorite space for hosting small-scale performances and banquets and appears frequently in his poems written in the first two decades of the seventeenth century.

46. For dating of the completion of *Lingyun ji*, see Luo, Preface to *Ming guben chuanqi* Lingyun ji, unpaginated.

47. Pan, "Daiyu xuan ji."

48. Zhang Xuan, "Zhulin xiaoji xu" 竹林小記序, in *Xiyuan cungao* 西園存稿, *juan* 16, 31a–35b. For *Xiyuan cungao*, there are photo reprints in the Gest Library in Princeton University, Hishi copy of the original in Naikaku Bunko, nos. 820–831; one facsimile reprint of the Naikaku Bunko edition is preserved in the University of Michigan Library, 1973, digitized version in the Hathitrust Digital Library. For an additional facsimile reprint of the National Library edition, see *Mingdai Shiwenji zhenben congkan* 明代詩文集珍本叢刊 (Beijing: Guojia tushuguan chubanshe, 2019), vols. 120–25.

Ming Zaju Dramas (*Mingdai zaju quanmu* 明代雜劇全目).[49] Deng was the magistrate of Changzhou 長洲 (present-day Suzhou) and Censor in Nanjing from 1598 to the early 1600s, and networked with famous local drama connoisseurs such as Zhang Fengyi and Xu Zichang 許自昌 (1578–1623). His friend Zhang Xuan acclaims his achievements in popular culture in the following words: "The play had prevailed in the pleasure quarters, making Deng's repute comparable to the Tang poet Wang Wei's mass popularity among Tang courtesans" 歌樓伎館無不如郵亭遊女歌王摩詰詩.[50] The thematic appropriateness of the play, to be staged in a brothel setting, is also striking: it tells of the ascension of a third-century literatus named Ji Kang 嵇康 to the Realm of the Immortals accompanied by his favorite courtesans.[51]

Consisting of a motley of southern and northern suites (eleven scenes in total), *The Bamboo Grove* bemused the critic Qi Biaojia in its unruly mix of the southern and northern: "It is unclear for what music categories *The Bamboo Grove* was written" 腔調不明.[52] The problem was that, like *Soaring the Sky*, Deng's play apparently conformed to routine practices in brothel *xiansuo* performances. These practices were considered unrecognizable literary digressions from the "norm." Qi's comment was consonant with the increasingly marginalized enterprise of *xiansuo* and with the unapologetic passion of writing for *kunqu* among literati since the late sixteenth century. By Qi Biaojia's productive years after 1631, the admiration in which Han, Deng, Pan, and other connoisseurs had bathed the courtesan who excelled in *xiansuo* singing had dried up. Concomitantly, the momentum of writing for the courtesan's *xiansuo* rendition had died down.

One of the last holdouts against the increasingly dominant *kunqu* style in the literary field is described in Zhang Xuan's 1632 preface, an account of a 1622 performance delivered by an itinerant troupe traveling from Wanling 宛陵 (present-day Xuancheng 宣城, Anhui province) to Boluo 博羅 (present-

49. See Wu Shuyin 吳書蔭, "*Zhulin xiaoji* zuozhe kao" 竹林小記作者考, *Wenxian* 文獻 1 (1992): 262–65. Fu Xihua, *Mingdai zaju quanmu* 明代雜劇全目 (Beijing: Zuojia chubanshe, 1958), 279. According to Zhang Xuan, "Baiyulou ji xu" 白玉樓記序 (*Xiyuan cungao*, *juan* 16, 51a–53b), Han Shanggui was the author of another play, *Qinglian ji* 青蓮記, completed before Deng's *Zhulin ji*. I suspect that this play was for *xiansuo* performance in nature, not to be confused with an earlier play of the same name written by Dai Zilu 戴子魯, whose five scenes appear in Hu Wenhuan's anthology in the *guanqiang/kunqu* catalogue (*juan* 14) and an additional scene was included in *Yuelu yin* 月露音 (preface 1616, comp. by Lingxu zi 淩虛子, facsimile reprint in *Shanben xiqu congkan*).

50. Zhang Xuan, "Zhulin xiaoji xu." Also see Wu, "*Zhulin xiaoji* zuozhe kao," 265.

51. Qi Biaojia, *Yuanshantang jupin* 遠山堂劇品 lists the play as anonymous under the rubric of "Good Plays" (*nengpin*). See *Zhongguo gudian xiqu lunzhu jicheng*, 6:189.

52. Qi, *Yuanshantang jupin*, 189.

day Huizhou 惠州, Guangdong province), where Zhang's garden estate was located.[53] The actors had presented Zhang with a letter of recommendation from his friend Tang Binyin 湯賓尹 (1569–1628; *jinshi* 1595), stating that "they do *kunqu*" 日此崑調也. Zhang had proceeded to assess their skills using *The Northern Elegance* that he had published twenty years before, a time capsule that defined his love for Double Virtue. He was delighted with the performers at first, and hurriedly provided a venue—likely his West Garden—for their staging, but soon concluded that "they were none but Siping-style actors [a minor branch of the 'vulgar' Yiyang style] who did a little better at cadence, articulation, and ornamentation" 亟為開場, 則四平調中稍知抗墜掩抑頂疊闗轉者. He could not help chuckling—why all the fuss about the special *kunqu*?—and wrote a reply to Tang 余因胡盧以報嘉賓. Zhang's preface goes on to compare *kunqu* with *xiansuo* in an unfair game that points out *kunqu*'s lack of viability and authenticity in rendering famous northern lyrics passed down from the Yuan and early Ming. This anecdote reveals the aesthetic clashes between Zhang's outdated taste for *xiansuo* and most literati's new favorite style, *kunqu*. But his mind was not only exactly the kind shared by those who cherished the courtesan's performance tradition but also a generative agent in the literary creativity needed for the new *xiansuo* plays.

The Courtesan's Dwindling Mental Storage of Yuan Libretti

A courtesan's memorial archive of northern drama had always been a matter of literary education because the *xiansuo* art required much more effort to master the lyrics than the music, especially for a (semi-)illiterate or blind singer. Unlike local genres of southern operas, *xiansuo* singing did not have a local dialect as a linguistic basis; the melodic contour of each tune pattern was relatively steady, not to be altered based on the linguistic tones of words. In comparison to southern operas such as *kunqu*, tune patterns rendered in the *xiansuo* style had a clearer musical identity, and each song suite had a much stabler sequencing. In the novel *The Plum in the Golden Vase*, in one client's dialogue with a courtesan, he disdainfully speaks of the *xiansuo* form as "the same couple of suites, as monotonous as a dog scratching at the door" 左右只是這兩套狗過門的.[54] When music was repetitive, training of singers focused traditionally on their mental storage of libretti rather than on mastery of the accompanying string instruments they would play.

53. Zhang, "Baiyulou ji xu," 51b.

54. *Jin Ping Mei cihua* (Hong Kong: Taiping shuju, 1993), chap. 32, 6a; David T. Roy, trans. *The Plum in the Golden Vase* (Princeton: Princeton University Press, 2001), 2:251.

Due to their argot of the Jurchen Jin and Mongolian culture, and to their lyrical nature, Yuan libretti proved to be a challenge for late Ming courtesans. We know virtually nothing about the levels of literary learning among late Ming theater women, whether full-fledged courtesans or younger singsong girls. The only clue about the existence of all-girl schools is, again, to be found in the novel *The Plum in the Golden Vase*. The protagonist's fifth concubine begins receiving an early education at the age of six, in a *nüxue* 女學 (female school) privately run by a *xiucai* 秀才 (scholar who holds the lowest/county-level degree in the civil service exams), and attends the school for three years. Very likely, the school functioned to train future singsong girls: she learns "to trace characters from books of sample calligraphy, so there are hardly any characters in the printed copies of poetry, lyrics, songs, rhapsodies that she doesn't know" 字仿也曾寫過, 甚麼詩詞歌賦唱本上字不認的.[55] She is sent to the girls' school at the juncture when her mother becomes an impecunious widow; being literate prepares her for the career of a singsong girl to support her family. She does not end up being a courtesan but is sold to a rich household to be a maidservant, sexually available to her master.

If we take this direct description to be naturalistic, as the novel's handling of other aspects of the late Ming pleasure life is, we can postulate that late Ming singsong girls may have had a few years of preliminary education, unlike medieval European monk-singers of church music who did not necessarily know what they were reciting in Latin and who eventually memorized the Psalter by rote.[56] Nonetheless, basic literacy was apparently not enough: in the 1570s, Yuan libretti met their rival in the domain of popular culture in the form of "small arias in vogue," or *shiqu* 時曲 /*shishang xiaoling* 時尚小令. Many courtesans abandoned the rigors of memorizing libretti and preferred instead to sing popular songs. Our best source on this phenomenon is the literatus He Liangjun 何良俊 (1506–1573), who declared his disappointment at the courtesan's literary retreat from sophisticated Yuan drama and embrace of the flashy *shiqu* lyrics. He complains that brothel performers of the day "no longer study and transmit ancient lyrics from *zaju* dramas" 雜劇古詞, 皆不傳習.[57] Such a contrast suggests that the courtesan's memorial archive shrank seriously during He's later years.

Walking proof of the courtesan's new literary choice in the 1570s is found in the figure of a male artist named Dun Ren 頓仁 (fl. 1510s–1570s), whom He Liangjun warmly called Old Dun and whom he hired as a music master

55. *Jin Ping Mei cihua*, chap. 78; Roy, *The Plum in the Golden Vase*, 4:612.

56. Carruthers, *The Book of Memory*, 106–11.

57. He Liangjun, *Siyouzhai congshuo* 四友齋叢說 (Beijing: Zhonghua shuju, 1983), 337; also in Yu and Sun, eds., *Lidai quhua huibian: Mingdai bian*, 1:464.

for his private female troupe. At the peak of Old Dun's professional career in 1519–1520, he had served in the royal troupe during Emperor Wuzong's (reign 1505–1521) infamous, extravagant last tour to the South. Subsequently he followed the troupe back to the court in Beijing, the center of "authentic" *xiansuo* music nourished by royal favoritism, where generations of court musicians had thrived by providing music in this style. After some years Old Dun returned home—to the Nanjing pleasure quarters—only to find that popular lyrics had invaded the traditional terrain of Yuan lyrics. "Having acquired such skills for fifty years" 懷之五十年, he told He Liangjun, "all that I was requested to sing during banquets were popular songs (*shiqu*); no one even asked about this kind of [*zaju*] aria" 供筵所唱，皆是時曲，此等辭並無人問及.[58] *Shiqu* here refers specifically to popular songs rendered in the *xiansuo* style. No brothel clients in 1570s Nanjing except for He Liangjun seem to have felt obliged to keep alive the "authentic" *xiansuo* style (which would be crowned today as an "intangible heritage" by UNESCO) by hiring Old Dun to teach his household actresses. He Liangjun could do nothing, however, to convince theater women in the public domain in Nanjing brothels to convert to the Yuan libretti.

Old Dun, like Nimble Beauty's father, belonged to the last generation of Nanjing musicians who were capable of Yuan lyrics in the *xiansuo* style and eager to bring them to daily entertainments if requested. A further decline in the next generation can be surmised in Han and Pan's lament of 1609 over having lost Nimble Beauty, who, in their eyes, was the last such courtesan in the field. In 1598, when the living tradition of Yuan libretti was broken and tutors such as Old Dun and Nimble Beauty's father were nowhere to be found even in Beijing, Zhang Xuan invented a hybrid method for training his favorite concubine, Double Virtue, by combining oral transmission and textual sources. He recounts this training process in detail in his preface to *The Northern Elegance*, a 1602 edition of Ming prince Zhu Quan's *Formulary for Correct Sounds in an Era of Great Harmony*. He first hired an old female vocal teacher in the neighborhood with a good record of giving private lessons in *xiansuo* singing.[59] Yet he was dissatisfied with her vocal skills, which were "hybrid and sometimes ornamented excessively" 本領既雜兼帶邪聲; worse still, the lyrics she sang "abounded in vulgar expressions" 所歌之詞又多俚語. His next strategy was to "seek after various ancient librettists' works and finally find *The Formulary for Correct Sounds in an Era of Great Harmony*" 因轉求諸古名家樂府小令，始得太和正音譜. He then asked

58. He, *Siyouzhai congshuo*, 340 (in Yu and Sun, 467).

59. Zhang, "Beiya tici," *Beiya*, 3a.

the vocal teacher to study Zhu Quan's formulary—so that the Yuan lyrics were thereupon transferred to bodily performance—and teach the songs to Double Virtue. The mark of Zhang's prestige derived both from his possession of the formulary and from the resurgence of a Yuan repertoire through his concubine's performance.

At the same time, the audiences in Beijing brothels shifted their interest and indulged in popular songs, or *shishang xiaoling*, rendered in the *xiansuo* style. Thanks to courtesans' musical intervention, a tune entitled *Rhythmic Singing "Sheep on the Mountain Slope"* (*Shulao Shanpo yang* 數落山坡羊), which originated in the northern borderlands, began to spread in Beijing in the Wanli reign (1573–1620), according to Shen Defu.[60] It was the Beijing courtesans who popularized the tune by "rendering it in the *xiansuo* northern style" 今京師技女, 慣以此充弦索北調. A favorite in the brothel repertoire, the song featured linguistic elements of the bawdy, the vulgar, and the rustic, surpassing even the ancient folk music that unabashedly portrayed lovemaking scenes 其語穢褻鄙淺, 並桑濮之音, 亦離去已遠. What Shen most feared, however, was not moral degeneration but that a courtesan who indulged in such popular songs would then *forget* her hard-earned knowledge about the *xiansuo* rendition of northern drama inherited from court musicians 而教坊所隸 . . . 則皆不知為何物矣. Competition with popular songs for the courtesan's mental storage space may even have motivated some new literati compositions such as Han Shanggui's *Soaring the Sky*.

For the tune *Rhythmic Singing "Sheep on the Mountain Slope,"* invented in the Beijing pleasure quarters, we have two salient examples from the novel *The Plum in the Golden Vase*. They belong to the repertoire of a low-ranking blind singsong girl who is independent of any licensed pleasure quarters and specializes in the subcategory of Rhythmic Singing (*shulao*). To take her second *shulao* song as an example, the prose content of its lyrics can be boiled down to this short narrative: "I am longing for you to come, but you must have been thwarted, and so I am waiting in vain." The lines are structured spirally, evolving around the central theme of unfulfilled erotic desire from the perspective of a young scholar in the love affair celebrated in *The Story of the Western Wing*. The literary style is characteristic of all popular songs of the time: erotic love running rampant in repetitive language, or, in He

60. Shen Defu, *Guqu zayan*, 647 (in Yu and Sun, 70). 北方惟盛愛【數落山坡羊】，其曲自宣、大、遼東三鎮傳來 For a very similar statement of popular songs (*liqu* 俚曲), especially *Rhythmic Singing, Sheep on the Slope*, see Gu Qiyuan 顧起元 (1565–1628), *Kezuo zhuiyu* 客座贅語 (colophon 1618) (Beijing: Zhonghua shuju, 1987), *juan* 9, 302. Also see Liu Tong 劉侗 and Yu I-zheng 于奕正, comps., *Dijing jingwulue* 帝京景物略 (pref. 1635) (Beijing: Beijing Guji chubanshe, 1980), *juan* 2, 58.

Liangjun's words, "diction made up with rouge and powder" 作調脂弄粉語.[61] Here is the full translation of the song by David Roy:[62]

> As for my loved one,
> The two of us are totally preoccupied.
> What obsesses me is that we are unable,
> To exchange looks with eyes and eyebrows.
> Once you departed, I have only my lonely pillow.
> The pillow is cold, the coverlet remains;
> Alone I confront my jasper-inlaid zither.
> My sick body is like a stick of kindling;
> My waist has become emaciated.
> I realize that it is difficult for you
>   to leave your mother's side,
> But this waiting only makes my heart
>   feel the more inebriated.
> I am all on tenterhooks as I keep company
>   with this unfeeling lamp.
> Come!
> On hearing the sound of the wind rustling the bamboo,
> I assume that my loved one has come,
> And hastily step out of my study.
> But it is only the gentle swaying of the flower shadows,
> In the moonlight that is as limpid as water.

> 意中人, 兩人里懸心挂意。
> 意兒里，不得和你兩個眉來眼去。
> 去了時，強挨孤枕。
> 枕兒寒，衾兒剩，瑤琴獨對，病體如柴，瘦損了腰肢。
> 知道你夫人行應難離，倒等的我寸心如醉。
> 最關心伴著這一盞寒燈來呵，又被風弄竹聲，只道多情到矣。
> 急忙出離了書幃，不想是花影輕搖，月明如水。

To He Liangjun, such lyrics are the type "pleasing to the ears of the vulgar" 諧於俗耳, an object of ridicule. In contrast, he sings the praises of the original Northern Version: "Its best lyrics are on a par with Li Bai's (701–762) poetry; in addition [to its poetic quality], it uses Jurchen Jin and

61. He, *Siyouzhai congshuo*, 338 (in Yu and Sun, 465).
62. Roy, *The Plum in the Golden Vase*, ch. 61.

Yuan expressions" 有妙處可比李白詩歌，又用金元胡語. Clearly, the remarkable poetry with ethnic flavors that he relished would have posed linguistic hurdles to a courtesan's memory. Yet *"The Western Wing" in Its Northern Version*—which is thematically related to erotic love, a staple in the courtesan's *xiansuo* repertoire—is far from being the most difficult play. Among many thematic variations of Yuan drama, those concerned with the loftier matter of Daoist solitude and seclusion, for example, could have been even more challenging.

No wonder there are many more popular songs than Yuan dramatic song suites in *The Plum in the Golden Vase*. To the popular tune of *Sheep on the Slope* alone, the novel incorporates nineteen stand-alone songs in full (excluding arias sung to this tune that are embedded in a song suite in chapter 44 and, later, in chapter 74). All these lyrics would have gone easy on the memory of the courtesan—no Jin/Yuan expression, no recondite metaphors, no classical allusions—and the prose content is full of erotic energy and relatable details of courtesan life, short but touched with soft humor. Four of the songs, sung by the prodigal son-in-law who uses the songs to flirt with the protagonist's fifth concubine (and eventually to have an affair with her), are slightly longer than other variations, consisting of lines in which the names of fruits, flowers, or coins are embedded. The lyrics are sexual in nature, simple in diction, spiced up with colorful puns, and narrated through the persona of a disappointed prostitute.[63]

The novelist also provides extraordinary details suggestive of a late Ming mentality that placed Yuan libretti on a higher level than popular songs within the aesthetic hierarchy. The blind singsong girl responds to the protagonist's inquiry about the size of her repertoire by saying "I have committed to memory about a hundred song suites" 小的大小也記百十套曲子 (chapter 61), which is certainly more than would be generally expected of a singer of her low rank. Even He Liangjun's most assiduous singer—his maidservant, who had a retentive memory under the tutelage of Old Dun—mastered only about fifty Jurchen Jin and Yuan song suites.[64] However, before proceeding to the two songs to the tune of *Sheep on the Slope*, the blind girl first sings two song suites from a lost thirteenth-century Yuan drama entitled *A Red Leaf Afloat in the Palace Moat*, as preserved in the *beiqiang* category of Hu Wenhuan's *Categorized Selections from Essential Dramas*.[65] Under social

63. Roy, *The Plum in the Golden Vase*, ch. 33, 2: 269.

64. He, *Siyouzhai congshuo*, 340 (in Yu and Sun, 467).

65. See Hu, comp., *Qunyin leixuan*, 1287–1468. Other versions of this suite with slight variations can be found in *Shengshi xinsheng*, 55–59; *Cilin zhaiyan*, 2:825–32; *Yongxi yuefu*, 2:32a–34b.

pressure to maintain her ties with a traditional, respectful form of music, the Yuan song suites must be heard first; yet they are somehow a distraction from singing the truly pleasurable newer repertoire to her patron.

The hierarchical order between song suites and popular songs becomes even more evident in a humiliating circumstance the singsong girl falls into in chapter 75 of *The Plum in the Golden Vase*: an ambitious maidservant in the protagonist's household, offended by the singsong girl's reluctance to sing, relentlessly reveals the tiny proportion of song suites in her repertoire, which contradicts her earlier boast of having memorized a hundred or so in chapter 61. "What kind of presentable song suites can you memorize? How dare you start putting on airs?" the maid asks, and continues, "You merely cast about with your oily mouth and canine tongue in search of lewd tunes. What else do you have beyond *Sheep on the Slope* and *Shrouding the Southern Branch*? Not up to par!"[66] This vivid, circumstantial description, though fictional, is a window through which we can see the dynamics between the two categories of lyrics in late Ming mundane entertainments.

He Liangjun and Shen Defu were accurate in blaming popular songs for occupying too much of the courtesan's mental space, and in ascribing the decline of northern drama to the subsequent dwindling memory storage of the courtesan-actress. That brothel performance was the main institution for public access to Yuan drama is reinforced by a survey of late Ming printing history. From the 1570s onward, supplying printed Yuan dramas became an increasingly profitable business, and marketing minds responded quickly to the massive appetite for Yuan plays by expanding the dramas' scale of publication. Before this point, the private libraries where hand-copied transcripts of Yuan dramas and other works were stored served as markers of social privilege. For those who lacked status and prestige, the brothel reserved an opportunity to listen to memorized lyrics sung in the *xiansuo* style. No doubt, the courtesan's performance was more accessible than were privately owned manuscripts. According to Sun Kaidi and Hajime Yagisawa's pathbreaking study of the surviving seven late Ming editions of Yuan drama, all Wanli printings are based on privately owned manuscripts that descend from one hypothetical ancestor—the transcription of the memories of court musicians and courtesans registered in the Court Entertainment Bureau (*jiaofang si* 教坊司) of the early Ming.[67] These manuscripts were not an authorita-

66. *Jin Ping Mei cihua*, chap. 75; Roy, *The Plum in the Golden Vase* 4:589.

67. Sun Kaidi 孫楷第, *Yeshiyuan gujin zaju kao* 也是園古今雜劇考 (Shanghai: Shanghai zazhi gongsi chubanshe, 1953), 150; Hajime Yagisawa, *Mindai gekisakka kenkyu* 明代劇作家研究 (Tokyo: Kodansha, 1959), 452–54; Lo Chin-T'ang, trans., *Mingdai juzuojia yanjiu* 明代劇作家研究 (Hong Kong: Longen shudian, 1966), 291.

tive canon inherited from the Yuan court; nor were they hand copies of Yuan bookshop imprints that survived the dynastic transition. Rather, they were by their very nature a transmission of the oral tradition passed down from the early Ming court.[68] All evidence has pointed to a textual archetype rooted in Beijing, called the "royal mansion editions," or *neifu ben* 內府本. Scribes copied out such palace scripts, which flew into the private libraries of those who had special connections with the royal family.[69]

Li Kaixian 李開先 (1502–1568; *jinshi* 1529) was the first scholar-official to open up to the public his literary treasures, which allegedly consisted of a collection of a thousand texts. He produced the earliest extant Yuan drama anthology of sixteen plays, published roughly between 1558 and 1568.[70] As Li puts in the preface, this publication aimed to allow "the commoner to be able to read Yuan lyrics and understand why these lyrics became famous" 欲世之人得見元詞，並知元詞之所以得名也.

Another high official with royal connections who boasted a large-scale collection was Liu Shouyou 劉守有 (military *jinshi* 1583), head of the imperial secret police department and the Wanli emperor's favorite. David Roy speculates that sometime between 1583 and 1584, Liu entrusted Tang Xianzu 湯顯祖 (1550–1616; *jinshi* 1583), crowned the best southern drama playwright of all time, with handpicking three hundred rare dramatic texts from Liu's

---

Komatsu points out differences between texts deriving from the *jiaofang si* and the *zhonggu si* 鍾鼓司 (Office of Bell and Drum). See Komatsu Ken 小松謙, "Min kan shohon kō" 明刊諸本考, in his *Chūgoku koten engeki kenkyū* 中國古典演劇研究 (Tokyo: Kyuko shoin, 2001), 198–231.

68. William Dolby imagines a Ming royal collection of texts passed down from the Yuan dynasty: "A large proportion of the scripts and editions of Yuan plays existing in the Yuan period must have found their way into the various huge libraries of Yuan *zaju* known to have existed in the Ming." See William Dolby, "Yuan Drama," in *Chinese Theater: From Its Origins to the Present Day*, ed. Colin Mackerras (Honolulu: University of Hawaii Press, 1983), 36. I disagree with Dolby's vision.

69. Komatsu Ken, "Naifuhon-kei shohon kō" 內府本系諸本考 in *Tanaka Kenji hakase sōshū kinen Chūgoku koten gikyoku ronshū* 田中謙二博士頌壽記念中國古典戲曲論集 (Tokyo: Kyuko shoin, 1991).

70. Li Kaixian, "Preface to *Gaiding Yuanxian chuanqi*" 改定元賢傳奇, facsimile reprint in XXSKQS, 1760:109–88. A modern typeset edition is provided in Bu Jian 卜健, *Li Kaixian quanji* 李開先全集 (Shanghai: Shanghai guji chubanshe, 2014), 3:2045–2179. On Li Kaixian's "courtly" connections and Zang Maoxun's 臧懋循 appropriation of a "courtly" approach, see Patricia Sieber, *Theaters of Desire: Authors, Readers, and the Reproduction of Early Chinese Song-Drama, 1300–2000* (Hampshire: Palgrave Macmillan, 2003), 83–122.

Beijing residence.[71] Tang may have benefited greatly from this service since he claimed to have a thousand *zaju* texts in his own collection. Tang's 1583–1584 selection was shipped to Liu's hometown in Macheng, Hubei province. Whereas Tang is not known to have published any of his collected Yuan texts, his friend Zang Maoxun 臧懋循 (1550–1616; *jinshi* 1580) visited Liu's son in Macheng and borrowed (or copied) these manuscripts in 1613.[72]

Emerging from Zang Maoxun's trip to Liu's private library in Macheng was the largest compendium of Yuan drama up to that time, published in 1615 under the title *Selection of One Hundred Yuan Plays* (*Yuanren baizhong qu* 元人百種曲). It was an unsurpassed commercial success, outperforming Chen Yujiao's 陳與郊 (1544–1610; *jinshi* 1574) *Northern Drama by Famous Ancient Playwrights* (*Gu mingjia zaju* 古名家雜劇), the second largest late Ming production of Yuan drama, produced batch by batch over three decades;[73] Xijizi's 息機子 (pseudonym) *Selection of Northern Drama from Past to Present* (*Gujin zaju xuan* 古今雜劇選, preface 1598);[74] and also Meng Chengshun's 孟稱舜 (1599–1684) *Famous Plays from Past to Present* (*Gunjin mingju hexuan* 古今名劇合選, preface 1633).[75] The profits Zang Maoxun received from publishing

71. David T. Roy, "The Case for T'ang Hsien-tsu's Authorship of the *Jin Ping Mei*," *Chinese Literature: Essays, Articles, Reviews (CLEAR)* 8, no. 1 (1986): 54.

72. In his letter to Xie Zhaozhe 谢肇淛 (1567–1624; *jinshi* 1592), Zang Maoxun indicates that he only took in twenty something plays from these Macheng manuscripts and that the rest of the compendium were based on earlier Ming editions. See Zang, *Fubaotang wenxuan* 負苞堂文選 in CMCS, vol. 168. Digital version, Chinese Text Project, https://ctext.org/library.pl?if=gb&res=3762

73. Between 1574 and 1592—years of his Beijing officialdom, Chen must have received good money from a Mr. Xu, a commercial publisher of Xin'an county in Anhui province, for his compilation work. The cooperation between Chen and the commercial publisher lasted over several decades into the early 1600s. The total number of plays published under this title is uncertain, but at least sixty-five plays survived into our century, be it printed texts or manuscripts copied out of the original imprints. Lo Chin-T'ang provided crucial evidence for dating Mr. Xu's publication activities of Yuan drama to as early as 1588. See Lo Chin-T'ang, *Zhongguo xiqu zongmu huibian* 中國戲曲總目彙編 (Xi'an: Shanxi shifan daxue chubanshe, 2021), 67.

74. Xijizi, comp., *Gujin zaju xuan*, original in the National Library in Beijing. Preface in Yu and Sun, 3:435. Fifteen out of twenty-six plays in this collection have facsimile reprints in *Guben xiqu congkan* under the title of *Zaju xuan* 雜劇選.

75. Wilt Idema, "From Stage Scripts to Closet Drama: Editions of Early Chinese Drama and the Translations of Yuan *Zaju*," *Journal of Chinese Literature and Culture* 3, no. 1 (2016): 175–202. Idema feels that there should have been a division between the scripts connected with the Ming court performance and those which were edited and attempted to be literature, initiated by Li Kaixian. I agree with the existence of

the first half of *Selection of One Hundred Yuan Plays* in 1615 provided enough funds for the second half to come out in 1616. Such lucrative payouts would have targeted a broader range of readers than playwrights.

At first glance these printing projects seem to have sought to rekindle public interest in *xiansuo* performance and to supplement the courtesan's dwindling memorial archive with the printed words' memorial utility. But no record shows any sign of a revival of Yuan libretti in the courtesan's repertoire despite the booming publications of Yuan dramas. The woodblock imprints in circulation did not, or were not meant to, remedy the downward spiral of Yuan libretti in brothel performance by providing textual aids for the courtesan's memory. The major challenge to late Ming courtesans—comprehending and memorizing Yuan lyrics that incorporated romantic lyricism, classical allusions, and Jin/Yuan colloquialisms—could not possibly be alleviated by supplying the brothel singers with written scripts. Moreover, scholars have agreed that both Zang Maoxun's and Meng Chengshun's compendiums feature notoriously substantive editing that marks a new era in the history of Ming readership of Yuan drama. Their heavy editing created a stand-alone textual genealogy that digressed significantly from the lineage of their hand-copied predecessors, which had been centered on early Ming royal manuscripts.[76] In fact, this literary deviation from the oral tradition, in complete contrast to the literary effort made by Han Shanggui, would have resulted in further alienation for the courtesan singer.

To summarize thus far, courtesans had to grapple with the constant pressure of both the market (which favored popular songs) and the traditional patronage of literati (who preferred lyrics with a variety of intellectual content). At the same time, the social hierarchy persisted in the entertainment

the division, but I argue that the second branch was meant to instill the essence of Yuan drama into southern drama, or to supply inspiring literary models for *chuanqi* playwrights.

76. Stephen West, "A Study in Appropriation: Zang Maoxun's Injustice to Dou E," *Journal of the American Oriental Society* 111, no. 2 (1991): 283–302. Stephen West looked in the textual differences between Zang's recensions and the earlier Ming editions for what new historicist Stephen Greenblatt calls "social energy" that engendered the alterations. Stephen Greenblatt, *Shakespearean Negotiations* (Berkeley: University of California Press, 1988), 1–20. Following this line of argument, Patricia Sieber asserts that Zang's editorial role is less performative in that it created a reading experience featuring "mental spectacles on an invisible courtly stage." She interprets this "readerly simulation of performance" as an outcome of Zang's vindication of elite male passion for "expanding the range of what constituted permissible literary representation." See Sieber, *Theaters of Desire*, 114–15, 121.

world: popular tunes lacked literary elegance and stylistic variety, whereas Yuan libretti could bring cultural prestige for singers. The insurmountable cultural inferiority of popular songs combined with the loss of classic lyrics from the courtesan's memorial archive created a vacuum within cultivated leisure, which was to be filled by the replacement model, *kunqu*, that emerged as a socially prestigious form among elite aficionados as early as the 1540s before rising to dominance in popular culture in the 1570s.

"Smuggling" the Diva's Part into Southern Adaptations

Southern adaptations of Yuan dramas have been studied as purely the playwright's business—that is, as belonging exclusively to the realm of literary decisions. In addition, the generic boundaries of music have been overemphasized, as though they evolved by themselves without being shaped by actors' subjective interventions. Overall, earlier scholarship has overlooked the performer's agency, especially the role that bodily performance played as a mnemonic device. Because courtesans were kinesthetic learners, their memory of Yuan libretti was facilitated not only by any basic literary education they may have received but also by their bodily experience. In this sense, bodily performance was one way of "writing" that transmitted and recorded information in her brain in a subjective manner. Any performance-driven written texts, consequently, can be expected to contain traces of such encoded information closely connected with the bodily experience of the courtesan.

During the complex process by which the southern dramas rose to dominance and the *xiansuo* style faded into marginalization, there was a great range in what was lost, reframed, recycled, or replaced. Though a comprehensive view of this dynamic process is hard to reach, we can begin by shifting our focus to the pleasure quarters as the cultural locus of powerful innovations, and to the courtesan as a vigorous actor and generic boundary-crosser. In the absence of continued full-scale staging of Yuan dramas such as the one Ma Xianglan mounted in Suzhou in 1604 and Nimble Beauty's 1609 performance in Nanjing, the golden age of *kunqu*-southern-drama (roughly from the 1570s on) found itself heir to the diva's voice in southern adaptations of Yuan dramas.

First, the legacy of the "northern" diva manifested itself transparently in the wholesale borrowing of an entire Yuan song suite to be integrated into a proper southern play. This epiphenomenon is characterized in Hu Wenhuan's categorized anthology as the "smuggling" (*touru* 偷入) of a *beiqiang* unit into a southern play. For example, Guan Yunshi's 貫雲石 (1286–1324) song suite in the courtesan's repertoire that portrayed the West Lake "was recently smuggled into *The Double Reds*" 近偷入二紅記,[77] Ma Zhiyuan's 馬致遠 (1250–1323) song suite "was recently smuggled into *The Jade Pendant*" 近偷入玉玦記, and a song suite from Qiao Ji's 喬吉 (ca. 1280–1345) *zaju* drama *Marriage Destiny over Two Lifetimes* (which appears in the courtesan's repertoire in *The Plum in the Golden Vase*) "was recently adapted and inserted into *The Jade Pendants*" 近改入玉環記. Anecdotal accounts prove the reliability of Hu's categorization. For example, Shen Defu suspected that scene 31 of *The Embroidered Cloak* (*Xiuru ji* 繡襦記) had been stolen from a Yuan work by the contemporary playwright Zheng Ruoyong 鄭若庸 (fl. 1530s).[78] Lacking adequate sources, however, Shen had no way to prove his theory and therefore turned to a widely respected drama scholar, who confirmed that he had once seen the scene in a Yuan drama. Through this transplantation of the courtesan's repertoire into full-length southern plays, the skilled courtesan vocalist acquired a reserved space in southern-style theater, which, in turn, sustained her rapidly shrinking memorial archive of Yuan libretti.

A second method of retaining the diva's voice in southern theater was through integration of northern song suites, newly written but strictly observing Yuan rules, into new southern plays. This method featured a double orientation: these northern song suites were musically compatible for both *beiqiang/xiansuo* and *kunqu* rendition at the time. The foremost playwright pioneering this innovation was Li Kaixian, whose two southern plays—*Ten Thousand Taels of Gold* (*Qianjin ji* 千金記, also known as *Dengtan ji* 登壇記 or *Ascending the Altar*)[79] and *The Precious Sword* (preface 1547)—provided multiple northern song suites that were performed in the *xiansuo* style. The former was included in Hu's *beiqiang* category or appear in chapter 70 of *The Plum in the Golden Vase*, and became staples of *kunqu*

77. It may refer to *Shuanghong ji* 雙紅記, attributed by Qi Biaojia to a Mr. Gengsheng zi 更生子 (pseudonym), which combines the stories of Ms. Red Whisk and Ms. Red Silk, hence named "Double Reds." Qi, *Yuanshantang qupin*, 587. It appears in Hu Wenhuan's anthology in the *beiqiang* catalogue (*juan* 5, 9a–10a). The next two suites appear in the same catalogue, in *juan* 5 (14b–15b) and *juan* 6 (16a–18a), respectively.

78. Shen, *Guqu zayan*, 648 (in Yu and Sun, 70).

79. Xu Fuzuo 徐復祚 (1560–after 1629), *Sanjia cunlao qutan* 三家村老曲談, in *Lidai quhua huibian: Mingdai bian*, ed. Yu and Sun, 2:257. It appears in Hu Wenhuan's *beiqiang* catalogue (*juan* 4, 16a–18a).

performance in future generations up to the present day. Other good examples found in Hu Wenhuan's *beiqiang* category are *The Decorated Pavilion* (also in chapter 20 of *The Plum in the Golden Vase*) and Liang Chenyu's landmark "*kunqu*" play *Washing Gauze*.[80] Due to the new compositions' resemblance in style to Yuan libretti, the courtesan was able to discover for herself the nature of these new *beiqiang* scenes and enact them in her own unique fashion of *xiansuo*.

The above two "smuggling" epiphenomena can be seen as part of the larger trend of adapting the familiar subjects of Yuan dramas into new southern plays, which was statistically a salient literary phenomenon throughout the Ming dynasty. Expert of the *chuanqi* genre Guo Yingde estimates that two-thirds of the extant Ming *chuanqi* plays before the 1570s are adaptations from earlier northern dramas, while the remaining one-third are scripts that tell new stories.[81] The ratio between adaptations and their northern "original" works dropped from 2:1 to 1:1 after the 1570s, when the scope of subjects and themes of new southern plays expanded to transcend the confines of Yuan drama.[82] These data suggest that interest in southern adaptations was sustained, albeit declining, throughout the Ming dynasty. But we need to be cautious about the reliability of the statistics: on most occasions, a nonextant Yuan drama is identified as the "original" of a *chuanqi* play based solely on the similarity between their titles. Contemporaneous drama critics who had both the originals and their adaptations at their disposal offered more precise knowledge when feasible, yet this kind of information remains scanty and speculative because after the 1570s, Ming scholars' pool of Yuan-drama resources was just as limited as ours is today. Full-length adaptations of Yuan dramas that can afford comparative studies are few: the most important pairs of works are the southern play *Praying to the Moon* (*Baiyue ting* 拜月亭) that can be read against Guan Hanqing's 関漢卿 (fl. 13th century) *zaju* version, studied by the inimitable Wang Guowei,[83] and the Southern versus Northern Version of *The Story of the Western Wing*.[84]

80. These two examples appear in Hu Wenhuan's *beiqiang* catalogue in *juan* 6 (19a–20a) and *juan* 4 (14b–16a), respectively.

81. Guo Yingde, *Ming Qing chuanqi shi* 明清傳奇史 (Nanjing: Fenghuang chubanshe, 2001), 48–49.

82. Guo's interpretation reads this data as a landmark of the maturation of the *chuanqi* genre and literary techniques associated with it—a vision in which a standalone art form cut off its umbilical tie with northern drama.

83. Wang Guowei, *Song Yuan xiqu shi* 宋元戲曲史 (Nanjing: Fenghuang chubanshe, 2010), 143–50.

84. Cong Jingwen 叢靜文 makes meticulous textual comparisons and has deduced

For a more direct source for tracing the courtesan diva's voice in the emerging southern music culture—and a third method that granted the courtesan leeway to participate in southern renditions—we may turn to thirty-seven southern song suites adapted from nontheatrical Yuan song suites by three literati: Shen Jing 沈璟 (1553–1610; *jinshi* 1574), his student Bu Shichen 卜世臣 (fl. 1610), and Shen Zan 沈瓚 (1558–1612; *jinshi* 1586).[85] They deploy three strategies, either separately or in combination: (1) slightly altering the original Yuan lyrics, (2) combining selected lines from different arias in the original into one southern tune, and (3) conveying the same idea with a new expression. Without exception, all the thirty-seven southern song suites express the erotic desire characteristic of brothel literature, falling into the subcategory of "boudoir emotions," or *guiqing* 閨情, in which the eroticized persona is that of a lovesick woman. Comparisons with their northern counterparts suggest that although the nature of the music changed, these thirty-seven song suites matched, if not surpassed, the Yuan works in their willingness and capacity to portray excessive erotic fantasy. Admittedly, there may have been a network of cultural agendas within which this repertory was located. For instance, they may have been a display of the three literati's cutting-edge, "increasingly virtuosic and deliberate technical innovations in musical form, including the 'southern' forms that dominated the popular stage of the time," as suggested by Yuming He in her in-depth study of Xu Wei's play.[86] One's first impulse is always to think that literary compositions are a kind of ingenious game played by brilliant minds, and that there is always a sense of playfulness in any adaptations. I do not claim that to channel the "northern" diva's part in the "southern" forms was the only rationale for these erotic southern song suites. But what they have in common in

five devices by which the adaptor turns the northern arias into the southern ones. See Cong, *Nan Bei Xixiang ji bijiao* 南北西廂記比較 (Taipei: Taiwan Shangwu yinshuguan, 1976). Comments on the Southern Version in comparison with the Northern Version abound in Ming sources. See Lu Cai, "Lu Tianchi Xixiang ji xu" 陸天池西廂記序, in *Lidai quhua huibian: Mingdai bian*, ed. Yu and Sun, 1:261; Liang Chenyu, "Nan Xixiang tici" 南西廂題辭, 1:475; Ling Mengchu, *Tanqu zazha* 譚曲雜劄, 3:192–93; and Qi Biaojia, *Yuanshantang qupin*, 3:576. Xu Fuzuo lists two southern adaptations of northern dramas, *Lianhuan ji* and *Nan Xixiang ji*. See his *Sanjia cunlao qutan*, 261.

85. Xie Boyang 謝伯陽, *Quan Ming sanqu* 全明散曲 (Jinan: Qilu shushe, 2016). The three authors—Shen Jing, Shen Zan, and Bu Shichen—are on pages 3248, 3309, and 4180, respectively. Cheng Yun 程芸 and Li Yanhua 李豔華, "Mingren 'fan beiqu' xianxiang chutan" 明人翻北曲現象初探, *Nanjing shifan daxue wenxueyuan xuebao* 南京師範大學文學院學報 3 (2015): 66–71.

86. He, "Difficulties of Performance: The Musical Career of Xu Wei's 'The Mad Drummer,'" *Harvard Journal of Asiatic Studies* 68, no. 2 (2008): 77–114, 103.

themes, persona, subjectivities, emotions, and expressive agenda undeniably points to codes of performance specific to brothels that had been inherited from the early Ming court performance.

A fourth method is to incorporate in new southern plays familiar acting skits from the courtesan's performance tradition. This method has everything to do with the *"The Western Wing" in Its Northern Version*, the most enduring staple in the courtesan's repertoire (reportedly last staged in its entirety in 1604), and hence the most familiar material to the mind of a courtesan performer. The Southern Version, instead, had been prominent in the repertoires of itinerant professional performers since its birth in the 1530s.[87] In terms of their expressive agenda of erotic pleasure, I agree with C. T. Hsia's observation that the Southern Version is a step forward toward the commonplace scholar-beauty romance often seen in later vernacular literature.[88] Yet the Northern Version is strongly informed by a specific sort of erotic imagery missing from the Southern Version. This distinction between the two different theatrical modes of erotic pleasure manifests itself in various episodes of a love story: the romantic encounter, the sexual act, the voyeur's pleasure, the patriarchal intervention, the love longing, and so on. In this sense, the two plays offered two models for later *chuanqi* playwrights, and which version to emulate was an active choice. Taking the lovemaking scene as an example, we see that the Northern Version drips with the blazing eroticism of male gaze, under which the heroine is observed and portrayed straightforwardly to the audience. Scholar Zhang, whose sexual desire has been thwarted several times before this point in the play, bursts with intense erotic energy. He begins by describing his own actions, while possibly acting out the action verbs in the lyrics: "I loosen the knotted buttons, untie her silken waistwrap; / Orchid musk spreads through my secluded study."[89] The heroine Oriole is silent on the page we read, but Scholar Zhang's lyrics allow for imagination of her actions: "Gently she adjusts her willowy waist, / And lightly splits the flower's heart: / Dew drips; the peony opens." He con-

87. Bibliographical evidence shows that *Nan Xixiang* was first completed in the 1530s, by a Cui Shipei 崔時佩 and later augmented by a Li Rihua 李日華, not to be confused with another Li Rihua (1565–1635; *jinshi* 1592), a preeminent art connoisseur and diarist. The earliest bibliographical record is the *Baichuan shuzhi* 百川書志 compiled by Gao Ru 高儒 with a preface dating from 1540 (*Zhongguo zhexueshu dianzihua jihua* 中國哲學書電子化計劃. https://ctext.org/wiki.pl?if=gb&res=182640&searchu=南西廂. Accordingly, the adaptation should have been printed and circulated before that year.

88. C. T. Hsia, *The Classical Chinese Novel: A Critical Introduction* (New York: Columbia University Press, 1968), 98.

89. Stephen West and Wilt Idema, trans., *The Story of the Western Wing* (Berkeley: University of California Press, 1995), 228–29.

tinues to reveal Oriole's actions in his eyes: "Partly resistant, partly eager to give, / Now alarmed, now full of love." The Southern Version has a distinct treatment of the same subplot: Scholar Zhang leads his virgin lover by the hand, and both exit, leaving the maidservant onstage, who solos to the audience about what she has observed voyeuristically. Both the northern and the southern versions offer the era's most erotic theatrical representations of sex, but in conspicuously different dramaturgical designs.

Tang Xianzu's 1598 masterpiece, *The Peony Pavilion* (*Mudan ting* 牡丹亭), is a good example of the literary recollection of the Northern Version's intense verbal eroticism, while retaining the southern convention of having the lovers go offstage and enter again after someone else has sung about their lovemaking scene. Here are the lyrics that depict the sexual intercourse in the famous scene 10, "Interrupted Dream":[90]

Male Lead (*in a low singing voice*): Open the fastening at your neck, loose the girdle at your waist; / while you / screening your eyes with your sleeve, / white teeth clenched on the fabric as if against pain, / bear with me patiently a while / then drift into gentle slumber.

(Female Lead turns away, blushing. Male Lead advances to take her in his arms, but she resists him.)

Male Lead, Female Lead: Somewhere at some past time you and I met. / Now we behold each other in solemn awe / but do not ay / in this lovely place we should meet and speak no word.

(Male Lead exits, carrying off Female Lead by force.)

Given that *The Peony Pavilion* belongs to the same dramatic genre as the Southern Version, Tang's decision to copy the lines from the Northern Version should not go unremarked. In fact, such hybrids that incorporate wisps of imitative brothel performance skits are not uncommon among *chuanqi* plays produced during the hedonistic 1570s–1600s, which coincided with the transitioning of the courtesan from being a "northern" diva into being an actress of the increasingly popular *chuanqi/kunqu* theater. Although literary borrowing and imitation of acting are deeply entangled and hard to

90. Adapted slightly from Cyril Birch, trans., *The Peony Pavilion* (Bloomington: Indiana University Press, 2002), 227.

distinguish on paper, vestiges of northern renditions in southern dramas should not be seen simply as the playwright's imitation of some Yuan dramatist. Instead, such vestiges should also be seen in the light of performance history, precisely because a late Ming courtesan who had inherited a performance tradition rooted in and nourished by Yuan drama was increasingly expected to build southern theatrical arias into her repertoire. The tendency to produce "northernized" hybrids in a long *chuanqi* play can thus be interpreted as one way of "smuggling" in familiar performances for the sake of the courtesan-actress.

Conclusion

The courtesan has been largely taken out of the genealogy of knowledge about Yuan drama, rendered invisible in literary history. It is our undue emphasis on printed knowledge that has erased both the courtesan-actress's agency and her ephemeral repertoire from our cultural memory of the genesis of knowledge production and transmission.

What this chapter restores is the role that the courtesan performed in preserving the *xiansuo* performance inherited from the early Ming court performance, or even the Yuan tradition of female performance. The courtesan's memorial archive greatly influenced many other cultural dimensions of theater, including Yuan drama printing and southern adaptations of Yuan drama. Evidence that supports this argument is gleaned mainly from drama, fiction, and song anthologies. To musicological evidence, however, I shall return in chapter 2.

The Wanli reign, beginning in 1573 and ending in 1620, stands out as a crucial period that witnessed the decline of the two mediums of Yuan drama—the courtesan's memorial archive and the scribal copying that built up the bibliophile's collections—that were to be replaced by printed Yuan dramas. At the same time, the main venue for oral performance of Yuan lyrics, the pleasure quarters, were gradually taken over by *kunqu*. By 1609, not only was Nimble Beauty a rarity among Nanjing courtesan-actresses, but Han's *Soaring the Sky* was an outlandish spectacle in the literary landscape. But *Soaring the Sky* was representative of a string of dramatic works that were written exclusively for brothel performances.

Nevertheless, interesting hybridization took place in both literature and performance. On the one hand, there was the northernization of some scenes in the *chuanqi* genre, as analyzed in the last section of this chapter.

On the other hand, the southernization of the rendition of Yuan libretti happened in the milieu of performance. As theater historian Pu Jiangqing puts it, since the mid-sixteenth century, "northern tunes in *chuanqi* demonstrate prosodic features and vocal renditions (*changfa* 唱法) that had already become 'southernized.'"[91] How the courtesan's training changed to accommodate this "southernization," how orality and music literacy interacted in a more complex way in the new favorite *kunqu*, and how these changes altogether influenced literary practice are the subject of the next chapter.

91. Pu Jiangqing 浦江清, *Zhongguo wenxue shigao: Ming Qing* 中國文學史稿：明清 (Beijing: Beijing chubanshe, 2018), 165–66.

CHAPTER 2

Improvisation and Musical Modernity

The Courtesan's Memory in the Transition from Xiansuo *to* Kunqu

The training of Nimble Beauty—arguably the last courtesan virtuoso of the "authentic" *xiansuo* 弦索 (lit., "string-instrument") style of *zaju* (northern drama)—had been focused on learning to quickly memorize and render new libretti, for which a solid literary education and a large repertoire of northern tunes were prerequisites (see chapter 1). She would have been able to easily match the lyrics and melodies of Han Shanggui's 韓上桂 (1572–1644) new *zaju* play *Soaring the Sky* (*Lingyun ji* 凌雲記) thanks to his accommodation of the living tradition of the courtesan's *xiansuo* repertoire. She delivered a costumed performance of the play every other night, a sure sign of her memory skills as a *xiansuo* singer. But the "notes and tones learned by heart" vocal pedagogy in which her former *zaju*-star father had trained her—which I shall unpack later—belonged to a medieval modality and had been replaced by *kunqu*'s innovative approach to memorization, which emphasized improvisation. Moreover, *kunqu*'s capacity for passionate improvisation brought a replacement model of vocal virtuosity into the arena of competition.

This chapter argues that at the dawn of musical modernity, the courtesan, powered by improvisation, chose an early modern approach to memorization over a medieval one. This decision, equally important to the literati's promotion of *kunqu* as high music culture, anticipated the obsolescence of *xiansuo* and boosted *kunqu*'s rise to a central part of the late Ming musical/theatrical universe. This argument flies in the face of the older elitist narrative of *kunqu* history, which envisions innovative ideas trickling down from an intellectual stratum of society to the less intelligent and less schooled. In this vision, the literatus-client's mind decided where the entertainer was going, and what and how s/he was being taught; the actress (or actor) had neither authority nor agency. I argue for the courtesan-actresses' active agency in appropriating and assimilating the ideas that they deemed suited to their own expressive agenda—and thus seek to reveal the untold story of *kunqu*'s emergence as the dominant strain.

To interpret *kunqu* as partially the courtesan's legacy is a distinctly feminist argument alien to, if not unheard of in, the traditional field of *kunqu* studies. The quasi-mythic history of *kunqu* boasts its continuous occupation of the terrain of Chinese "classic music," over the span of six centuries, up to the present day—tracing the rise of this musical form to a small group of fourteenth-century elite aficionados. According to this view, *kunqu* came of age in the mid-sixteenth century under the leadership of the saint-like reformer Wei Liangfu 魏良輔 (fl. sixteenth century), and was championed by a circle of literati-aesthetes of vocal music who are considered the pioneering fathers of China's national music/theatrical form and UNESCO-designated "intangible cultural heritage." By obliterating *kunqu*'s low-life associations with prostitution, the standard histories avoid the moral dangers of imagining professional *kunqu* teachers such as Wei Liangfu luxuriating in the company of swindlers, pimps, and prostitutes—and of imagining the brothel, a place of daily hedonism and debauchery, as a cultural contingency for the emergence of *kunqu*.

Elsewhere I have debunked the standard view by placing Wei Liangfu back in the lineage of professional music teachers hired by the bawdy houses as either "guest artists" playing the supporting roles in brothel theaters or private tutors of *kunqu*.[1] I have argued that as practitioners of *kunqu*, prostitutes financed *kunqu* teachers, and were an essential part of the broad musical/theatrical panorama of the field of *kunqu*. In turn, professional teachers/procurers supplied courtesans with *kunqu*-related education as a form of cultural capital. This chapter offers more musicological evidence for understanding the vernacular dimension of such knowledge and training, thereby further collapsing the divide between high and low culture. Centering on the key notion of memory that historians of European cultures have investigated, I pursue an intrinsic musicological explanation for the courtesan's willingness to be steeped in *kunqu* vocal music. As such, I offer an alternative

1. Peng Xu, "The Music Teacher: The Professionalization of Singing and the Development of Erotic Vocal Style During Late Ming China," *Harvard Journal of Asiatic Studies* 75, no. 2 (2015): 259–97.

interpretation for the rise of *kunqu* other than the courtesan's desire to cater to higher social organizations whose members favored it.

I. *Xiansuo* versus *Kunqu*: Two Memory Habits in Contrast

It is crucial to compare the mnemonic practices of *xiansuo* with those of *kunqu* if we are to understand the divide which we have discerned between the "premodern" and the "modern." But the evidence is scanty, especially for the medieval mnemonic methods of *xiansuo*. To glimpse the thickly veiled medieval memory habits, I begin with a ninth-century anecdote that tells of a low-life street singsong girl named Double Red (Zhang Honghong 張紅紅), a genius with both an astounding natural memory and brilliant mnemonic techniques.[2] Crucial to her success is a period of apprenticeship under her husband Wei Qing 韋青, a great music connoisseur and vocalist from the nobility. Yet it is a single performance event that catapults her to celebrity like a springboard, resulting in her leaving her husband and becoming an imperial concubine.

The story begins with a male professional singer regurgitating an older song in the guise of a new one, with merely rhythmic variations that put on a pretense of novelty 加減其節奏. This variation is not simply a general change in the tempo range, or *tempo rubato* in Western music terminology, defined in *Stainer and Barrett's Dictionary of Musical Terms* as "Time occasionally slackened or hastened for the purposes of expression."[3] Rather, he presents the song to Wei Qing as a "new sound" (*xinsheng* 新聲). Suspicious of the nature of the new song, Wei has arranged to hide Double Red behind a screen. She "uses a few boxes of red beans to mark the song's rhythms" 以小豆數合記其節拍, and memorizes the entire song. "I have a female disciple who learned this very song by heart long ago," Wei Qing declares to the boaster, "(by which I judge that) this is not a new composition." Then from behind the screen comes Double Red's voice presenting the whole song without "missing a single note" 一聲不失, leaving the charlatan "composer" ashamed and subdued. In late Ming diction, the word "a master behind the screen" (*pinghou shi* 屛後師) denotes female music teachers, alluding to Double Red and her mastery of the art of memory.

This anecdote is valuable because of its unconscious and unscreened

2. Zeng Xianfei 曾獻飛, ed. *Yuefu zalu shuzheng* 樂府雜錄疏證 (Nanchang: Jiangxi jiaoyu chubanshe, 2015), 36.

3. Revised edition by J. Stainer and W. A. Barrett, *Stainer and Barrett's Dictionary of Musical Terms* (London, 1898), 439.

nature. The ninth-century author's intention may well have been to write a eulogy for his contemporary aesthete Wei Qing: Wei was able to discern the genius of the lowly singsong girl by overhearing her singing outside his mansion (she happened to be begging for coins by singing for passersby); he then took her in as a disciple and concubine, transmitting his splendid music expertise to her. The tragic ending of their story discloses Double Red's love: upon hearing of Wei's death from the emperor, Lady Best Memory for Songs (*Jiqu Niangzi* 記曲娘子), as she is now known in the palace, dies suddenly of heartbreaking grief. The main purpose of the author of the tale was not to supply us with information about the mnemonic techniques in vocal art of the day. That is why his brief description—the use of "a few boxes of red beans to mark the song's rhythms"—is a telltale detail that suggests the significant role of memory techniques in musical training vis-à-vis Double Red's inborn advantage in recording rhythmic patterns in her mind.

This glancing reference to the medieval use of red beans to encode rhythms in singing sent me dipping into late Ming courtesans' biographies and anecdotes about their musical talents in the hope of finding descriptions of red beans. The only account I located comes from Zhang Xuan's 張萱 (1558–1641) memorializing preface to a northern song formulary that his mistress Double Virtue (Shuangcheng 雙成) compiled, based on the Ming prince Zhu Quan's 朱權 (1378–1448) work, under the new title *The Northern Elegance* (*Beiya* 北雅).[4] This 1602 preface tells in detail how Double Virtue had been trained to become a *xiansuo* virtuoso. I have already cited the preface lavishly in chapter 1, but did not quote the important detail of the *absence* of beans in her training, of which Zhang was quite proud. "My girl had always been versed in reading and superbly bright," he declaims, "and was able to repeat whatever the old lady (teacher) taught upon hearing the demonstration once. She would never bother to count beans" 兒故通翰墨, 穎悟絕倫, 一聞媼歌輒能, 不煩數豆.[5] Zhang further stresses the importance of her reading ability, a skill that her teacher lacked, in helping her skip the bean-counting stage and become a mature singer. Clearly, bean-counting was a typical method for beginners of *xiansuo* singing, whereas privileged students who could understand rhythms notationally could bypass it.

How would Double Red and her late Ming fellow singers—other than the courtesans who read notations—have used beans to assist their memory? We

4. Zhang Xuan, "Beiya tici" 北雅題詞, *Beiya*, 3a. The original in the National Library, Beijing; another copy of the same edition preserved in Naikaku Bunko, Tokyo. *Beiya* is a posthumous publication of Double Virtue's compilation in 1602 in commemoration of her untimely death several years ago.

5. Zhang Xuan, "Beiya tici," 2b.

are told a detail crucial to our understanding of Double Red's rapid memorization of the altered older song: its supposedly new composer changes the original rhythmic pattern. My reading is that he "robbed" time from some pitches and added the "stolen" time values to other pitches. Some notes of the fake new song received the expanded time, while others were contracted. Hypothetically, the relative temporal emphases of the song were changed, but the pitch notes and their sequence per se were intact. Because Double Red's memory had already stored the overall sequence of the pitch notes in the preexisting song, she was able to restore the distorted temporal order by using a notation method that made references to the duration of each pitch. The easiest way to do so would be to designate one bean for each pitch note in the new song and place it in its adequate metrical position. This method translates the rhythmic identity of the music into a space demarcated by even blocks. Let us call this rhythm-centered notation, or Approach No. 1.

Imagine that Double Red has fifty empty, white porcelain saucers of equal size, each representing one-quarter note, or one beat in time in a 4/4 measure. While listening to the singing, she would place bean(s) in the saucers as a way to note down the temporal value of each pitch. A saucer that has three beans, for example, denotes three pitches sung within the time frame of one beat. Needless to say, the more beans she places in one saucer, the more complicated the time value of each bean/pitch would become, and the more demanding it is for her memory. Despite this rhythmic flexibility, this method can dictate the change in rhythmic patterns and facilitate the singer's memory effectively when pitches and their sequence in the original song remain largely the same. I am inclined to think that this ingenious use of red beans to denote rhythmic patterns was not invented on the spot to cope with the con artist's presentation of the "new" song, but instead may have been the central pillar of the vocal pedagogy by which Wei Qing enhanced his concubine/student's memory skills.

A less likely but second plausible way to record the rhythms with beans would be to designate one saucer to one syllable/character (Chinese is monosyllabic), which can be called Approach No. 2. The preexisting tune that the con artist adapts in the story is called *The Birthday Girl from the West River* (*Changming xihenü* 長命西河女). Its standard formula has thirty-nine syllables—so thirty-nine saucers would fit the bill.

Although neither of these two approaches can precisely mark the duration of each pitch, Approach No. 1 defines the shape of time spatially. In pedagogy and criticism, its depiction of metrical progression would be more precise because it operates at the micro level of individual pitches rather than at the larger unit of syllables. All Double Red would have had to do was memorize the new metrical positions of the pitch notes in the original sequence and arrange them within a web space built with saucers. Imagine that the fifth pitch note *re* (or 尺 in her day), which originally takes place toward the end of the second beat (i.e., the second saucer), is now moved to the beginning of the third beat (i.e., the third saucer) and hits a downbeat. The change of metrical positions is the only focus of Double Red's memory; the seemingly daunting task of memorizing every aspect of the "new" composition is therefore reduced to a single memory task. This notational approach would demand fewer beans in each saucer, but it requires more saucers, that is, a larger space. Had it been transferred to a page layout, it would increase the cost of paper due to running blocks that visualize the saucers on paper.

The divide between the rhythm-centered Approach No. 1 and the syllable-centered Approach No. 2 would have been associated with two distinct memory habits—the medieval and early modern ones, respectively—which would then inexorably translate into two kinds of print layouts among music scores. My use of music scores as historical evidence for studying memory habits is determined, first, by the limitations of documentary evidence of the period. Little primary source material about the training processes has survived. Second, I am convinced that the distinction between the two notation systems provides a vital clue for understanding two different kinds of performance practices. We cannot expect to get a precise picture of how Double Red's brain processed rhythms without being able to give her a modern lab trial. But it is worth looking into the uncharted area of different notation methods' relevance to a vocalist's memory, thereby conducting an experiment in thinking about the types of memory techniques by means of examining those of music scores. I owe gratitude to but deviate significantly from two lineages of Chinese scholarship—those of scholars trained at Nanjing University and at Sun Yat-Sen University in Guangzhou, respectively—which have expanded the field of Chinese textual criticism to include music scores, song formulas, and songbooks, yet treat them as a single source of information deprived of their performance contexts.[6] My disparate use of this source as one of many kinds of evidence aims not at restoring order among these texts but at an inquiry into historical human

6. Representative scholars in the two lineages are Wu Xinlei 吳新雷 and Yu Weimin 俞為民 and Huang Shizhong 黃仕忠. See Wu Xinlei, *Zhongguo xiqu shilun* 中國戲曲史論 (Nanjing: Jiangsu jiaoyu chubanshe, 1996); Yu Weimin, *Quti yanjiu* 曲體研究 (Beijing: Zhonghua shuju, 2021); Huang Shizhong, "Taihe zhengyinpu yandu jihua jiqi shishi qingkuang" 太和正音譜研讀計劃及其實施情況, *Xiqu yu suwenxue* 戲曲與俗文學 1 (2019): 1–15.

consciousnesses. At the center of my concern is how courtesans might have approached these texts in actual usage, and how, in turn, these texts helped them become better at singing from memory.

The medieval rhythm-centered memorial pattern has only three examples. In contrast to the scarcity of Approach No. 1, instances of Approach No. 2 abound because it was the prevailing print layout in numerous early modern *kunqu* scripts. It is sufficient to use two comparative examples of the same aria to the tune of *Welcome Drumming in the Village* (*Cunli yagu* 村裏迓鼓), both from the Yuan drama *The Story of the Western Wing* (*Xixiang ji* 西廂記).

My examples do not follow a chronological order. This is because, in the field of music publication, early release dates do not necessarily suggest closer proximity to an earlier music reality. There was a fundamental divide between the late Ming editorial audacity and inclination toward popular renditions and High Qing antiquarian scholarly pursuits in book-making. Qing scholars who sought authorial intention often accused Ming editors of frivolously bending to contemporary tastes and practices. Thus it is not surprising that a late Ming *xiansuo* score uses Approach No. 2 (see fig. 5 below), whereas two Qing *xiansuo* scores use Approach No. 1 (see figs. 3 and 4).

My first example of Approach No. 1 is *Mr. Wei's Music Score* (*Weishi yuepu* 魏氏樂譜), a 1768 Japanese edition that allegedly records the tradition started by the late Ming refugee Wei Shuanghou 魏雙侯 (1617–1689), better known in Japan by his style name Shien 之琰, who moved to Japan in the 1660s. According to the postscript of the 1768 edition, Shien was a Fujianese official who fled from Ming China to Nagasaki during the dynastic transition.[7] In another Japanese account, which is perhaps more reliable, he was the owner of a Chinese junk that engaged in trading with Vietnam.[8] He had been to Japan many times. On his 1666 trip returning from Vietnam, he stopped by Nagasaki. After several years of sojourning there, he finally decided to settle down and acquired the Japanese surname Ōga 鉅鹿 in 1672. That same year he went to Kyoto and performed for the emperor. About a century later, in 1768, his great-grandson Wei Hao 魏皓 (1728–1774) compiled *Mr. Wei's Music*.[9] It is true that the hundred years from the late Ming, the great-

7. See Monishi Miyaki 海西宮奇, Postscript to *Weishi yuepu*. Digitized version, original in Peking University Library. https://ia600306.us.archive.org/13/items/02095092.cn/02095092.cn.pdf

8. *Nagasaki-shi shi: Kinsei* 新長崎市史·近世編 (Tokyo: Kyosei, 2012), 818–20.

9. "Kimiyama Sensei Den" 君山先生傳 in Tsutsui Iku 筒井郁, *Gishi gakki zu* 魏氏樂器圖 (1780), see Qian Renkang 錢仁康, "*Weishi yuepu* kaoxi" 魏氏樂譜考析, in *Qian Renkang yinyue wenxuan* 錢仁康音樂文選, ed. Qian Yiping 錢亦平 (Shang-

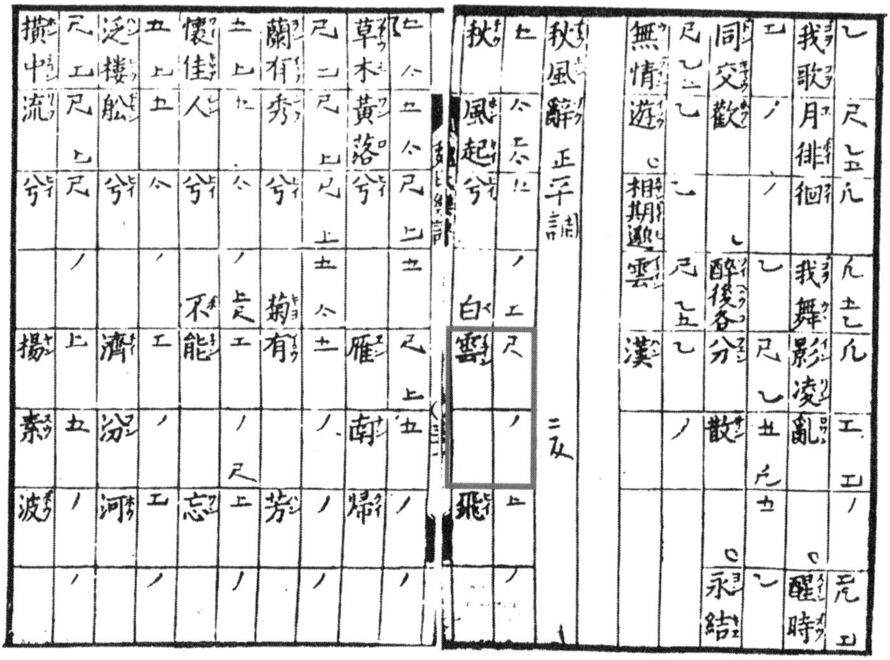

Fig. 2. *Mr. Wei's Music Score* (*Weishi yuepu*), an eighteenth-century score that displays a medieval modality of memorization. (Reprinted from *Xuxiu siku quanshu, zibu:* "the arts," vol. 1096 [Shanghai guji chubanshe, 2002].)

grandson and his disciples' mnemonic distortions, and Japanese influences may come to some extent between the surviving edition of *Mr. Wei's Music Score* and Wei Shuanghou's memorized Ming music. But there can be no doubt that this score tells us more about a medieval Chinese mental habit in singing than anything else we have at our disposal. At the core of this memorial technique are orders of even blocks with pitch notes in them that were memorized in the order defined by the melodic contour of a preexisting tune. This eighteenth-century score displays a medieval modality of memorization. Figure 2 shows a sample page.

The four highlighted blocks in the sample page shown in figure 2 exemplify how temporal value is expressed through spatial means. To the syllable *yun* 雲, meaning "cloud," one would sing for two beats (two saucers

hai: Shanghai yinyue chubanshe, 2013), 133–54. Also in Qi Mingjing 漆明鏡, *Weishi yuepu lingyunge liujuanben zongpu quanyi*《魏氏樂譜》凌雲閣六卷本總譜全譯 (Guilin: Guangxi shifan daxue chubanshe, 2017), 58–61.

in Approach No. 1, or the saucer hypothesis). The character 尺 in the right block next to 雲—equivalent to the pitch *re* in a movable *do* rendition—is a pitch note in the *gongche* 工尺 notation system. The curvy "/" sign below 尺 means the duration of the same note for a second beat. The small signs squeezed into the same block with 雲 are Japanese *hiragana*, glossing the Chinese pronunciation of 雲. The blank block underneath 雲 suggests continued articulation of this syllable. The way in which rhythm is defined spatially on paper here, I contend, corresponds to Double Red's memorization of a revised rhythmic pattern by spatially arranging red beans.

It is no coincidence that all the extant seventeenth-century publications of *xiansuo* music scores are for the same play, *The Story of the Western Wing*—the essential, enduring piece in the late Ming courtesan's *xiansuo* repertoire. My second example of spatializing rhythm in musical notation (fig. 3) comes from *A Lute Score of "The Story of the Western Wing"* (*Pipadiao Xixiang ji qupu* 琵琶調西廂記曲譜), the 1749 recension of a 1718–1719 edition as part of *A Heritage Passed Down from Mythic Time* (*Taigu chuanzong* 太古傳宗), a compendium in various fields commissioned by Qianlong Emperor (r. 1735–1796).[10] When referring to the lute score, musicologists conventionally use the general title of the compendium (hereafter *A Heritage*) rather than the full title of the specific volume. They do not agree on how authentically the score represents the *xiansuo* style prior to the rise of *kunqu*.[11] Despite the lack of internal evidence, it may be tempting to conjecture that *A Heritage* could retain traces of a "southernized," *kunqu*-ish rendition of *xiansuo*, reflecting the seventeenth-century musical reality, due to its hundred-year distance from the end of the *xiansuo* era. The intellectual context, however, suggests otherwise: namely, that *A Heritage* can be a valid source of information for glimpsing a medieval modality of memory associated with the late Ming courtesan's *xiansuo* performance. Its compilation, ranging from 1718 to 1749, coincided with the High Qing intellectual trend of evidential studies, or *kaoju*, which tended to preserve heritages without overt editorial interventions. To my knowledge, *A Heritage* is the earliest, if not the only, *xiansuo* score that strictly observes the

10. Compiled by Qianlong Emperor's music bureau called *Lülü zhengyi guan* 律呂正義館, completed 1718–1719.

11. Tan Xiong 譚雄, "Dui *Taigu chuanzong* yu *Nashuying qupu* zhong *Xixiangji qupu* de bijiao yanjiu" 對太古傳宗與納書楹曲譜中西廂記曲譜的比較研究, *Tianjin yinyue xueyuan xuebao* 天津音樂學院學報 2 (2006): 37–44; Wu Dan 毋丹, "Nanqu xiansuo hua: Ming Qing xiqu shouzhong de qingxiang ji nanbeiqu shenglü zhi bianqian, yi *Bei Xixiang* gongche pu weili" 南曲弦索化：明清戲曲受眾的傾向及南北曲聲律之變遷——以《北西廂》工尺譜為例, *Wenhua yichan* 文化遺產 4 (2018): 70–78.

rhythm-centered layout we have seen in the 1768 Japanese edition of *Mr. Wei's Music Score*. The 1749 editors of *A Heritage* sang the praises of the editors of the 1718–1719 recension for their treatment of the arrangement of pitch notes, which they characterized as being "extremely proper" 工尺譜至為妥協. In the prefatory essay "How to Read This Book" (*fanli* 凡例), the 1749 editors acknowledge that they "slightly altered some padding words that do not fit the prosodic rules" 添換襯字之間平仄不甚叶處, while leaving "the rest of the old score intact" 餘者悉依舊譜.[12] There is no doubt that the music score per se, together with its spatially luxurious design, was considered to be something "authentic" that deserved to be preserved for antiquarian taste.

As the sample in figure 3 shows, *A Heritage*'s print layout closely approximates the first example from *Mr. Wei's Music Score* (see fig. 2), except that the borders of the blocks are rendered invisible, and the size of each block is thus less even. In addition, the aria here is more melodic, so there are more pitch notes in a single block/saucer. But the mental habit required to read this notation would be not unlike that of the reader of *Mr. Wei's Music Score* and that of Double Red. To make it visually clear, figure 3 highlights a four-block unit for the single syllable *xia* 下, which runs eight beats. This particular syllable has been highlighted simply for its spatial proximity to the earlier example 雲 in figure 2. I intentionally chose this aria to the tune title of *Welcome Drumming in the Village* (*Cunli yagu*) because it occurs in four of the five samples illustrated in this section—figures 3 through 6—that is, in two examples of Approach No. 1, and two of Approach No. 2. It is an aria from the last suite of the first act in the northern version of *The Story of the Western Wing*. The aria portrays, in a fast-cutting fashion, how the protagonist Scholar Zhang is given a tour of a temple by a monk until the moment he encounters—and immediately falls in love with—the heroine Oriole.

In figure 3, the traditional spatial design is maintained, but the characters are much more widely spaced in comparison with figure 2 because the aria is more melodious. For example, in figure 3 the syllable *seng* 僧, the character to the left of 下, takes up to six blocks, sprawling over a large space on the paper. The chief merit of this design, therefore, does not make much economic sense but lies in its temporal clarity: it conveys a clear sense of temporality defined by space, which would better serve those who memorized the melodies spatially. For *xiansuo* players/singers, it must have

12. "Fanli," *Taigu chuanzong*, 1a, facsimile imprint in Liu Chongde 劉崇德, ed., *Zhongguo gudai qupu daquan* 中國古代曲譜大全, vol. 1 (Shenyang: Liuning renmin chubanshe, 2009.)

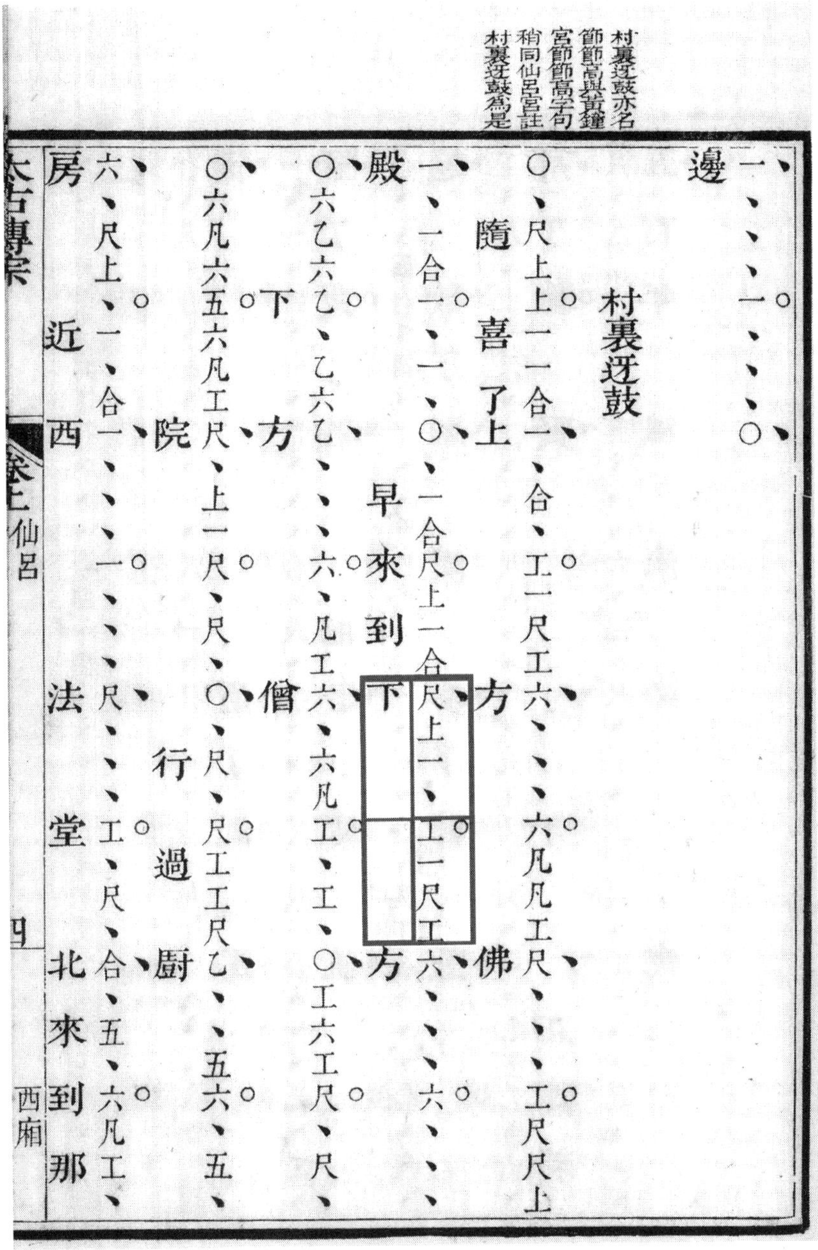

Fig. 3. *A Heritage Passed Down from Mythic Time* (*Taigu chuanzong*), whose print layout closely approximates the example from *Mr. Wei's Music Score* (fig. 2), 1749. (Courtesy National Library, Beijing.)

accommodated their spatially oriented memory habits better than syllable-centered notation did.

My last example that loosely maintains the spatial design, but with signs of erosion by southern habits, is a 1657 *xiansuo* music score (fig. 4), Shen Yuan's 沈遠 (fl. seventeenth century) *Collated and Corrected Xiansuo Scores of "The Western Wing" in Its Northern Version* (*Jiaozheng Bei xixiang xiansuo pu* 較正北西廂弦索譜). It shows a sample of the aria *Welcome Drumming in the Village*. The rhythm-centered notation system is compromised to handle florid rhythmic patterns. The highlighted four-square block has been transcribed by the modern musicologist Zhang Shibin into the following rhythmic pattern: |x xx x͡|xx x·x|, which I think grapples well with how this music works.[13] To accommodate this rhythm, the score borrows many marks from the printing conventions of late Ming *kunqu* notation books. First, the middle bar in |x xx x͡|xx x·x| is marked by the small horizontal bar "–" between the note 才 (specific symbol for the lute player's hand gesture) and the pitch notes 乙乙 (*ti* in a movable *do* scale) in the lower register of the block. This symbol denotes a *diban* 底板 (a beat sound from the clappers in the middle of a syllable's duration) in standard *kunqu* notation terminology. No such terms existed in authentic *xiansuo* performances, which relied on string instruments instead of clappers to signal beats. Second, it provides phonetic assistance for southerners, who were used to singing in the *kunqu* style. A small circle "o" is placed on the upper left corner of entering-tone syllables, such as the ones circled in figure 4—佛, 法, and 北—to remind some of the score's target readers of the differences between the local dialects of individuals with and without entering tones. Upon seeing these signs, readers whose native dialect had glottal endings (i.e., /p/, /t/, or /k/) for these words would hopefully have resisted the temptation to sound out a glottal ending, as they would have done in daily speech. The earlier usages of this mark are found in popular *kunqu* songbooks published between 1616 and 1623.[14] Thus, the 1657 *xiansuo* score is a mix of an arcane spatial layout designed for medieval memory habits and contemporaneous marks borrowed from an up-to-date notation method associated with *kunqu* practices.

The music scores sampled in figures 2–4 offer explicit examples of how

13. Zhang Shibin 張世彬, *Shen Yuan Bei Xixiang xiansuopu jianpu* 沈遠北西廂弦索譜簡譜 (Hongkong: Zhongwen daxue chubanshe, 1981), 4.

14. For example, Zhou Zhibiao 周之標 (fl. 1610–47), comp., *Wuyu cuiya* 吳歈萃雅, preface 1616, facsimile reprint in *Shanben xiqu congkan*, vols. 12–13, ed. Wang Qiugui 王秋桂; Xu Yu 許宇, comp., *Cilin yixiang* 詞林逸響, preface 1623, facsimile reprint in *Shanben xiqu congkan*, vol. 17; Ling Mengchu, comp., *Nanyin sanlai* 南音三籟, 1620s, facsimile reprint in *Shanben xiqu congkan*, vols. 52–53.

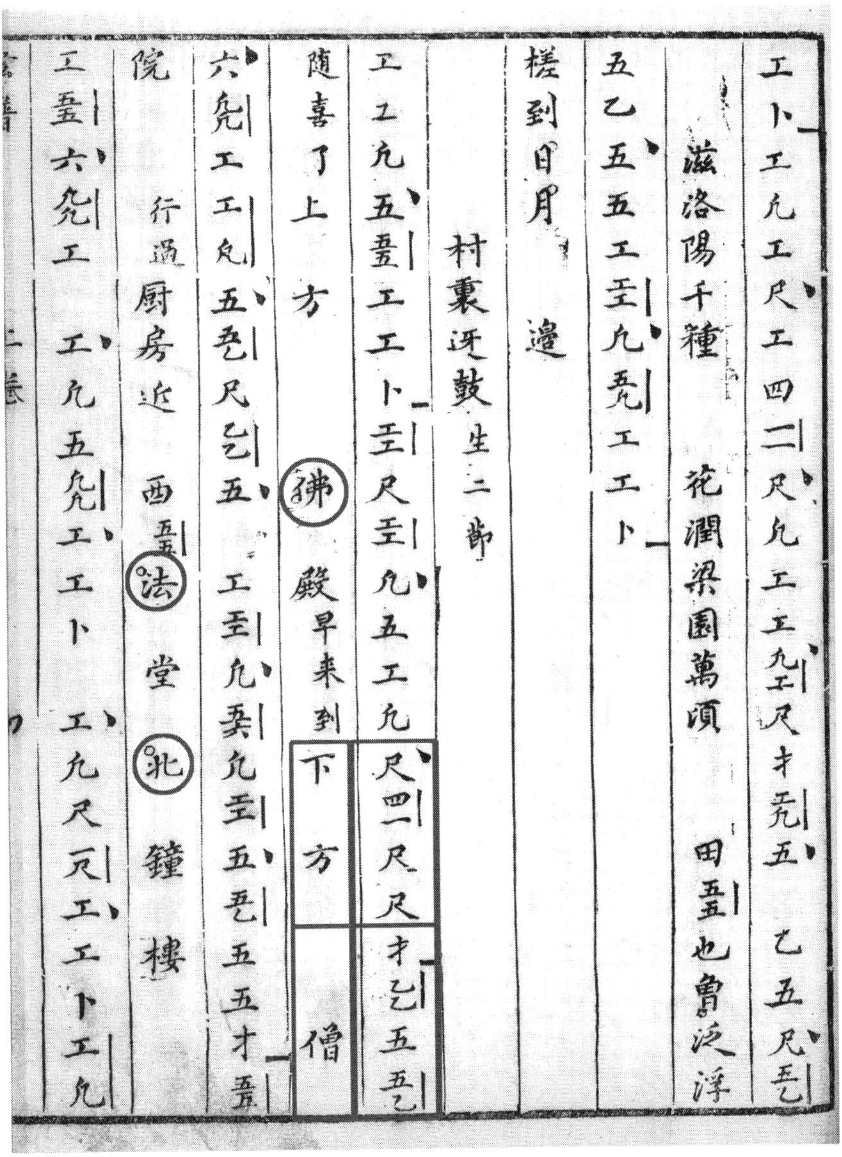

Fig. 4. *Collated and Corrected Xiansuo Scores of "The Western Wing" in Its Northern Version* (*Jiaozheng Bei xixiang xiansuo pu*), preface 1657. (Courtesy National Library, Beijing.)

marked meter weighed heavily in the medieval mnemonic techniques inherited by *xiansuo* performers of the late Ming. Despite small variations, they share an emphasis on pitch notes instead of words as reference points, with Chinese characters being relegated to the sidelines and distanced from each other unevenly. Pitch notes occupy more of the reader's attention, though usually printed in smaller fonts.

In contrast, the two examples of the syllable-centered method (Approach No. 2) for the same aria, *Welcome Drumming in the Village* (figs. 5 and 6), display vertical lines of words distributed evenly, with a flourish of pitch notes clustering by their side. The shaping of time is shifted from spatial means to linguistic means, and the steady metric flow at the center of the reader's attention is now replaced by the acoustic performance of a literary text, with music being rendered as an auxiliary extension of the printed lyrics. Behind the two distinct governing principles in printing—the melody framed by metrical blocks (Approach No. 1, in figs. 2–4) and the lyrics ornamented by pitch notes (Approach No. 2, in figs. 5 and 6)—are two different models of perception of time in musicking and memorization.

The example shown in figure 5 comes from Hu Zhoumian's 胡周冕 (fl. seventeenth century) *Examination and Correction of "The Western Wing" in Its Northern Version* (*Bei Xixiang dinglü* 北西廂訂律). It was released during the reign of the last Ming emperor, Chongzhen (r. 1628 to 1644), and is hence the earliest available *xiansuo* music score. According to the modern scholar Wu Dan's sight-reading, this score is in close proximity to Shen Yuan's 1657 score, and both scores operate entirely within the paradigm of *kunqu* vocal music, suggesting a full "southernization" of the northern genre *xiansuo*.[15] A comparison of figure 4 (1657) and figure 5 (1628–1644), however, shows a dichotomy in both page layout and musical content that is at variance with Wu's conclusion. To take the word 僧 as an example: it runs for six beats/blocks, with florid pitch notes in figure 4 (similar to figure 3 from the eighteenth-century *A Heritage*), but with approximately one-and-a-half beats in figure 5, with the singular note 五 (*la* on a movable *do* scale) stroked three times on the lute. It is thus a myth that an unbroken chain of *kunqu* vocal tradition was committed to writing in these two *xiansuo* scores. The only connection is found in their deployment of similar printing techniques in producing phonetic marks, something easily produced by book workshops specializing in *kunqu* songbooks. Hu Zhoumian is more thorough in this respect. There are three elocutionary symbols, including (1) the raindrop-

15. Wu Dan, "Nanqu xiansuo hua," 70–78.

shaped "ᴏ" indicating a velar ending of the syllable, (2) the small circle "o" suggesting that the reader should suppress a guttural ending—both (1) and (2) being added to the upper left corner of some characters—and (3) the big circle crossing a character, such as ㊂, meaning that the character 參 should be rendered with the ending of a labial sound /m/. These symbols collectively prescribe that the text is to be pronounced in a northern way, that is, with the enunciation of the "Central Plain" (*Zhongyuan yinyun* 中原音韻), which would have benefited southern singers whose native tongues had evolved to differ from standard Yuan-drama articulation.

What makes the 1628–1644 edition stand out is its strange positioning of the beat marks—not on the pitch notes but on the characters, resulting in a significant blurring of the rhythmic identity. Time distribution among the multiple pitch notes assigned to one character is much more flexible, and the relationship between one note and another is not detailed. This arrangement, at the expense of *gongche* notation's usual rhythmic rigidity, nonetheless catered to those who were accustomed to reading *dianban* 點板 notation—that is, rhythmic notation with no pitch notes but metric markings. During Hu Zhoumian's preparation for his *xiansuo* score in the first half of the seventeenth century, *dianban* notation enjoyed perhaps the largest reading community, as a popular form taken by most *kunqu* songbooks, *chuanqi* drama imprints (in different southern musical genres) for a wider audience, and song formulas for aspiring *chuanqi* playwrights. This was a strong enough reason for borrowing the trendiest music printing format.

To show its approximation of *dianban* notation, I juxtapose the northern aria *Welcome Drumming in the Village* in Hu's book with its southern equivalent from scene five of *"The Western Wing" in Its Southern Version* (*Nan Xixiang* 南西廂) in Ling Mengchu's 凌濛初 (1580–1644) *Three Kinds of Southern Sounds* (*Nanyin sanlai*, ca. 1620s). Though evidence shows that the southern adaptation had been completed for a different southern music style prior to the golden age of *kunqu*, it served, in effect, as the literary foundation for *kunqu* aficionados to render it in the "pure singing of the Wu folks" (*Wuren qingchang* 吳人清唱).[16] Li Yu's 李漁 (1611–ca. 1680) 1671 treatise on drama also maintained that the compositional principles of *kunqu*, as opposed to some other southern music styles, somehow rigidly resisted the original fourteenth-century text 不便強施於崑調.[17] Comparisons of the layouts between the two samples suggest that, with reference to print layout, the

16. Ling Mengchu, "Tanqu zazha" 譚曲雜劄, in *Nanyin sanlai*, 6b.

17. Li Yu, *Xianqing ouji* 閑情偶寄, in *Lidai quhua huibian: Qingdai bian* 歷代曲話彙編清代編, ed. Yu Weimin and Sun Rongrong 孫蓉蓉 (Hefei: Huangshan shushe, 2009) vol. 5, *juan* 3, 257.

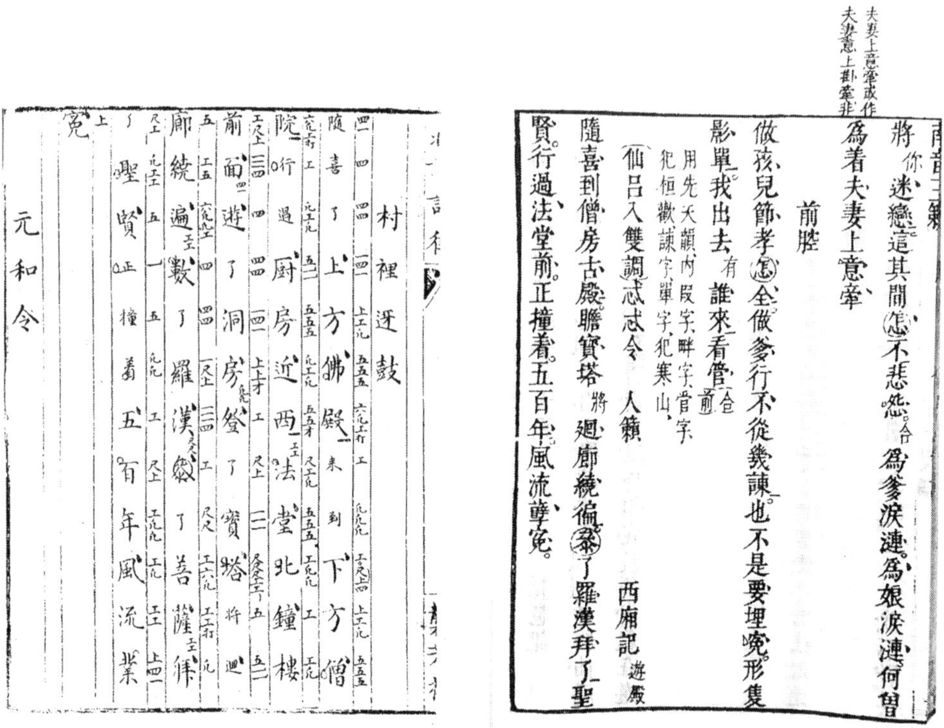

Fig. 5. Comparison between the northern aria *Welcome Drumming in the Village* (*Cunli yagu*) in Hu Zhoumian's *Examination and Correction of "The Western Wing" in Its Northern Version* (*Bei Xixiang dinglü*), published between 1628 and 1644, and its southern equivalent from scene five of *"The Western Wing" in Its Southern Version* (*Nan Xixiang*), published in the 1620s. (*left*, Courtesy of Library of Chinese National Academy of Arts, Beijing; *right*, Fudan University Library.)

1628–1644 edition (fig. 5) is literally a *dianban* notation with inserted vertical lines of pitch notes placed to the right of the characters.

The longtime prevalence of *dianban* notation, as well as the very late advent of precise pitch notation in the site of *kunqu* vocal art, deserves an explanation. *Gongche* notation of instrumental music scores appeared as early as in the 1580 woodblock edition of an encyclopedia.[18] It was therefore absolutely not the lack of printing techniques that led to the widespread reluctance to add pitch notes to *dianban* notation for *kunqu* for some three

18. Xu Huiying 徐會瀛 (fl. sixteenth century), comp., *Xinjuan Yantai jiaozheng tianxia tongxing wenlin yaobao wanjuan xingluo* 新鐫燕臺校正天下通行文林要寶萬卷星羅, 1580 edition, facsimile reprint in *Beijing tushuguan guji zhenben congkan* 北京圖書館古籍珍本叢刊 (Beijing: Shumu wenxian chubanshe, 1988), 75:25.

centuries. There is a crucial difference between the mindset in which no one felt the need to notate the pitches and the mindset in which their absence was a device for musicality. *Dianban* notation may well have served as the basis for elaboration, leaving ample blank space that functioned to urge the reader to improvise. The earliest surviving *kunqu* vocal scores with pitch notes, which put an end to the domination of *dianban* notation from the early seventeenth to late eighteenth century, are *kunqu* master Ye Tang's 葉堂 (ca. 1724–ca. 1799) *Music Scores from the Room of Stored Books* (*Nashuying qupu* 納書楹曲譜), published between 1792 and 1794. Ye's sizable publication projects provided rhythmic symbols marked on *gongche* pitch notes, albeit with all the elocutionary markings removed, for four full-length *chuanqi* dramas in Tang Xianzu's 湯顯祖 (1550–1616; *jinshi* 1583) oeuvre, and for numerous scenes excerpted from a great variety of southern plays. From the perspective of performance history, the Ye Scores (*Ye pu* 葉譜) marked the transition to a new era that called for less accidental, less arbitrary rhythmic performance in *kunqu*.

Eight years before the publication of these *kunqu* scores, in 1784, Ye Tang had published *A Complete Music Score of "The Story of the Western Wing" from the Room of Stored Books* (*Nanshuying Xixiang ji quanpu* 納書楹西廂記全譜), experimenting with setting in score his personal *kunqu* rendition of the fourteenth-century northern drama. Half a century after the publication of Qianlong Emperor's antiquarian investment in *xiansuo* music, *A Heritage*, Ye's popular rendition was destined to supersede any preceding *xiansuo* scores and reached a broader audience. As discussed in chapter 1, "authentic" *xiansuo* renditions of the northern version had fallen into obsolescence in the early seventeenth century, with the exceptions of a few live performances delivered by courtesan troupes; and the southern adaptation rendered in *kunqu* was the thing to listen to or view onstage. Most drama critics thought it regrettable that the musical charm of the southern version, whose literary merit was far less profound than that of the original Yuan drama, had led to the inevitable neglect of the original drama.[19] According to a local gazetteer, Ye Tang was motivated to revive the popular interest in the medieval play by setting its lyrics to *kunqu* music of his own style. The goal was achieved: there was a bounce-back of the northern drama after the 1784 release of its

19. Drama critics who held the same view with Ling Mengchu and Li Yu include Lu Cai 陸采 (1497–1537), Liang Chenyu 梁辰魚 (1519–1591), Qi Biaojia 祁彪佳 (1602–1645), Li Diaoyuan 李調元 (1734–1803), and Wu Mei 吳梅 (1884–1939), etc. Their comments can be found in Lu's "Lu Tianchi Xixiang ji xu" 陸天池西廂記序, Liang's "Nan Xixiang tici" 南西廂題辭, Qi's *Yuanshantang qupin* 遠山堂曲品, Li's *Juhua* 劇話, and Wu's *Guqu zhutan* 顧曲麈談, respectively.

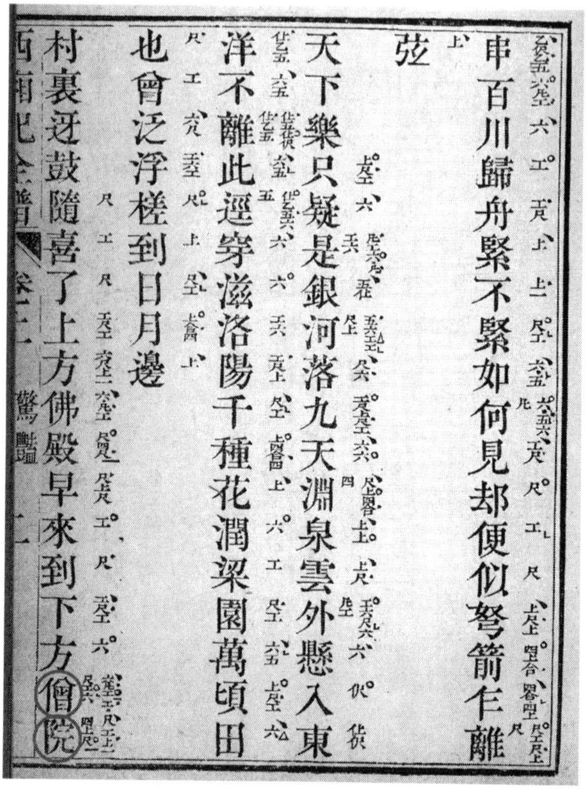

kunqu scores.[20] Following the publishing conventions of the preceding *xiansuo* scores, the scores present the music in *gongche* notation. The successive *kunqu* scores published from 1792 to 1794 spontaneously followed suit in their choice of *gongche* notation over the traditional *dianban* notation—in this sense the 1784 scores served as a cushion against the breakthrough in completely abolishing *dianban* notation for *kunqu*.

One crucial moment in the publication history of this score deserves our attention: Ye compromised in response to the popular demand for more detailed rhythmic signs and published a new edition in 1795, which speaks

20. Cao Yunyuan 曹允源 and Li Genyuan 李根源, comp., *Minguo Wuxian zhi* 民國吳縣志, *juan* 75, in *Zhongguo defangzhi jicheng: Jiangsu fuxianzhi ji* 中國地方誌集成·江蘇府縣志輯 (Nanjing: Jiangsu guji chubanshe, 1991), 12:526.

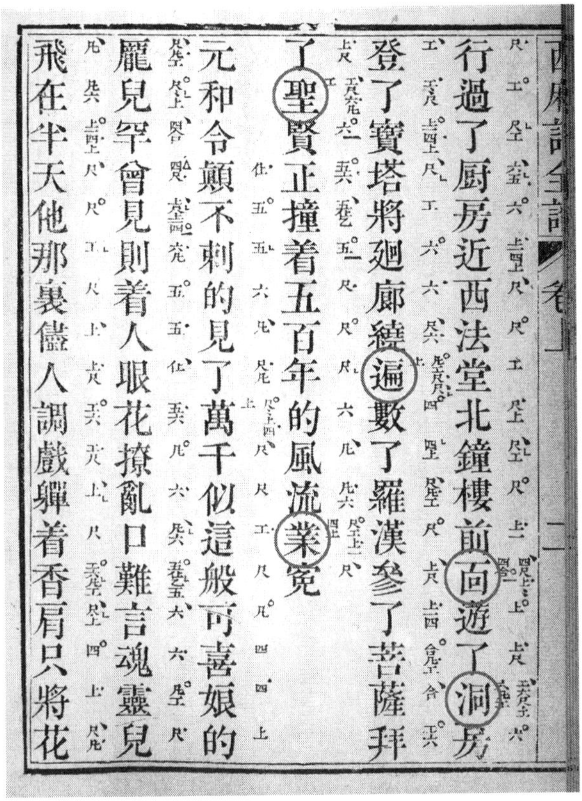

Fig. 6. (*above and facing page*): *A Complete Music Score of "The Story of the Western Wing" from the Room of Stored Books* (*Nanshuying Xixiang ji quanpu*), 1795. (Courtesy Fudan University Library.)

volumes about the changing practice in rhythmic performance at the time. Full rhythmic notation, lacking in the 1784 edition, was a norm established by the ensuing southern drama scores, which apparently sold better. Ye mentions his financial pressure in his preface to the 1795 recension: the 1784 imprints were not selling well 購者寥寥.[21] He explains that "this [addition of rhythmic details] was imposed on me by the wish of the masses" 不得已從俗, so that he deviated from his original plan, which had been designed to maintain the desirable vitality of the music by allowing for rhythmic variations depending on the singer's personal understanding (*huoban* 活板). As shown in figure 6, in the 1795 recension, next to each large Chinese character there is a square-shaped space of equivalent size filled with pitch note(s), most

21. Ye Tang, preface to the 1795 edition of the *Xixiang ji quanpu*, 9.

of which are marked with complicated rhythmic marks. Some words, such as 僧, 院, 面, 洞, 遍, 聖, and 業, highlighted in circles (see fig. 6), have their notations squeezed into the busy traffic of double vertical lines.

The popular demand for detailed rhythmic-notation marks allows us to shed light on a particular mode of reading—namely, the reading of the musical imprint as an authorial if not definitive composition, potentially enacted out loud for a selected group of listeners. Indeed, by 1794, the series of *kunqu* scores of southern dramas that stressed the stylistic beauties of Ye's personal vocal style had established his wide reputation as the founder of his own *kunqu* vocal school. Master Ye's ownership of the scores, particularly his rhythmic characteristics, was valuable on the market. Consumers wanted to flesh out the rhythmic details in the exact manner of the Ye style. They preferred to be constrained by Ye's full transcriptions, which he had initially refused to offer and had condemned as "lifeless" rhythms (*siban* 死板), than to welcome the freedom he had granted them to punctuate the music themselves. They preferred musical stability over the instability brought about by the common seventeenth-century practice of improvisation. In this sense, the Ye Scores not only ended the age of *dianban* notation but also erased the arbitrariness of the seventeenth-century musicians, alongside the fad of exercising one's musical intelligence by improvising.

As the very first *gongche* notation of *kunqu*, the late eighteenth-century Ye Scores became the model for publishers of *kunqu* scores in the centuries that followed. Some later *gongche* notation would slant the vertical linear pitch notes into diagonals in the hope of better visual clarity, especially for the sake of making out the rhythmic marks. No invention other than this slight amendment has since been added to this type of textual aid for *kunqu* singers. Two salient features of this lineage of music scripts are its fidelity to a singing master of genius (though different masters might have different renditions) and its dismissal of the seventeenth-century appreciation for improvisation. The suppression of microlevel rhythmic choices is the heritage principle of *kunqu* vocal art handed down to students of *kunqu* to this day, myself included. I began my own *kunqu* training in the late twentieth century, with modern scores of *gongche* notation. As a native speaker, I took the syllable-centered layout to be self-evident; at the time I first encountered the rhythm-centered notations, they looked merely old-fashioned, if not primitive, at best, and had a peculiar period charm. I had difficulty accepting the idea that they might represent a long tradition of memorial reconstruction in singing. Such different memory habits, after all, are not only scarcely mentioned in written documents but have also long been out of practice in the oral tradition.

It was the account of Double Red's red beans that enlightened and thrilled me: I started to search among the early modern *xiansuo* music scores for connections between the spatially lavish notation system and the medieval memory skills that had existed for centuries prior to the age of *dianban* notation. Admittedly, music prints in early modern China are a specialist area that increasing numbers of scholars are working on, and this chapter does not pretend to summarize their work or to follow the field's antiquarian tendencies. To recover a lost vestige of vocal training and memory skills in singing, I have tried to read music archives within the interpretive framework devised by cultural historians of memory. No previous scholarship has read the two kinds of scores as manifestations of two different systems of transcribing musical reality onto paper, and, further, as two different mental pictures imprinted on the courtesan singer's memory. The examples listed here, inevitably sketchy, are nonetheless worth looking at carefully to understand how neatly they can be divided into two major types of engagement with human memory—the rhythm-centered Approach No. 1 (figs. 2–4) and the syllable-centered Approach No. 2 (figs. 5–6), respectively—with a rough sense of evolution. The dichotomy reminds us of the importance of *dianban* notation in generating both a new sense of the shaping of time in music and a new memory habit that symbolizes the break with the medieval past. Our study of the late Ming courtesan's musical performances must attend to the way in which her memory habits mutated in reaction to the changing musical forms and contents during the transition from *xiansuo* to *kunqu*.

In this section, comparisons with musical practices anterior or posterior to the heyday of *dianban* notation (i.e., the long seventeenth century) have allowed us to see the relative rhythmic flexibility in *kunqu* singing once upon a time. Besides rhythmic variations, evidence in the next section will show that *kunqu* melodies in the age of *dianban* notation also enjoyed more freedom due to their capacity for passionate improvisation.

II. "Fixed Melodies" of *Xiansuo* and Its Replacement Model in *Kunqu*

Courtesans who performed at the moment when *kunqu* renditions of northern arias (北曲 *beiqu*), such as *Welcome Drumming in the Village* from *The Story of the Western Wing*, were growing increasingly popular, faced the drastic change in their training from the spatially oriented memorative learning to the syllable-centered memory habit. Far from pushing *xiansuo* aside and concentrating on *kunqu* alone, courtesans had embraced both in their repertoire. Courtesans with solid training in *xiansuo*, such as Nimble Beauty, became good *kunqu* singers. The juxtaposition of two drastically different forms performed by the same group of people was characteristic of the programming at the time. I turn to the courtesan's mixed performance events as the context for this merging in the next section. In this section, however, my focus remains musicological, centering on how the two forms differed essentially on compositional principles and on how such differences changed the definition of the new generation of virtuosic singers.

We lack aural access to "authentic" *xiansuo* rendition of northern tunes, notwithstanding the knowledge to be gained from the above-mentioned scores.[22] But the living tradition of *kunqu* includes an entire reservoir of operatic scenes written in northern song suites. Concomitantly, the early modern *kunqu* culture, saturated with early modern ideas and rules, has brought about a misconception that has confused scholars since the late Ming—namely, the assumption that the original *xiansuo* renditions of northern arias and their *kunqu* counterparts were the same, in other words, the belief in an ideal continuity between medieval and early modern practices of *xiansuo* singing.

It is common knowledge to modern *kunqu* singers that northern arias (*beiqu*) as a literary category are rendered in a more melodious manner than southern arias (南曲 *nanqu*), for two reasons: (1) *beiqu* are in the seven-tone rather than five-tone mode (with *nanqu* missing *fa* and *ti*); and (2) they have the capacity for addition of time to one syllable (again, we must apply a strictly syllable-centered logic), as long as the inserted time does not affect the metric positions of other syllables. For example, adding four beats in a 4/4-meter composition, or adding two beats in a 2/4-meter composition, will not alter the overall structure in terms of syllable-beat correspondences. Imagine a long rubber band nailed on the wall, with the nails forming a rigid pattern but the band between two nails stretchy enough for additional weight. A reader who is more used to reading staff notations

22. For the living tradition of *xiansuo* performance passed down from the Manchu royal family, see *Xiansuo rensheng* 弦索人生 (Shanghai: Shanghai yinyue chubanshe), forthcoming 2025. The recordings feature the performances of a music professor Tan Longjian 談龍建 (1952–) at the Central Conservatory of Music in Beijing and those of her disciples. Tan's master was Aisin Gioro Yuhuan 愛新覺羅·毓峘 (1930–2003), the fifth generation in the lineage of Daoguang Emperor (1782–1850), who started at the age of eight learning *xiansuo* performance from a eunuch and a blind player specializing in teaching *xiansuo* (*menxian'er* 門先). No other contemporary performers than Tan and her disciples, that I know of, can claim the heritage of the authentic *xiansuo* tradition. I thank Professor Lei Liang, who initiated and sponsored this important publication project, for bringing it to my attention.

can also imagine that the singer is welcome to add a bar or two of melody within the duration of a syllable to heighten this particular syllable emotionally. The additional time on particular syllables granted to the singer as s/he likes is called *zengban* 贈板 (lit., "gifted beats"), or "ornamental beats." In *gongche* notational practice, the structural beats and the ornamental beats are marked differently for theoretical clarity. Differentiating the structural from the ornamental beats notationally means that the singer must have the shape of the "skeleton" structure memorized before fleshing out the melodies. In this way the unitary identity of each tune pattern remains clear no matter how florid the musical rendering becomes. To summarize, having ornamental beats is a rhythmic characteristic that distinguishes *beiqu* from *nanqu* in *kunqu* practice. By contrast, each *nanqu* melody in *kunqu* has a set number of beats, and that number is an unbreakable taboo. This distinction is held by towering modern *kunqu* scholars such as Wu Mei 吳梅 (1884–1939) and is applied to early modern practices ahistorically.[23]

The main reason for the anachronistic theory that ignores the late Ming *kunqu* improvisation may perhaps be the legacy of Ye Tang's *gongche* notation, which replaced *dianban* notation as the model for *kunqu* scores in the 1790s. Many dramatic effects must have been lost as a result, including what Ye Tang called the "vitality of music through rhythmic variations" (*huoban*) that involved the *zengban* technique, as well as basic compositional skills of "flowing" with linguistic tones. Modern *kunqu* differs greatly from the late Ming practice in this respect. It is a common mistake not to see the living tradition differing from *kunqu* practices in the era of improvisation after the traces of the improvisation-era practices were erased in the prevalent *gongche* notation of *kunqu*.

The triumphant story of *kunqu* trickling upward from its humble origins in brothels to reach the highest levels of social organizations—the gentry and royalty—must be seen within the context of improvisations. Our most valuable evidence for the musical trend of improvisation during this period is a songbook edited and published between 1629 and 1644 by a few aficionados of *kunqu* under their pseudonyms, entitled *Music Scores of Black Snow* (*Xuanxue pu* 玄雪譜).[24] Modern *kunqu* singers would regard this score as completely unperformable, since it bears neither *gongche* nor *dianban* notation. Its editors' explanations for the lack of any musical markings thus qualify as the core tenet in favor of improvisation with extreme freedom:

23. For a typical narrative of the difference between *nanqu* and *beiqu* in the *kunqu* tradition, see Wu Mei, *Guqu zhutan* (Taipei: Taiwan shangwu yinshuguan, 1973), 56.

24. Facsimile reprint in *Shanben xiqu congkan*, vols. 50–51.

"Beats . . . are fundamentally something in a gray zone when it comes to musical rules. With extraordinary finesse one could even skip notes and rush on some words without violating the rhythmic rules. The most virtuosic courtesans can spontaneously adapt their singing to the newest fashions and display classy finesse" 板 . . . 原在有定無定之間, 最妙於偷腔促字而仍合於拍, 善歌紅雪, 自能與時偕變而入於妙. The compound Hong Xue 紅雪 (here glossed as "most virtuosic courtesans") alludes to two medieval courtesans expertly versed in singing, Hong'er 紅兒 and Xueniang 雪娘, respectively.[25] To the male amateur compilers, no skillful courtesan would have needed to be shown rhythmic markings.

Freedom in adding beats led to the finest nuances, originality, and spontaneity in expression that would carry the singer to the heights of fame at singing festivals, the most famous festival being the grand annual singing competition in Tiger Hill (present-day Huqiu, Suzhou). Improvisation of ornamental beats with enhanced coloratura must have been considered the most difficult part of execution: the singer who exhibited these skills in astonishing ornamentation for fifteen minutes on a single syllable 每度一字, 近乎一刻, as recounted with awe by Yuan Hongdao 袁宏道 (1568–1610; *jinshi* 1591) and Zhang Dai 張岱 (1597–ca. 1679), was crowned the laureate singer of *kunqu*.[26] Though we have lost the aural access to such dazzling effects, there is no doubt that improvisation through *zengban* was the sine qua non of *kunqu* singing techniques in the late Ming.

Yet it is crucial that the late Ming and the medieval practices of *xiansuo* not be confused with each other. By no means were *beiqu* as a literary category rendered flexibly in the literatus He Liangjun's 何良俊 (1506–1573) musical ideal of *xiansuo*. On the contrary, he writes that what marked the whole "authentic" *xiansuo* tradition before the 1570s was its lack of flexibility. As a conservative musical cognoscente, He had a personal preference for the melodic rigidity of *xiansuo*, which contributed both to antiquarian effects and to the legitimacy of a *xiansuo-nanqu* hierarchy he insists on throughout his treatise. He quotes his private *xiansuo* adviser Dun Ren 頓仁 (fl. 1510s–1570s), a veteran royal *xiansuo* musician for Emperor Wuzong (reign 1505–1521), as saying that "[*Beiqu* or *xiansuo*] all have fixed rules, and

25. A clearer reference of the two names Hong'er and Xueniang to courtesan singers appear in Xiaochizi's 笑癡子 preface to *Xuanxue pu*: "Hong'er's teeth are by nature fragrant . . . Xueniang's tongue is by nature agile" 紅兒之齒自香 . . . 雪娘之舌本慧, *Shanben xiqu congkan*, 50:16.

26. Qian Bocheng 錢伯城, ed., *Yuan Hongdao ji jianjiao* 袁宏道集箋校 (Shanghai: Shanghai guji chubanshe, 1981), *juan* 4, *Jinfan ji* 錦帆集 (dated 1596–1597), 157–59. Zhang Dai, *Tao'an mengyi* 陶庵夢憶 (Taipei: Kaiming shudian, 1978), *juan* 5, 69–70.

therefore it is much easier to set music to new lyrics" 皆有定則, 故新曲要度入亦易, and also that "[now that *nanqu*] lack fixed rules to observe, one can feel the notes [on one's instrument in the accompaniments] in playing improvisationally" 既無定則可依, 而以意彈出.[27] As already mentioned in chapter 1, He Liangjun stuck to this rather stubborn position in the teeth of the popularity of *kunqu* not only in Nanjing (where he lived) and Suzhou, but also in other urban centers with flourishing pleasure quarters. It is probable that much of the popularity of *kunqu* was generated by the passion and capacity for improvisation of its practitioners—professional teachers, courtesans, and aficionados.

Beiqu in He Liangjun's terminology is, in the musical rather than literary sense, the equivalent to *xiansuo*; so is the term *nanqu*. His disfavor of *nanqu* is not about the literary features of "southern arias" as a literary category but about the "southern *manner*" of singing or composition, that is, improvisation. Improvisation on vocal parts, as I have emphasized elsewhere, was a highly developed skill, which not only demarcated virtuoso singers from ordinary ones but was the incentive for courtesans and aficionados to hire professional *kunqu* teachers with better skills.[28] In contrast to *xiansuo* renderings of *beiqu* lyrics with fixed melodies, two innovative musical modalities of *kunqu* are key to heightening improvisations on *beiqu* texts.

The first crucial technique is, in Dun Ren's words, "bending operatic melodies to follow the linguistic tones of the lyrics, which was done by people of our generation" 後人依腔按字打將出來, as opposed to *xiansuo* compositions with "fixed melodies" handed down to his generation.[29] The verb Dun uses for "compose" in the Western sense is *da* 打, or "to strike," which remains in the modern *kunqu* lexicon *da puzi* 打譜子, meaning to arrange pitch notes in the *kunqu* style.[30] This means that each Chinese character can serve as a unit indicating a certain melodic contour. Fitting the syllables into a preexisting tune with improvisations and ornaments was the job of

27. He Liangjun, *Siyouzhai congshuo* 四友齋叢說 (Beijing: Zhonghua shuju, 1983), *juan* 37, 342.

28. Peng Xu, "The Music Teacher."

29. He, *Siyouzhai congshuo*, *juan* 37, 342.

30. From He Liangjun's perspective, the traditional treatment of Chinese words with musical elements in composition, as was discussed by modern scholars Yuen Ren Chao and Rulan Chao Pian, was an unwelcome early modern invention, breaching the "fixed melodies" rule of Yuan music. See Chao, "Tone, Intonation, Singsong, Chanting, Recitative, Tonal Composition, and Atonal Composition in Chinese," in *For Roman Jakobson: Essays on the Occasion of His Sixtieth Birthday* (The Hague: Mouton, 1956), 52–59; and Pian, "Tone and Tone: Applying Musical Elements to Chinese Words," *Journal of Chinese Linguistics* 28, no. 2 (2000): 181–85.

the singer. The librettist and the singer meet halfway in their musical minds, sharing the obligations of a composer in the Western sense.

If the modern *kunqu* singer (myself included) finds the more musically detailed *beiqu* in the *kunqu* repertoire today more compelling than its *nanqu* arias, the vast body of improvisations of historical *kunqu* singers since the sixteenth century must have been one of the contributing factors to this aesthetic effect. The flourishes that were once indications of the singer's virtuosity or individuality have been selected, narrowed down, prescribed in *gongche* notations, and passed down to us by tradition. Precision in execution (some modern scores come with signs to breathe) vis-à-vis spontaneity in improvisation has become the new standard for virtuosity today, but our modern cultural attitude toward improvisation should not stand in the way of our understanding of historical performance.

Beyond this word-tone relationship, the second factor that enabled ornaments-qua-improvisation in *kunqu* singing was the actual reign of clappers in music, as opposed to the trivial role that clappers played in *xiansuo* singing. In visual and literary representations of musicking scenes from the late Ming, clappers exist almost everywhere; they cannot be taken as tokens of any particular music genre. Despite the superficial similarities between the clappers used in *xiansuo* and those in *kunqu* performances, their functions in the temporal dimension of the music diverge radically. In *kunqu* and other southern genres, temporalities are organized by the clappers, a bit like the conductor's baton, whereas in *xiansuo*'s "fixed melodies," the ensemble works within a unified temporality are defined principally by the string instrument. This contrast, again, is emphasized in Dun Ren's remarks on the *xiansuo/nanqu* dichotomy: "[In *nanqu*] the wind instruments can vary the length of certain notes but still stay within the normal range of metric performance, whereas for *xiansuo* music if one strikes the strings one time extra, or one time short, the rhythmic pattern will be in utter disorder" 笛管稍長短其聲, 便可就板; 弦索若多一彈, 或少一彈, 則汆板矣.[31] Dun's statement needs further interpretation, and here is mine: Under no circumstances in *xiansuo*, at least the "authentic" type advocated by He Liangjun and his peers, were there ad libitum passages because it was an "instrumental" genre designed for a chorus, rather than a "singing," touching, and expressive one for soloists. Judging by whether or not they have an ad libitum opening passage, the five examples in figures 2–6 can be grouped under the category of "authentic" or "phony" *xiansuo* renditions as follows: Example 1 (*Mr. Wei's Music Score*) and Example 2 (*A Heritage*) both have all the pitch notes mapped on

31. He, *Siyouzhai congshuo*, *juan* 37, 342.

rhythmic grids, whereas Example 3 (Shen Yuan's 1657 score) and Example 4 (Hu Zhoumian's 1628–1644 score) open with the first three syllables—隨, 喜, and 了—having free temporal durations until the arrival of the first downbeat, marked by "、" on the fourth syllable 上. In Example 5 (the Ye Scores), the first sound of the clappers is not heard until the fifth syllable. The silence of the clappers denotes ad libitum. Modern *kunqu* singing, from my experience, relies on the drummer's finesse to hit that first downbeat, which leads the singer to "enter the metric performance from ad libitum" (*shangban* 上板) at the right moment.

Based on his study of *A Heritage* and Shen Yuan's 1657 score, musicologist Liu Chongde speculates that *xiansuo* singing had no place for *sanban qu* 散板曲, or short tune-patterns rendered in an arioso style (imagine recitatives in a typical Wagner opera, but with the melodies maintaining recognizable tune identities). Certainly, this diverges dramatically from the modern *kunqu* practice of *beiqu*, in which almost every suite begins with a *sanban qu*. The rationale for the lack of *sanban qu* in *xiansuo*, Liu postulates, was that "the singing must fit in the *pipa*-lute's meters measured by the number of the player's plucks: sixteen plucks form a unit, distributed evenly among eight beats, and every eight beats one heard the clappers once."[32] Liu further characterizes such a rhythm as the persistence of rhythmic performance in "authentic" *xiansuo* inherited from the song lyrics of the Tang and Song dynasties (roughly the seventh to thirteenth centuries).

The all-important clappers in *nanqu* (southern music genres), once relocated to a *xiansuo* performance circumstance, would immediately lose their significance and become ornamental. The best summary to date of the kernel of the whole matter is found, unsurprisingly, in He Liangjun's words: "To northern tunes, the key to powerful rhythmic performance is the strings; to southern tunes, it is the clappers" 北力在絃, 南力在板.[33] This dictum gained currency after being quoted by a more politically influential and culturally prominent figure, Wang Shizhen 王世貞 (1526–1590; *jinshi* 1547).[34] The diminished importance of the clappers is used as a rhetorical device in the sixteenth-century novel *The Plum in the Golden Vase* (*Jin Ping Mei*

32. Liu Chongde 劉崇德, *Yuan zaju yuepu yanjiu yizhu* 元雜劇樂譜研究譯注 (Shijiazhuang: Hebei jiaoyu chubanshe, 2003), 1:18. He changed his assessment in *Yanyue xinshuo: Tang Song gongting yanyue yu ciqu yinyue yanjiu* 燕樂新說: 唐宋宮廷燕樂與詞曲音樂研究 (Hefei: Huangshan shushe, 2011), 389.

33. He, *Siyouzhai congshuo*, *juan* 37.

34. Wang Shizhen, *Quzao* 曲藻, *Zhongguo gudian xiqu lunzhu jicheng* 中國古典戲曲論著集成 (Beijing: Zhongguo xiju chubanshe, 1959, rpt. 1980), 4:27.

cihua 金瓶梅詞話).[35] In the pornographic chapter 27, the sixth wife, whose wealth, beauty, and kindness have made her the source of envy in a polygamous family, is forced by the fifth wife into a marginal position in a female ensemble by being relegated to playing the clappers. The performance event takes place when the protagonist asks his concubines to temporarily form a band and sing a northern tune in chorus. The third and fifth wives both have some training in a specific string instrument, but refuse to begin unless the sixth wife joins to play a pair of clappers and sing along. Their sour intention to provoke her embarrassment in the ensemble has easily skipped critical attention. The anonymous novelist who created this subtle drama of jealousy must have had in mind what He Liangjun and Wang Shizhen had stated about the "power" (*li* 力) in *xiansuo* performances residing in the strings, not the clappers. The distinction between *xiansuo* and *kunqu* is thus crucial to reaching a deeper reading of this vignette of music-making, followed as it is by the protagonists' two love-making scenes: with the innocent sixth wife, it is a consoling act for the embarrassment she has just endured; with the jealous fifth wife, it is a ferocious punishment.

The best evidence of how high levels of improvisational skills empowered the new generation of *kunqu* musicians to accommodate irregularities in the lyrics is the case of the literary genius Tang Xianzu's *chuanqi* masterpiece, *The Peony Pavilion* (*Mudan ting* 牡丹亭, 1598). Three contemporary adaptors of the play all ascribed their entire raison d'être to an effort to better serve the singer—in their narratives, Tang's lyrics, whether in the *nanqu* or *beiqu* category, are ill-suited to the purpose of singing.[36] The majority of modern scholars have speculated that there was a "literary war for *kunqu* music" started by the adaptors, experts on *kunqu* hailing from its cultural center, the Wu area, among whom the most influential fighter was Shen Jing 沈璟 (1553–1610; *jinshi* 1574). Aoki Masaru famously coined the phrase "Rivalry between Tang and Shen" (*Tang Shen zhi zheng* 湯沈之爭) in 1930 to describe the *kunqu* experts' ostracizing of the inlander, Jiangxi native Tang Xianzu.[37] But the experts' condescending rescues of Tang's masterpiece seem to have

35. *Jin Ping Mei cihua* (Hong Kong: Taiping shuju, 1982), vol. 2, chap. 32, 6a–b; David T. Roy, trans., *The Plum in the Golden Vase* (*Jin Ping Mei cihua*) (Princeton: Princeton University Press, 2001), 2:136–37.

36. Catherine C. Swatek, *Peony Pavilion Onstage: Four Centuries in the Career of a Chinese Drama* (Ann Arbor: Center for Chinese Studies, University of Michigan, 2002, 2012), 25–67.

37. Aoki Masaru, *Shina kinsei gikyokushi* 支那近世戲曲史 (Tokyo: Kobundo shoten, 1930), Chinese translation entitled *Zhongguo jinshi xiqushi* 中國近世戲曲史, trans. Wang Gulu 王古魯 (Shanghai: Shangwu yinshuguan, 1936), 211–12.

failed to attract *kunqu* singers at the time. Rather, it is Tang's original text that remained in the living repertoire of *kunqu*, triumphantly receiving Master Ye Tang's detailed scores in the late eighteenth century. From a literary historian's perspective, the only acceptable interpretation of *The Peony Pavilion*'s staying power in the *kunqu* repertoire is that it derives from a genius literary mind's conquest of musical rules—a sure sign of canonical literature's triumph. It is easy to forget that Tang's work was chosen to remain in the repertoire by the lowly, invisible men and women in the demimonde who were empowered by the new system of composition. By means of highly skillful improvisations, *kunqu* gained the capacity to overcome obstacles posed by contemporary playwrights who may have sacrificed musical and prosodic rules for the sake of literary merits or ideological agendas.

Once *kunqu* began to take over *beiqu* texts and set up its improvisation-oriented compositional rules both for lyrics that had heretofore been sung in the *xiansuo* style and for new plays, the outcome of the competition was self-evident. *Chuanqi* playwrights understood the attraction of the florid melodies of *beiqu* rendered in the *kunqu* style and never failed to make room in their new plays for northern song suites. A 1624 anthology, *Pure Notes from Ten Thousand Ravines* (*Wanhe qingyin* 萬壑清音), supplied *kunqu* lovers with excerpted *beiqu* scenes from thirty-seven plays in the theater repertoire of the time, all notated with *dianban* rhythmic marks.[38] The compiler, writing under the sobriquet Layman of Stopping the Clouds (Zhiyun jushi 止雲居士), regrets not being able to include his contemporary playwrights' most recent creative efforts and anticipates that a sequel of northern song suites from newer *chuanqi* dramas will be published soon.[39] Notably, besides drawing from numerous southern plays, he also includes two scenes from the northern version of *The Story of the Western Wing*.[40] This was an unprecedented phenomenon in printing history, and may suggest a new operatic practice—namely, rendering the fourteenth-century lyrics in *kunqu* long before Ye Tang's *gongche* scores came out late in the eighteenth century. The unusual incorporation of a *zaju* play in a *chuanqi* anthology signals the strength of the impulses toward and confidence in *kunqu* musicians' improvisational skills in the early seventeenth century. Evidence suggests that by

38. Full title, *Xinjuan chuxiang dianban beidiao Wanhe qingyin* 新鐫出像點板北調萬壑清音. Original manuscript with Kyoto University, facsimile print in *Shanben xiqu congkan*, vols. 48–49.

39. Zhiyun jushi, "Fanli" to *Wanhe Qingyin*, in *Shanben xiqu congkan*, 48:26.

40. The two scenes are "Huiming Delivers a Letter" (*Huiming daishu* 惠明帶書) and "Startled Dream at the Thatched Bridge" (*Caoqiao jingmeng* 草橋驚夢). *Wanhe qingyin*, *juan* 3, in *Shangben xiqu congkan*, 169–88.

the 1620s, when the *Pure Notes* anthology appeared, rendering the northern version of *The Story of the Western Wing* in *kunqu* was not simply a whimsical idea on the part of its compiler but a practice, albeit a less common one than it was to become in the late eighteenth century. In the preface to his poem *On the Boy Singers in the Mi Household* (*Ti Mijia tong* 題米家童), written sometime between 1613 and 1625, for instance, Fan Jingwen 范景文 (1587–1644; *jinshi* 1613) describes a private performance in the *kunqu* aficionado Mi Wanzhong's 米萬鍾 (1570–1628) household in Beijing. The preface reveals Mi's ownership of the *kunqu* music that his boy singers performed:[41]

> It was written on the playbill "The Story of the Western Wing." I figured it must have been the [southern] adaptation by [Li] Rihua since [Wang] Shifu's play had never been performed in the southern fashion. Yet listening carefully, I realized that the performance was entirely based on [Wang's] original lyrics, yet rendered in *kunqu*. I inquired about it and learned that it had been composed by Zhongzhao [Mi Wanzhong's style name]. While listening to and watching the performance, I thereupon changed my outdated understanding.
>
> 開題西廂，私意定演日華改本矣。以實甫所作，向不入南弄也。再一傾聽，盡依原本，却以崑調出之。問之，知為仲詔創調。於是耳目之間，遂易舊觀。

The poem that ensues contains some musicological details about how this music produced its effects: "Where the music was about to gallop up [in the *xiansuo* renditions], the tempo nevertheless slowed down; when it approached the end, the aria introduced a refrain" 每當轉處聲偏慢, 將到停時調入雙. The first line of the couplet means that in Mi Wanzhong's hands, the excitingly fast tempo was replaced by ornamental filigree and vocal display. The second line may refer to the *heqian* 合前 convention in southern arias, the juncture at which a soloist who has finished the main body of an aria was joined by another singer in a refrain. The preface further indicates the resulting boost in Fan Jingwen's understanding of *kunqu* music and his admiration for Mi Wanzhong's deep connoisseurship, testifying to the success of the composition as an intellectual game between the intelligent composer and listeners with the aptitude to perceive the musical adaptations. In the last line of the poem, Fan Jingwen anticipates that this novelty would be

---

41. Fan Jingwen, *Wenzhong ji* 文忠集, in *Siku quanshu* 四庫全書, *juan* 9. Digital access: https://zh.m.wikisource.org/wiki/文忠集_(范景文,_四庫全書本)/卷09#題米家童

emulated by others and evolve into a convention, and that "from now on the light clappers [of *kunqu*] will accompany the singing of 'the great gushing Yangtze River' [an anonym for northern arias in the Ming poetic diction]" 恐人倣此翻成套, 輕板從今唱大江.

A Beijing courtier since 1613, Fan Jingwen was not necessarily aware that by the 1620s it had become a norm in Nanjing brothels to render *beiqu* lyrics in the *kunqu* style. The sixth of Shen Defu's 沈德符 (1578–1642) sixteen poems that portray young male singers in the Nanjing pleasure quarters, written in 1627, seems to have recycled some words and phrases from Fan Jingwen's poem.[42] It seems plausible to say that these two brief sources, sharing so many similar words, refer to the same recent trend:

> In the new fashion, they improvised, sitting in a pair.
> Iron clappers in harmony with string instruments accompanied the singing of "the great gushing Yangtze River."
> Overhearing [the music], travelers from the northern lands of the Beijing area found it astonishing—
> As the northern lyrics sounded feminine and delicate, being rendered in *kunqu*.

> 新聲翻出坐成雙
> 鐵板和弦唱大江
> 竊聽頓驚燕趙客
> 北詞雌輭作崑腔

This Nanjing brothel band seems to have featured a typical composition of a *xiansuo* ensemble—namely, the reigning string instruments and symbolic heavy clappers. The northerners in the audience, upon seeing these familiar instruments, would expect a familiar *xiansuo* performance. Had Mi Wanzhong's private troupe used such a novel band, Fan Jingwen would not have failed to mention it in his poem or its preface. Instead, as indicated by Fan's use of the term "light clappers" 輕板, Mi probably used the more traditional *kunqu* accompaniments without string instruments.

This new Nanjing fashion of emulating the *xiansuo* band in emphasizing string instruments must have been initiated in Wei Liangfu's mature years during the late Jiajing reign (1522–1566), when he was widely known

42. Shen Defu, "Qinhuai ye'er qu" 秦淮冶兒曲, in *Qingquantang ji* 清權堂集, 22 *juan* in vol. 1377 of XXSKQS, *juan* 5, poem no. 6, 8b.

among the gentry aficionados for his treatise on singing.[43] It must not have been too long after this period that he and his like-minded cohorts set out to enrich accompaniment instruments for *kunqu* by borrowing string instruments from *xiansuo* performance. This innovation allowed *xiansuo* performers—mostly courtesans and male brothel singers—a smooth entry into the *kunqu* business, triggering what Pan Zhiheng 潘之恆 (1556–1622) later nostalgically referred to as the "death of northern tunes (*beiqu*)," that is, of the old manner of *xiansuo* singing.[44] Legend has it that Zhang Yetang 張野塘, a criminal banished to Wei's hometown near Suzhou during the Jiajing reign, adapted a *xiansuo* string instrument into a long-neck lute with a smaller sound box, probably an equivalent of the *sanxian* 三弦—one of the important string instruments in modern *kunqu* bands.[45] Detailed musical realities of the Ming, bafflingly rich and never ceasing changing for very long, are unlikely to be pursued due to the patchy sources. The 1780 illustrations of Ming musical instruments, however, offer a glimpse into that shadowy domain—a "Moon Banjo" or *yueqin* 月琴 with four strings (instead of three), long neck, and a small sound box could be similar to *sanxian* (fig. 7). Wei Liangfu, also an outstanding *xiansuo* singer by training, discovered Zhang's creativity and musicianship in *xiansuo* music and married his daughter to him. Near the end of the Wanli reign, as Shen Defu remarked, *sanxian* had become indispensable to a full band in the Wu area (where *kunqu* was the prevailing musical genre), with the more

43. Wei Liangfu, "Nanci yinzheng" 南詞引正. For the discovery of the manuscript in the early 1960s among the collections of the modern scholar Lu Gong 路工, see Wu Xinlei, "Guanyu Mingdai Wei Liangfu de qulun Nanci yinzheng" 關於明代魏良輔的曲論《南詞引正》, *Hebei shiyuan xuebao* 河北師院學報 1 (1993): 68–72; see also Wu Shuyin, *Zhongguo xiqu shilun* 中國戲曲史論 (Nanjing: Nanjing daxue chubanshe, 1997), 272–81. The manuscript itself is in fact lost but was transcribed and published with annotations by Qian Nanyang 錢南揚 and first published as Qian Nanyang, "Nanci yinzheng jiaozhu" 南詞引正校注, *Xiju bao* 戲劇報 7, no. 8 (1961): 58–66; a slightly revised edition appears in Qian Nanyang, *Han shang huan wencun: Liang Zhu xiju jicun* 漢上宧文存: 梁祝戲劇輯存 (Beijing: Zhonghua shuju, 2009), 81–100.

44. Han Shanggui, "Pan Jingsheng xiansheng *Luanxiao xiaopin* xu" 潘景升先生鸞嘯小品序 [Preface to *Luanxiao xiaopin*], in Pan Zhiheng, *Luanxiao xiaopin* 鸞嘯小品, 1628 edition in the Shanghai Library, 2a–b.

45. Ye Mengzhu 葉夢珠 (ca. 1623–ca. 1690s), *Yueshi bian* 閱世編, *juan* 10, in *Biji xiaoshuo daguan* 筆記小說大觀 (Taipei: Xinxing shuju, 1974), 222. I have corrected Ye's account based on Pan Zhiheng's when there are discrepancies. Pan claims that he knows Zhang Yetang, a *pipa*-lute player, his son Zhang Xiaotang 張小塘, a *tiqin*-fiddle expert, and the grandson Zhang Pinfu 張聘夫, who specializes in *sanxian*. Wang Xiaoyi, ed., *Pan Zhiheng quhua*, 80; Pan Zhiheng, *Luanxiao xiaopin*, *juan* 2, 10a–b.

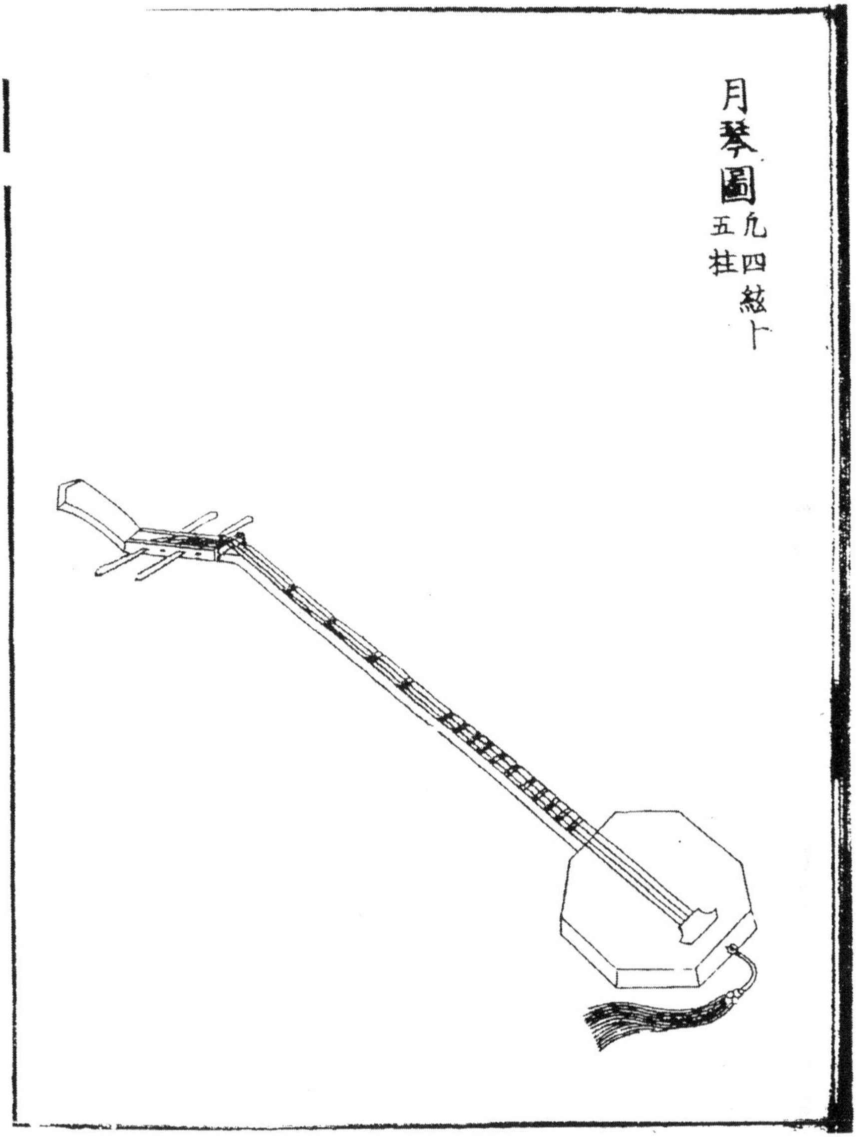

Fig. 7. Moon Banjo (*yueqin*). Woodblock illustration to Tsutsui Iku, comp. *Illustrations of Mr. Wei's Musical Instruments* (*Gishi gakki zu*), 1780. (Reprinted from Qi Mingjing, *Weishi yuepu lingyunge liujuanben zongpu quanyi* [Guilin: Guangxi shifan daxue chubanshe, 2017].)

traditional flutes on the side 今吳下皆三弦合南曲，而又以簫管叶之 (fig. 8).[46] To those *xiansuo* musicians who had humble social associations with the pleasure quarters—courtesans and male professional musicians such as Wei Liangfu and his son-in-law Zhang Yetang—the use of the *sanxian* as the chief instrument must have eased their way into *kunqu*.

With *sanxian* joining the *kunqu* orchestra, the *kunqu* rendition of northern lyrics, previously exclusive to *xiansuo* performers' repertoires, could now be embraced as natural and proper. This merging must have signaled the blurring of the boundaries between the two musical spheres on the site of *beiqu* lyrics. As early as the 1602 foreword to a *kunqu* songbook entitled *Red Corals from the Music Bureau* (*Yuefu hongshan* 樂府紅珊, imprint of 1800), we find castigations of the confusion of *xiansuo* and *modiao* 磨調 (a term designated for *kunqu* after the Wei Liangfu reform) as being "like a square tenon for a round mortise" 近來有弦索調唱作磨調，又將南曲配入弦索，誠為圓鑿方穿.[47] By 1602, therefore, the binary opposition between *xiansuo* and *kunqu* had already become quite unstable in reality, their distinction a piece of arcane knowledge on paper. That *chuanqi* and *zaju*, the two distinct literary genres, could not possibly carry the same type of music is a modern prejudice prevalent in the literary history of Chinese drama. *Kunqu* had evolved to be able to set any northern arias to music no later than the end of the sixteenth century, the age of *The Peony Pavilion* and edited Yuan dramas quickly becoming popular; as a result, staging a *zaju* play was anything but an "improbable dream."[48]

As we have discussed in chapter 1, textual aids for *beiqu* singing—or large compendia of Yuan drama—mushroomed from the 1590s onward, which potentially provided a foundation for *kunqu* improvisation. The trend of compiling Yuan drama compendia from private collections peaked in 1615 with the publication of Zang Maoxun's 臧懋循 (1550–1620; *jinshi* 1580) *Selection of One Hundred Yuan Plays* (*Yuanren baizhong qu* 元人百種曲). The coincidence between this publishing boom and the widespread presence of *kunqu* improvisation, however, has gone unremarked in scholarly writings. Now that

46. Shen Defu, "Guqu zayan" 顧曲雜言, in *Lidai quhua huibian: Mingdai bian*, ed. Yu and Sun, 3:61–62.

47. *Qinhuai Moke* 秦淮墨客, "Fanli ershitiao" 凡例二十條, *Yuefu hongshan*, 16 *juan* in *Shanben xiqu congkan*, 10:7–13.

48. Yuming He, "Difficulties of Performance: The Musical Career of Xu Wei's *The Mad Drummer*," *Harvard Journal of Asiatic Studies* 68, no. 2 (2008): 110, 89, 112. I disagree with the presumption that in the late Ming, the southern *zaju The Mad Drummer* and other plays of the same literary genre were "closet dramas" unenacted in *kunqu*. They did not have to wait until the late eighteenth century to have a stage life.

Fig. 8. The woodblock illustration of a scene from the novel *The Plum in the Golden Vase* that portrays the protagonist enjoying two courtesans' music-making with his five wives. (Reprinted from *Xinke Jin Ping Mei cihua* [Guyi xiaoshuo kanxinghui, 1933].)

the Yuan lyrics had become widely available (after previously being confined to oral transmissions of the courtesan and other professional genealogies), they must have tickled the compositional interest of those who had mastered improvisational skills at a high level. Making music was no longer simply a game for playwrights but a game in which "composers" began to delight as well. The earliest known *kunqu* score of *beiqu* lyrics, *Scores of Northern Arias* (*Beici pu* 北詞譜), was compiled by two *kunqu* masters, Xu Yushi 徐于室 and Niu Shaoya 紐少雅, of whom we know little except that they were admirers of Wei Liangfu hailing from the Suzhou area.[49] After the fall of the Ming dynasty in 1644, *chuanqi* dramatist Li Yu 李玉 (ca. 1590–ca. 1660), another Suzhou native, acquired and revised the compilation into *Scores of Northern Arias, Expanded and Corrected* (*Beici guangzhengpu* 北詞廣正譜).[50] Both scores applied *dianban* notation typical of *kunqu* to the northern lyrics. One familiar misinterpretation of the *dianban* action of Li Yu and his Suzhou cohort, misled by the same confusion as Zang Maoxun's, sees it as an antiquarian effort to restore *xiansuo*, the lost medieval art, rather than as an exciting, fashionable musical experiment.[51] But as modern scholar Li Jialian points out, the historical significance of Li Yu's scores "lies in the fact that *dianban* practices were mostly inherited by later important *kunqu* scores."[52]

Example 6 (fig. 9) is a sample of the same fourteenth-century aria to the northern tune *Welcome Drumming in the Village* that we have seen in Examples 2–5 (figs. 3–6). We must bear in mind the drastic differences between Example 6 and all the others: the score displays no sophisticated structure with specific pitch notes that would be jeopardized if a performer altered a single note. What carries the glory, or raison d'être, of the composition is no longer the prima donna's memory of a set piece of someone else's composition, but the technical virtuosity of improvisation required of the *kunqu* singer performing this page. Anywhere between two downbeat symbols "、" there could be vocal ornaments filling the enjoyable moments of excess. If there was a band, instrumental accompaniments would follow the singer's melodious flows up and down.

Concomitantly, among Ming intellectuals we find tendencies to amal-

49. The sole copy of the manuscript of *Beici pu* is preserved in the National Library in Beijing. Wang Gang 王鋼, "Ji Xu Qingqing de *Beici pu*" 記徐慶卿的北詞譜, in *Wen Shi* 文史 (Beijing: Zhonghua shuju, 1988), 31:303–10.

50. Zhou Weipei 周維培, *Qupu yanjiu* 曲譜研究 (Nanjing: Jiangsu guji chubanshe, 1999), 67–70. Li Jialian 李佳蓮, *Li Yu* Beici guangzhengpu *yanjiu* 李玉《北詞廣正譜》研究 (Taipei: Guojia chubanshe, 2012), 57.

51. Zhou Weipei, *Qupu yanjiu*, 77–78.

52. Li Jialian, *Li Yu* Beici guangzhengpu *yanjiu*, 267–73.

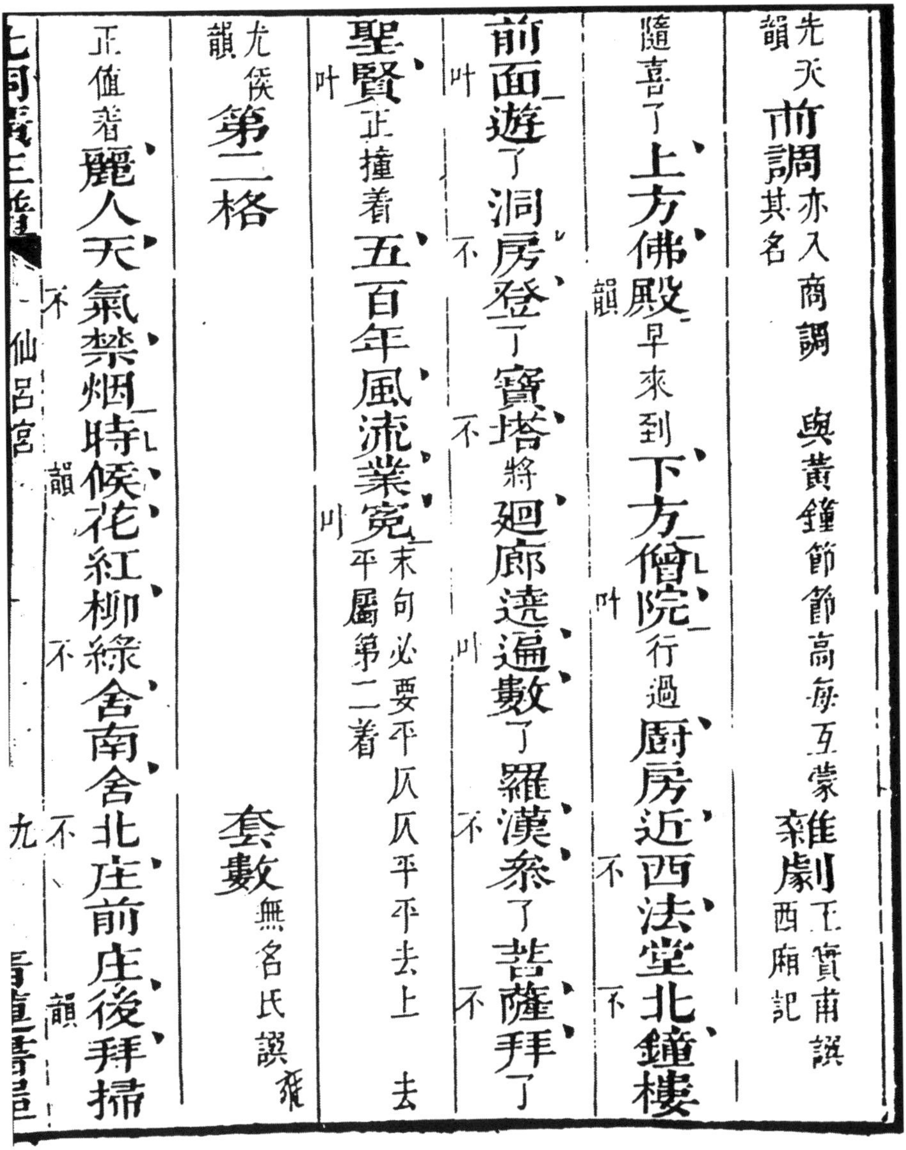

Fig. 9. *Scores of Northern Arias, Expanded and Corrected* (*Beici guangzhengpu*), ca. 1645–ca. 1660. (Courtesy Fudan University Library.)

gamate historical *xiansuo* practice and their contemporaneous *kunqu* renditions of northern arias. In his preface to *A Hundred Brocades to Courtesan Singers* (*Chantou bailian* 纏頭百練), a songbook of various music genres targeting brothel visitors and readers, Ling Mengchu defines *xiansuo* simply as "the most often performed northern arias [in popular entertainments]" 北曲之最傳者, 亦云弦索.[53] The emphasis on contemporaneous brothel practices, rather than on *xiansuo*'s connections with the Yuan dynasty, sharply contrasts with the conservative mindset represented by He Liangjun and Wang Shizhen. This mentality is, again, manifested in the songbook's supplies of *dianban* notation to these *beiqu* lyrics. Another example is Shen Chongsui's 沈寵綏 (?–1645) self-sponsored 1639 publication *Correcting Errors in* Xiansuo *Singing* (*Xiansuo bian'e* 絃索辨訛). Even though *xiansuo* appears in the title of the treatise, Shen aims not to train the listening ear to distinguish the dying form of *xiansuo* from *kunqu* but, rather, to assist a new evaluative system in discerning "good" *beiqu* music aligned with *kunqu*. Clearly, *xiansuo* was treated as a synonym of "northern arias in the *kunqu* repertoire," and Shen's book provides guidance on how to sing them correctly.

Indeed, things had become so confused that Shen Chongsui felt the need to clarify the concept of *beiqu*, which, as he reveals, had become a site of contestation in seventeenth-century music criticism. Shen's other treatise on *kunqu* singing and composition, *What You Must Know About Singing* (*Duqu xuzhi* 度曲須知), was also published in 1639. In it, Shen's particularly revealing essay, "The Survival and Downfall of the Rhythmic Rules of *Xiansuo*" (*Xianlü cunwang* 絃律存亡), discloses how contemporaneous *kunqu* practices had led to conflicting understandings about the rhythms of *xiansuo*. Shen portrays this contradiction by juxtaposing Wang Shizhen's famous remark and Zang Maoxun's sarcastic rebuttal:[54]

> Wang Shizhen once remarked on dramatic music: "To northern tunes, the key to powerful rhythmic performance is the strings; to southern tunes, it is the clappers." Yet Zang Maoxun from Wuxing derided Wang's theory as [manifesting] "ignorance of how music works." Zang said, "Northern tunes are accompanied by string instruments; similarly, southern tunes by flutes. These accompanying instruments can do nothing more than follow the voice; they do not follow any

53. Ling Mengchu, "Chantou bailian xu" 纏頭百練序, in Chonghe jushi 冲和居士, *Yi chun jin* 怡春錦, 6 ji 集, in *Shanben xiqu congkan*, 19:6. *Yichun jin* was another name for *Chantou bailian*.

54. Shen Chongsui, "Xianlü cunwang," in *Duqu xuzhi*, *Zhongguo gudian xiqu lunzhu jicheng*, 5:239–41.

existing rules. Suppose Wang is right that 'to northern tunes, the key to powerful rhythmic performance is the strings,' then isn't it reasonable to deduce that southern tunes' rhythmic prowess relies on the flute? As for using clappers to devise metrics, northern tunes actually do the same. How could he have attributed clappers to southern tunes only?"

> 昔日王元美評曲, 謂北筋在絃, 南力在板。而吳興臧晉叔譏為不知曲理, 且謂北之被絃索, 猶南之合簫管, 不過隨聲附和, 非有成律可憑, 若云北筋在絃, 將謂南力在管可乎?至板以節曲, 則北亦有力, 奚獨稱南? ......

Shen then openly scorns Zang's confusion of the medieval and the early modern modalities of *beiqu*, which may have become rampant in the popular culture of the early seventeenth century but which is a wrong notion that he is eager to clarify in his treatise. Wang Shizhen died in 1590, so he could not have responded to Zang's remarks (likely made in the 1610s). But Shen imagines that, "had Wang Shizhen heard [Zang's] comments, he would certainly have laughed at them with scorn" 此論出而元美要當齒冷矣. Shen continues to elaborate on the distinction between the two modes of *beiqu* performance with tremendous lucidity and pointed logic, especially concerning the idea of classical *xiansuo*'s "fixed melodies" (*dingpu* 定譜):

> The *xiansuo* performances in ancient times were different from today. Nowadays we do not distinguish between different modes of music. Nor do we have fixed melodies. When singers go up in scale, the string musicians strike high notes to accompany them. When the melodies take a low turn, they then follow with low notes. Indeed, it is like the way flutes are played to accompany southern arias. There are no rigid rules to define [melodic] borders from the outset. It is Zang Maoxun who used contemporary practices to gauge ancient ways, thereby supposing the latter to be an unorthodox practice. As for the ancient style of *xiansuo*, lyrics needed to comply with the instrumental music, and it was absolutely taboo to improvisationally play the instrument to accommodate the [linguistic tones of the] lyrics. All the tune patterns had been written down in *gongche* notation before the birth of lyrics. The modality in which *gongche* notes worked for song lyrics or dramatic libretti resembled how the *qin*-zither served to accompany [new compositions of] classic *shi*-poetry. Alternatively, it was also like scores of vertical flutes in the accompaniments, such as in the tunes entitled "Waves Carrying away Sands" and "Buying Good Wine,"

> with no lyrics but pitch notes only. These are set as formulas. . . . The finger positions were already fixed before the literati came to fill out the lyrics based on the formulas. The singer tuned their instruments and sang [the lyrics]. The sonic performance of the singing was supposed to match precisely the notes emitted from the instrument. For each tune title, there could be endless new arias. But no matter how words changed, the hand gestures and techniques were never different. This is similar to how we sing the regional tunes of the Wu area in the accompaniments of string instruments: lyrics in different refrains and songs do not remain the same, but the music repeats itself like a thousand pieces in the same tune. It always complies with the governing principles concerning finger positions summarized in four sentences. . . . Isn't it true that despite the vast number of the song texts [of *xiansuo*] there are not many tune patterns, and that even if the words are changed, the melodies are not?
>
> 古之被絃應索者，於今較異。今非有協應之宮商，與抑揚之定譜，惟是歌高則彈者亦以高和，曲低則指下亦以低承，真如簫管合南詞，初無主張於其際，故晉叔以今泥古，遂訾為曲之別調耳。若乃古之絃索，則但以曲配絃，絕不以絃和曲。凡種種牌名，皆從未有曲文之先，預定工尺之譜，夫其以工尺譜詞曲，即如琴之以鉤剔度詩歌，又如唱家簫譜，所為【浪淘沙】【沽美酒】之類，則皆有音無文，立為譜式者也。……指下彈頭既定，然後文人按式填詞，歌者準徽度曲，口中聲響，必仿絃上彈音。每一牌名，製曲不知凡幾，而曲文雖有不一，手中彈法，自來無兩，即如今之以吳歌配絃索，非不疊換歌章，而千篇一律，總此四句指法概之。……曲文雖夥，而曲音無幾，曲文雖改，而曲音不變也哉？

From a literary historian's perspective, the *beiqu* lyrics of both *xiansuo* and *kunqu* observe the same set of prosodic rules, except in those heterodox plays that follow the courtesan's oral tradition (the subject of chapter 1). Therefore, it takes a radical shift of mindset, from literary history to performance history, to perceive the divergence of the *kunqu* rendition of *beiqu* from the medieval tradition. Shen Chongsui's 1639 publications were written in part to clarify the muddled, unspoken distinction between the two musical forms—one a dying kind, the other, prevailing.

Thus far, we have presented tangible evidence of (1) the two different memory habits associated with "authentic" *xiansuo* and *kunqu*, and (2) the two distinct *beiqu* renditions in *xiansuo* (i.e., fixed melodies) versus *kunqu* (i.e., improvisation). Yet the boundaries between these domains became blurry and misled scholars, from Zang Maoxun in the early seventeenth century down to modern *kunqu* scholars. Having restored the binary opposition between these two modalities, I will, in the next section, hypothesize that the courtesan's mental stores of both musical genres, built during their training processes, provided the context for the rise of *kunqu*.

III. The Courtesan's Varied Curricula and the Problem of *Kunqu* Music Literacy

Courtesans seem to have been particularly able practitioners of navigating between the two chief genres of *xiansuo* and *kunqu*. Shen Defu's four poems written in 1629, entitled "Thoughts After Listening to Courtesans in Suzhou" (*Wuzhong tingji yougan* 吳中聽伎有感), record how diversified their training and performances were. Though the *xiansuo* music he listened to in 1629 was in the *kunqu* rendition rather than an "authentic" one (Shen lamented in his other writings that by 1604 authentic renditions were dying out), he nevertheless lauded the courtesans' diligent exercises in playing string instruments: "How delicate and adroit those young hands in the Suzhou area are! In the green bowers, plucking in *xiansuo* music has frequently been taught. Gradually I feel that these southern women become capable of northern music, making me fantasize about living in Handan [in the northern land] and meeting zither players there" 吳中新手巧多端, 弦索青樓每教彈; 漸覺南姬能北技, 恍逢挾瑟住邯鄲.[55]

The courtesans' great variety in training, beginning with wind and string instruments and ending with dance, is displayed proudly in the courtesan-authored southern play *Life After Life: The Jade Hairpin* (*Sansheng zhuan Yuzan ji* 三生傳玉簪記), written between the 1560s and 1593 (and probably completed at a later date).[56] Its preeminent author, Ma Xianglan 馬湘蘭 (1548–1604), had her own private female troupe in her compound, located amid other high-end brothels near the Qinhuai river in Nanjing.[57] The play

55. Shen Defu, "Wuzhong tingji yougan," in *Qingquantang ji*, *juan* 7, poem no. 2, 40b.

56. The only reliable late Ming reference to this lost *chuanqi* play is Lü Tiancheng's 呂天成 (ca. 1580–1618) drama catalogue *Qupin* 曲品. See Wu Shuyin 吳書蔭, ed., *Qupin jiaozhu* 曲品校注 (Beijing: Zhonghua shuju, 1990), 390–91. Excerpted scenes without spoken parts are included in Hu Wenhuan's 胡文煥 (fl. 1596) *Qunyin leixuan* 群音類選 in photo reprints (Beijing: Zhonghua shuju, 1980), *juan* 18, 930–33.

57. Accounts of the Ma household in the Nanjing pleasure quarters can be found in various books, including Shen Defu's *Wanli yehuobian*; Qian Qianyi's 錢謙益 (1582–1664) *Liechao shiji* 列朝詩集; Feng Mengzhen's 馮夢禎 (1548–1606; *jinshi*

dramatizes a young courtesan's training in a scene entitled "Learning to Sing and Dance" (*Xuexi gewu* 學習歌舞); specifically, it focuses on four musical skills for providing brothel entertainment—the playing of wind instruments (*chui* 吹), the playing of string instruments (*tan* 彈), singing (*ge* 歌), and dancing (*wu* 舞). The courtesan-dramatist gives each skill two arias, sequenced in a highly patterned aria structure, alternating between a southern and a northern aria. For example, for the skill of *chui*, a northern aria to the tune of *New Water* (*Bei Xinshuiling* 北新水令) begins with a line that discloses the subject instrument as the horizontal flute: "The beauty, with a jade horizontal flute, plays a new song" 麗姝橫玉奏新聲. This is followed by a southern aria to the tune of *Dainty Gait* (*Nan Bubujiao* 南步步嬌), whose opening line goes: "Switching to a new musical mode, she next plays the vertical flute" 換羽移宮再把簫韶整. Forming the same northern-southern opposites, the *pipa*-lute and the zither are paired up in the next two arias, portraying how the courtesan gets ready to perform the string parts in an ensemble.

The even distribution of songs describing the training in the four skills has been interpreted as the courtesan-dramatist's effort to draw attention to the hardships a courtesan would endure and the high professional standards she faced on her path to distinction.[58] But there is part of Ma Xianglan's agency in her self-representation that is erased in this self-contained analysis. I would like to stress that it was self-empowering to present the courtesan-heroine's training in singing and dancing by means of the four arias that highlight the brothel theater's most self-reflexive moment. The northern-southern opposites are self-consciously put into the two musical categories—the northern aria was to be rendered in the "authentic" *xiansuo* style, the signature of the courtesan's tradition, which was then musically contrasted with *kunqu* singing of the southern aria. According to Shen Defu, Ma Xianglan's troupe was the one that provided the last full-fledged "authentic" *xiansuo* performance of *"The Story of the Western Wing" in Its Northern Version*. Therefore, the highly patterned structure of this scene, categorized as *guanqiang* 官腔 (another term for *kunqu*) in Hu Wenhuan's musically categorized anthology of drama around the early 1590s, was very likely consciously designed to showcase the specialty of Ma Xianglan's troupe. For example, the northern tune of *Wild Geese Landing* (*Bei Yan'er luo* 北雁兒落) induces the image of a big-voiced soprano singing at the top of her range, using all chest: "She raised up [the larynx in] the throat, opened her mouth

1577) *Kuaixuetang riji* 快雪堂日記; and Liang Chenyu's *Jiangdong baizhu* 江東白紵.

58. Hua Wei 華瑋, "Ma Xianglan yu Mingdai houqi de qutan" 馬湘蘭與明代後期的曲壇, *Xiqu xuebao* 戲曲學報, 2 (2007): 55–82; also *Zhonghua xiqu* 中華戲曲 37 (2008): 151–77.

to the full, and discerned between the voiced and unvoiced sounds" 動歌喉綻榴房識重輕. In contrast, the southern aria to the tune of *Shrill Cries* (*Nan Jiaojiaoling* 南僥僥令) begins with a line signaling the musical genre in which the song was sung, through props and gestures typical of a female *kunqu* performance: "A singer's fan in the shape of the full moon danced as though seeking the shadows of the moon" 歌扇團圓尋月影. Beyond these textual clues, we must keep in mind that the music that we can no longer hear was an equally critical contributor, besides the lyrics per se, to the production of meaning. The courtesan-dramatist Ma Xianglan, who is known to have trained her whole troupe in the "authentic" *xiansuo* style while writing for *kunqu*, gives a unique voice to the fledging courtesan by creating this musically self-reflexive scene.

For Ma Xianglan's troupe to train and rehearse in the delivery of rhythmic accuracy, both of the medieval (rhythm-centered, spatially oriented) and the early modern (syllable-centered, improvisational) approaches, would have demanded two different methods of communication and instruction. It must have taken much more strenuous effort to master the two distinct musical languages and memory habits than the training that Ma Xianglan sketches in *Life After Life* as the expeditious path to success. There are two other plays, each dramatizing one mode of learning, that emphasize the difficulties courtesans faced in their singing lessons of *xiansuo* and *kunqu*, respectively—Tang Xianzu's *chuanqi* play *The Purple Flute* (*Zixiao ji* 紫簫記), completed in Nanjing around 1578, and Kong Shangren's 孔尚任 (1648–1718) *chuanqi* play *The Peach Blossom Fan* (*Taohua shan* 桃花扇), completed in 1699, set in the late Ming Nanjing pleasure quarters.[59]

In *The Purple Flute*, Tang Xianzu goes to great lengths to highlight the significance of memorizing all the melodies in the courtesan's *xiansuo* training. In a scene entitled "Studying Music" (*Shenyin* 審音), the importance of a courtesan's arcane knowledge of music could hardly be further underscored in the singing lesson delivered by the famous Tang courtesan singer and *pipa*-player Bao Sixian 鮑四絃, also known as Lady the Fourth 四娘.[60]

59. For Xu Shuofang's dating of *The Purple Flute*, see his "Tang Xianzu pingzhuan" 湯顯祖評傳, in *Xu Shuofang ji* 徐朔方集 (Hangzhou: Zhejiang guji chubanshe, 1993), 30–34.

60. More commonly referred to as Bao Siniang 鮑四娘, but there is no doubt that the prototype is the Tang courtesan Bao Sixian, the protagonist of the anecdote of "exchanging one's beloved concubine for a fine horse" recounted in a Tang collection of short stories, *Taiping guangji* 太平廣記, *juan* 39. In scene 20 of *Zixiao ji*, the heroine refers to her as Bao Sixian, a revealing moment of truth. See Xu Shuofang, ed., *Tang Xianzu quanji* 湯顯祖全集, vol. 3, drama (Beijing: Beijing guji chubanshe,

Her seemingly tedious lecture onstage elaborates on a single skill that a fledging courtesan must master—namely, how to discriminate between different northern tunes that belong to different music modes (*gongdiao* 宮調), as a way to inherit a long tradition that she proudly traces back to great antiquity:

> Maidservant: What Lady the Fourth teaches is much too [lewd] for us.
>
> Lady the Fourth: Nonsense! All you want to achieve is to sound professional. Your Ladyship, be seated and listen to me. To sing well there are three keys: first, know the melodies well by heart; second, keep to the beats; third, use all the chest to reach the highest volume.
>
> Ms. Jade (the heroine): How many tunes are there altogether?
>
> Lady the Fourth: It is hard to enumerate everything in one go. Generally speaking, there are twenty-four tune patterns under the rubric of the *Huangzhong* mode, twenty-five in the *Zhenggong* mode, twenty-one in *Dashidiao*, five in *Xiaoshidiao*, forty-two in *Xianlü*, thirty-two in *Zhonglü*, twenty-one in *Nanlü*, one hundred in *Shuangdiao*, thirty-five in *Yuediao*, sixteen in *Shangdiao*, six in *Shangjiaodiao*, and eight in *Banshediao*, adding up to three hundred thirty-five in total. These are the twelve modes that have been passed down since the Yellow Emperor codified music into seventeen modes. Note that different terms could refer to the same tune. For example, *Yizhihua* and *Zhanhuakui* are literally the same. [She goes on to list forty-four more, omitted here due to space constraints, to explain how one tune could be assigned two different names.] Also, beware of the same tune titles that carry different musical contents. For example, *Shuixianzi* appears in both the *Huangzhong* and the *Shuangdiao* modes. [She lists four more examples of this phenomenon.] The singer is not supposed to confuse them. There are some tune patterns flexible with the number of words, such as *Duanzhenghao*, *Huolang'er*, *Hunjianglong*, *Houtinghua*, *Qingge'er*, *Meihuajiu*, *Xinshuiling*, and *Zheguiling*. Words can be added to or subtracted from them. All that aside, we have yet to mention the *Daogong*, *Gaoping*, and *Xiezhi* modes. When it comes to *Zimudiao*, the so-called "string of dragon pearls," see to it that you don't get undesirable vocal breaks.

1999), 1808. I briefly discuss the image of Bao Sixian rendered in the Qiu Ying 仇英 (ca. 1494–1552) style popular in the late Ming marketplace and its relation to brothel staging in another essay, "The Courtesan's 'Role Portrait': Brothel Performances and the Qiu Ying Models in Late Ming Suzhou," *Ars Orientalis* 55 (2025), forthcoming.

浣紗：四娘教的曲子唱不得。
四娘：說哪裏話？只要在行。郡主端坐，聽俺道來。唱有三緊：一要調兒記得遠，二要板兒落得穩，三要聲兒唱得滿。
小玉：調兒有許多？
四娘：一時數不起，略說大數：黃鐘二十四章，正宮二十五章，大石調二十一章，小石調五章，仙呂四十二章，中呂三十二章，南呂二十一章，雙調一百章，越調三十五章，商調十六章，商角調六章，般涉調八章，共三百三十五章。自軒轅黃帝制律一十七宮調，至今留傳一十二調。中間又有音同名不同的，假如：【一枝花】便是【占春魁】……又有名同音不同的，假如：黃鐘、雙調都有【水仙子】…… 唱不得廝混。又有字句多少都唱得的，相似：【端正好】【貨郎兒】【混江龍】【後庭花】【青哥兒】【梅花酒】【新水令】【折桂令】，這幾章都增減唱得。中間還有道宮、高平、歇指。又有子母調 "一串驪珠"，休得拗折嗓子。

Lady the Fourth floods her students with befuddling tune titles and theories that are based on medieval guides to singing, such as *Sounds and Rhymes from the Central Plain* (*Zhongyuan yinyun* 中原音韻), completed in 1324.[61] Tang Xianzu certainly thought of Lady the Fourth as a true heir of the "authentic" *xiansuo* singing. This characterization is also reinforced in Tang's musical arrangement in scene 4, in which he assigned her seven northern arias enveloped by six southern arias distributed among three male characters.[62] There is no doubt about her identity as a virtuosic but old-fashioned *xiansuo* performer in the "authentic" courtesan tradition.

Yet Tang Xianzu arranges a surprising turn in tone after the female teacher demonstrates a northern song. The heroine/disciple Ms. Jade seems unimpressed with Lady the Fourth's musical erudition, but remarks nonetheless, with hints of sarcasm, on *xiansuo*'s erotic content that lacks lyrical or intellectual depth. "Well done, indeed," she exclaims, "but this is a song for dandies and wantons, not for gentlemen or poets" 唱便唱得好, 此乃遊童艷婦之篇, 非上客幽人之操.[63] She then asks for contemporary poetic works so that she can "render them into the vocal style of the courtesan" 寫入秦樓聲一派.[64] This request seems to me more than sufficient to suggest Ms. Jade's departure in taste from the traditional *xiansuo*, which embraces erotic lyrics and burdens her memory with endless fixed melodies.

61. Yannan Zhi'an 燕南芝庵 (fl. 1330s), *Changlun* 唱論, in *Zhongguo gudian xiqu lunzhu jicheng*, 1:159–66; Zhou Deqing 周德清 (fl. 1330s), *Zhongyuan yinyun*, 169–285.

62. Xu, *Tang Xianzu quanji*, 3:1727–32.

63. Xu, *Tang Xianzu quanji*, 3:1737.

64. Xu, *Tang Xianzu quanji*, 3:1739.

Eleven scenes later, a simple accident but a moment imbued with symbolic meaning takes place—Ms. Jade stumbles upon a vertical flute, the chief accompanying instrument for *kunqu*. Due to practical concerns, she keeps the discovery to herself. Tang Xianzu may have meant to allude to the association between the flute and the courtesan. Around 1578, the year of the play's completion, Nanjing singsong girls were facing choices between musical preferences and specializations, despite the all-around training they had received as beginners. Later in the scene, an imperial concubine is in charge of investigating the captured heroine's true identity, and she notices the prop flute held in the heroine's hand. Is the heroine a palace lady secretly seeking a lover who truly appreciates her flute music? Or is she an imperial courtesan registered in the Pear Garden who specializes in the flute? Although the heroine wittily debunks both guesses by pointing out that her outward appearance (such as her clothing) differs from that of both these categories of women, her rank in the aristocratic society is clearly a zone of ambiguity. Given that she has learned *xiansuo* music from Lady the Fourth, Ms. Jade is clearly in the lineage of courtesan-singers, a truth that lies behind any and all appearances. It is difficult to shed her former birth identity as a courtesan-musician simply by physically replacing her clothing and adopting the title of Lady, recently bequeathed to her by her birth father, who is a prince. In the world of the play, written at the height of *kunqu*'s power permeating the Nanjing brothels, the purple flute is the carrier of the kind of music that is the opposite of the music of the traditional *xiansuo* genre. In this sense, Tang Xianzu seems not far from Ma Xianglan in embedding self-reflexive moments into his play that reflect on the Nanjing-brothel music life.

My reading of the symbolic meaning of the purple jade flute—as a symbol of the musical changes in Nanjing brothel entertainment—is reinforced by its bizarrely poor narrative significance as the key prop, which would usually appear repetitively as a love token, according to the *chuanqi* convention. This structural convention was well observed by the same playwright in another *chuanqi* play featuring the same protagonists, *The Purple Hairpin* (*Zichai ji* 紫釵記, ca. 1587), finished about nine years later. Unlike the purple hairpin, however, the purple flute appears and disappears abruptly, unattached to the main storyline: in the existing thirty-four scenes of *The Purple Flute*, it is not seen again after being found by the heroine, bequeathed to her by the emperor, and brought home by her.[65] This has always been puzzling to modern scholars, and its interpretations remain a matter of conjecture.[66] I

65. Xu, *Tang Xianzu quanji*, vol. 3, scenes 17–19, 1927–33.

66. For a reading of the purple flute as a poetic euphemism for an erect penis, see

am therefore emboldened to suggest that the purple flute bears vestigial witness to the demimonde theater's transitioning from the *xiansuo* mode (inherited by the older courtesan Lady the Fourth) to the *kunqu* mode (the newer fashion embraced by the heroine-disciple Ms. Jade). If this assumption is true, then Lady the Fourth's lecture on *xiansuo* in scene 6 becomes revealing of the burdens that the "authentic" *xiansuo* style placed on the courtesan's memory, an undesirable feature from the perspective of courtesan-singers of the younger generation.

Because the "authentic" *xiansuo* designates metrical performances at the level of pitches rather than syllables, it allows more rhythmic precision for *xiansuo* chamber groups and ensembles, but at the same time provides no freedom for the singer's rhythmic choices. The opposite was true in *kunqu*, however. At the expense of the certainty that one felt about *xiansuo*, *kunqu* greatly increased the dramatic effect through its capacity for improvisation. The change in pedagogy evoked by *kunqu*'s impulse toward improvisation offered a more effective mnemonic device in comparison to the one used in the *xiansuo* pedagogy. With fewer restrictions on melodies, teachers would correct an error only when a syllable failed to occur on its designated beat. Our second example is a dramatic representation of this phenomenon in instruction on singing.

In the historical drama *The Peach Blossom Fan*, we see how the instructor of a courtesan-to-be uses syllables as points of reference to facilitate her memory. At the beginning of the scene entitled "Teaching Singing" (*Chuange* 傳歌), we are informed that the fledging disciple has just begun to study a scene from Tang Xianzu's *The Peony Pavilion* under the tutelage of a famous *kunqu* master. He enters the stage and begins the class by asking her: "Have you learned by heart the song I taught you yesterday?"[67] He then interrupts her singing to shout, "Wrong! Wrong! The character *mei* 美 should be on a downbeat, and the character *nai* 奈 should be on a downbeat. Don't slur them with adjacent characters."[68] It can be imagined that in *kunqu* singing lessons guided by *dianban* notation, the chance occurrence of rhythmic incongruity was unacceptable only when it violated the syllable-beat correspondence established by the notation. Guided by this relatively loose conception of rhythmic performance, the singer was given the relative

David T. Roy, "The Case for T'ang Hsien-tsu's Authorship of the *Jin Ping Mei*," *Chinese Literature: Essays, Articles, Reviews (CLEAR)* 8, no. 1 (1986): 56–61.

67. 昨日學的曲子, 可曾記熟了 (italics added). Kong Shangren, *Taohua shan*, ed. Wang Jisi 王季思 et al. (1959; rpt., Beijing: Renmin wenxue chubanshe, 1997), 18.

68. 錯了錯了, 美字一板, 奈字一板, 不可連下去. Kong Shangren, *Taohua shan*, 18.

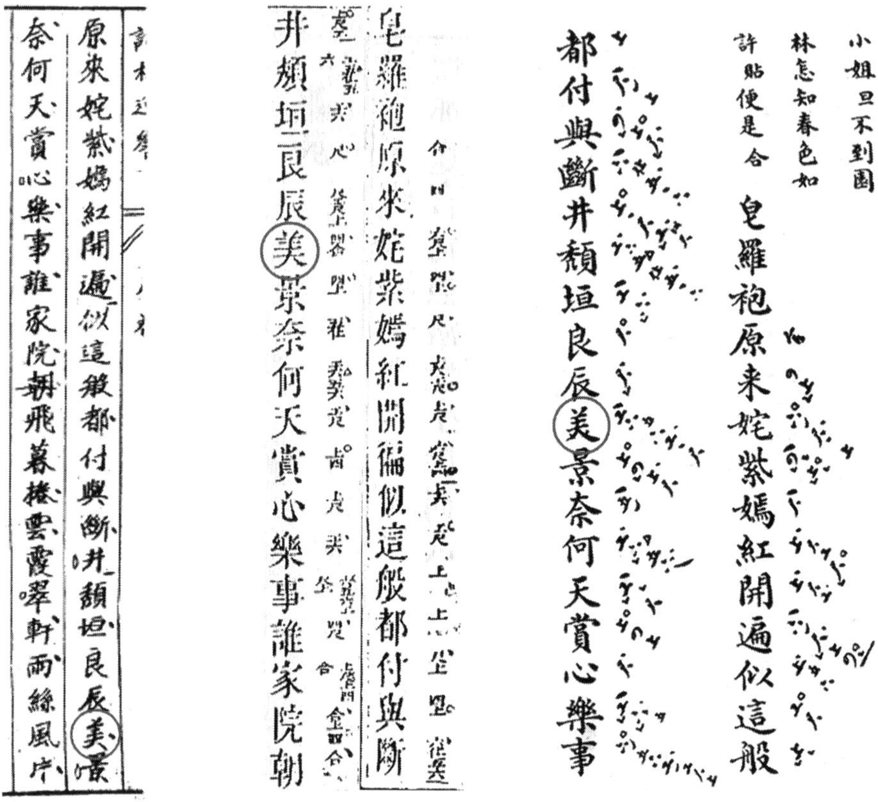

Fig. 10. Notations for the lyrics of the song learned by the courtesan-to-be disciple in *The Peach Blossom Fan* from three music imprints, published in 1623, 1792, and the 1980s, respectively.

freedom of variegating rhythmic details, and even excessive ornaments, in between two designated beats. This allowance for improvisation was to be extinguished in the late eighteenth century, which witnessed the *dianban* tradition being replaced by *gongche* notation system in the field of *kunqu* music prints. Figure 10 juxtaposes notation for the lyrics of the song learned by the courtesan-to-be disciple in *The Peach Blossom Fan* from three music imprints, published in 1623, 1792, and the 1980s, respectively. Beat signs increased over time, but the syllable-to-strong-beat correspondences (such as *mei* on a strong beat) have remained relatively stable.

From the learner's perspective, *kunqu*'s merit lies in its releasing performers from the stressful memorative learning of precise *gongche* pitch notes and their exact rhythmic positions, as required in *xiansuo*. The close word-music relationship in *kunqu* meant that the processes of "composition" and memorization became intertwined, thereby prompting a crucial change in the role of memorization—namely, incorporating memorization (of the words) as part of the musical creativity, which, in turn, enhanced memorization itself. Thus improvisation placed more power in the hands of the courtesan as a musician and "composer," which was sufficient reason to justify her preference for *kunqu*.

The expectations for music literacy imbued *kunqu* with new scholarly value and social prestige and helped enshrine it as a symbol of post-Yuan-drama intellectual culture. I have argued elsewhere that professional teachers were employed by the majority of courtesan-singers, whose selling of their voices, potentially combined with prostitution of their bodies, may have been profitable enough to sustain such educational expenses. Courtesans skilled at improvisation were lauded for virtuosity; undoubtedly their appeal derived largely from their peers' lack of similar accomplishments.[69] At the same time, adding *kunqu* to the courtesan's traditional repertoire may have entailed a more diversified and thus more prolonged training program, which could be a substantial investment. Evidence of the diversified curriculum designed to train courtesans is completely absent. But we can still glean a little information from accounts of how boy actors specializing in *kunqu* were taught. Pan Zhiheng recounts the first performance he saw of Tang Xianzu's *The Peony Pavilion*, which took place in the Nanjing pleasure quarters (certainly with courtesans in the audience). The boy actors belonged to Pan's *kunqu*-connoisseur friend Wu Yueshi 吳越石. To train them to be able actors for new *chuanqi* plays, a special formula involved three interlocking steps (emphasis added):[70]

> First, find a renowned intellectual to explicate (word by word) the lyrics of a play; and then *engage a song specialist to fit the words to pre-existing tunes in the play*; at the last, hire a theater expert to establish a model of performance.
>
> 先以名士訓其義，繼以詞士合其調，復以通士標其式.

69. Peng Xu, "The Music Teacher."

70. Pan Zhiheng, "Qingchi" 情痴, in *Genshi* 亙史, "Miscellaneous," *juan* 4, reprint in *Siku quanshu cunmu congshu* 四庫全書存目叢書 (Jinan: Qi Lu shushe, 2001), *zibu*, 193:532; also in *Luanxiao xiaopin*, *juan* 3, 7a; Wang Xiaoyi, ed., *Pan Zhiheng quhua*, 72.

The second of these three steps—namely, the extra effort to contrive word-music harmony in a preexisting tune—marks the improvisational nature of the late Ming *kunqu* training, for it was missing from the medieval modality. Whether or not the disciples were capable of reading *dianban* notation, a "song specialist" or a professional music teacher was indispensable for the staging "without leaving a single word out" from Tang Xianzu's notoriously difficult lyrics 一字不遺. Differing from *gongche* notation, the unwritten part in *dianban* notation generated market value for the professional teacher. Beyond the comprehension of the lyrics and the accurate pronunciation that a literary education could provide, what distinguished able *kunqu* actors from actors in the *xiansuo* style was their mastery not of improvisational techniques used merely to ornament composed melodies, but of elaborations that evolved into melodies per se. This extra "compositional" work may have exceeded most courtesans' already burdensome mental storage capacities, given their all-around training programs that embraced various genres.

Notably, the age of *dianban* coincided with the rise to dominance of *kunqu* and the late Ming printing boom.[71] Most commercial full-drama imprints, however, far from being servile copies of the professional teacher's handwritten script, took the liberty of daubing rhythmic symbols beside the vertically arranged lyrics, thereby randomly punctuating the lyrics simply to feed the fashion of printing, like a stylish mask covering nothing. The large quantity of such texts with pseudo-notation suggests the advent of musical modernity, which featured a new vocal pedagogy that touted music literacy. The sudden flourishing of *dianban* songbooks beginning in the 1610s might be seen as a countermovement that stressed accuracy against the widely available full-drama imprints with pseudo-*dianban*-annotation. *Sounds of Jade Pendants* (*Shanshan ji* 珊珊集, 1617), for example, commissioned the renowned *kunqu* songbook editor Zhou Zhibiao 周之標 (fl. 1610–1647) to touch up the entire volume and put his name at the front of each chapter, to enhance the songbook's credentials in accurate *dianban* notation.[72] Zhou's preface claims: "The errors of *dianban* notation have come from the engraver's carelessness, with symbols either daubed on wrong characters or missing. [Earlier editors] were too tired to collate and rectify them, and for this rea-

71. For scholarly observations of patterns of woodblock publishing in the late imperial period in general, see Cynthia J. Brokaw and Kai-Wing Chow, eds., *Printing and Book Culture in Late Imperial China* (London: University of California Press, 2005), 23–34; Tobie Meyer-Fong, "The Printed World: Books, Publishing Culture, and Society in Late Imperial China," *Journal of Asian Studies* 66 (2007): 787–817.

72. *Shanshan ji*, facsimile reprint in *Shanben xiqu congkan*, vol. 14.

son, mistakes have accumulated. This edition sets out to correct them one by one" 點板之訛緣刻手信意, 或錯或少, 疲於校讎, 遂相因仍, 此刻一一訂正.

Conclusion

This chapter restores the courtesan's two distinct modes of memory associated with *xiansuo* and *kunqu* before the latter integrated northern arias into its expanded repertoire. It also explores the vernacular dimension of *dianban* notation within the context of the courtesan's training. During the rise of *kunqu*, I argue, the courtesan was the context as well as the agent of this change. Her memory faced not only the daunting task of accommodating two kinds of memory habits in training but also an enlarged *beiqu* repertoire with variegated renditions. In comparison to the "authentic" *xiansuo*, *kunqu* earned its practitioners' favor because it upheld a new memory habit and new aesthetics that encouraged improvisation.

Although Wei Liangfu has typically been heralded as the progenitor of *kunqu*, such simplistic lineages ignore the broader musical ferment taking place in late sixteenth-century Jiangnan brothels. I speculate that the reason the newer, expanded approach of *kunqu* training replaced the narrower one in the *xiansuo* tradition was that it substantially reduced the pain of rote memorization of lyrics. Though my suggestions may be patchy and highly provisional, I nevertheless trust they provide evidence that the courtesan did not blindly follow the cultural elite's taste for the putatively high-end artistic form of *kunqu*. On the courtesan retreat from sophisticated Yuan drama being responsible for making *xiansuo* a dying kind of vocal art, I agree with He Liangjun (see also chapter 1). Yet it remains easy to forget that courtesans were trained in both forms, and that it was in their memory banks that courtesans were given the opportunity to meld the two. It is unfortunate that such a crucial role in late Ming drama has been erased.

It was the work of these courtesans who were capable of both styles that made possible the emergence of mixed and overlapping soundscapes, in which the literature rendered in *kunqu* gained a new kind of fetishized musical eroticism. Through brothel performers, *chuanqi* drama rendered in *kunqu* became sexually charged, surpassing Yuan drama's erotic poetry. Musical eroticism is the subject of the next chapter.

CHAPTER 3

Musical Eroticism and the Evolution of Taste

In chapter 2, we saw that, as part of the courtesan's varied curriculum and repertoire, the two modes of performance known as *xiansuo* and *kunqu* melded within the context of the pleasure quarters. Given this context, I suggested that an essential reason for the courtesan's pro-*kunqu* preference resided in its memorable yet improvisation-based arias. In the present chapter I first explore another crucial factor that contributed to the rise of *kunqu* in the late Ming pleasure quarters—namely, its musical eroticism, associated closely with an intimate formula in performance and *kunqu*'s special sonic environment. I then submit that within several decades the tastes for musical eroticism evolved rapidly: in literati accounts from around the time of the Ming-Qing dynastic transition (1618–1683), for example, the intimate formula typical of the courtesan's *kunqu* performances became a stereotypical, if not banal, occurrence. Concomitantly, although *xiansuo* had long been vestigial by this time, the new appetite for musical eroticism took a paradoxical turn toward favoring the vigorous style reminiscent of *xiansuo*.[1]

I. The Musical Eroticism of *Kunqu*

It has gone unnoticed that late Ming terminologies evolved to make distinctions between *xiansuo* and *kunqu*. The term which acknowledges the

1. For a more generous discussion of the interrelations between words, music, and eroticism in late Ming texts, see Joseph Lam, "Reading Music and Eroticism in Late Ming Texts," *Nan Nü* 12, no. 2 (2010): 215–54.

northern origins of the *xiansuo* genre is *Liangzhou* (written as 涼州 or 梁州, denoting the northwestern borderland or a northern tune title inherited from medieval music, respectively); the one which emphasizes the Suzhou origins of the *kunqu* genre is *Wuyu* 吳歈 (lit., "songs from the Suzhou area"). In late Ming poetic diction, *Liangzhou* indicates a shrill, sad quality, yet at a fast tempo. The Suzhou gentry dramatist Zhang Fengyi 張鳳翼 (1527–1613), for example, portrays a beautiful female musician's *pipa*-lute performance as such: "All of a sudden she rotated the pegs (to reach a higher range) and created accelerando effects; her vocal style switched to *Liangzhou*, sounding melancholy and shrill" 忽焉撥柱轉促急，腔轉涼州半淒邑.[2]

The term *Liangzhou* also appears repeatedly in the many poetry collections of the music connoisseur Zou Diguang 鄒迪光 (1550–1626; *jinshi* 1574), to indicate a style that was the opposite of the full-fledged staging of southern plays (with music perhaps in the *Wuyu/kunqu* style). There is no doubt that Zou used the term *Liangzhou* to create a clear division between the music specialties of his boy singers (he never recruited female singers for his private troupe). Some of Zou's boys specialized in singing in the *Liangzhou* style, which Zou occasionally refers to instead as *Yizhou* 伊州 or *Chile* 敕勒 (two place names that were geographically and musically associated with medieval northern tribes); other boys were versed in staging southern plays. Evidence abounds. One of Zou's accounts is particularly revealing of the high-pitched voices employed in *xiansuo*. Sometime between 1593 and 1602, he ascended to the Floating Clouds Pavilion in a temple at dusk, drank with his hangers-on using huge wine vessels, and listened to the songs of his boy singers. Feeling utterly delighted, he describes their high-pitched voices in the following couplet: "All because of a song in the *Liangzhou* style, none of the floating clouds can overpass us" 只因一曲梁州調，遏盡行雲総不流.[3] Zou embeds a witty pun here: the musical notes are soaring high to stop clouds from passing by the Floating Clouds Pavilion.

In contrast to the high-pitched, shrill vocality of *Liangzhou/xiansuo*, the *Wuyu* style offered an explicit eroticism in which the diarist Li Rihua 李日華 (1565–1635; *jinshi* 1592) could unabashedly revel. In his diary entry for the eighteenth day of the seventh month (lunar calendar) in 1612, Li describes

2. "He Luwang ting pipa ge" 和魯望聽彈琵琶歌 in Zhang Fengyi, *Chushitang jixuan* 處實堂集選, *juan* 1, 34a–b. Original Ming imprints in Shangdong Library (*juan* 1–3, *juan* 10–12) and Naikaku bunko (*juan* 1–9), photoprints in the Hishi collection at the Gest Library, Princeton University.

3. "Rimu deng Shangfang si Liuyun ting yu ke fu dadou ming shi'er changge bujue kuaishen" 日暮登上方寺流雲亭與客浮大斗命侍兒唱歌不覺快甚, in Zou Diguang, *Yuyilou ji* 鬱儀樓集 (pref. 1604), *juan* 22, 13a. Hishi collection.

an evening of banqueting and musicking on a pleasure boat in Jiaxing, Zhejiang province.[4] Two courtesans had traveled from Yangzhou to entertain the guests. The program began with "string instruments and vocal cords competing against each other" that well conveyed the style of *Liangzhou* (i.e., *xiansuo*) 絲肉競發, 頗有涼州風調. As time went by, the guests all became drunk and the moon rose in the sky. The banquet seems to have been over by this time, so everyone left for the Misty Rain Pavilion. Probably from a lookout point there, the literati "sang in high-pitch notes without any accompanying music" 清嘯.[5] At that point:

> The two courtesans switched to the new fashion of *Wuyu* [i.e., *kunqu*]. The notes were graceful and long, truly tugging at my heartstrings.
>
> 二伎更爲吳歈新聲，殊柔曼攬人也。

Evidence of this kind shows that in a typical courtesan performance of the day, one would first have experienced the opulent, multivoiced *Liangzhou/xiansuo* style, followed by the individualistic ethos and "jazzier" style of *Wuyu/kunqu* solos. It seems that banquet sequences involving courtesans began with *Liangzhou* music at the feast—where courtesans also served up wine, wit, and banter—and went on to include *Wuyu* solos in the post-banquet, late-night quietude of collective inebriation. Despite the lack of audio files, such evenings clearly accommodated these clashes of musical strategies and aesthetics—the disciplined versus the willful, the predictable versus the extravagant, the standardized versus the idiosyncratic. This sequence was, therefore, a characteristically late Ming musical experience.

Sometimes male *kunqu* experts would replace courtesans in the post-banquet *kunqu* recitals, but the musical eroticism was equally strong. In another account written about five months earlier, the same diarist, Li Rihua, reports in detail his first encounter with "the vocal technique of *Wuyu*" 吳歈之伎, albeit sung by a Buddhist monk rather than the courtesan whom the host had invited from Nanjing.[6] The gathering took place at a monastery in Hangzhou, where the virtuosic monk Jingxiu 靜修 (lit., "silent cultivation")

4. Tu Youxiang 屠友祥, ed., *Weishuixuan riji* 味水軒日記 (Shanghai: Shanghai yuandong chubanshe, 1996), *juan* 4, 247.

5. For my reading of the word *xiao* 嘯 as a reference to literati singing in the late Ming as opposed to a medieval heritage of whistling, see Peng Xu, "Courtesan versus Literatus: Gendered Soundscapes and Aesthetics in Late Ming Singing Culture," *T'oung Pao* 100 (2014): 417–27.

6. *Weishuixuan riji*, *juan* 4, 221. The diary item of the twenty-first day of the second month in 1612.

surprised Li with his riveting vocal finesse: "[His voice] is as lithe as a raw silk thread, his breath like a thin ground stream—[the sounds are] pure, bright, lonely, polished, reserved, deep, intoxicating, and fragrant. At each juncture he sang with full seductive energy, I shall expire [with pleasure]" 曳如□繭, 吐若伏流, 清亮孤圓, 溫涵醞馨, 每一騁態, 令人欲絕. I assume that the phrase "*chengtai*" 騁態, translated here as "sang with full seductive energy," refers to moments of long improvised passages, reminiscent of the Tiger Hill champion's slow tempo, excessive coloratura, and sentimental intensity referred to in chapter 2.[7] Li's blatant portrayal of Jingxiu's astonishing musical eroticism is reinforced by his identifying the monk singer as the homosexual lover of a certain Mr. Fan the Third 狎友范三郎君賞者. Young and inebriated, Jingxiu's behavior had already grown carnivalesque before he began singing 酒態狂縱, a state in all likelihood appreciated or shared by his listeners. His virtuosity was by nature an agile, showy vocality with outstanding ornamentation and the finest timbre needed to stir feelings, both sentimental and amorous.

The singing mood was, in general, melancholy and hypnotic, the effect often bringing the audience to tears. Commenting on a concert held at Tiger Hill in Suzhou during the eighth month of 1613, which featured a courtesan and a gentleman from the Ye clan, renowned for producing avocational *kunqu* singers, Ye Shaoyuan 葉紹袁 (1589–1648) writes: "Singing in the Suzhou style [reminiscent of the lascivious music of the Zheng Kingdom] was originally decadent, and now the singers [deliberately] make it even more cadenced and delicate" 鄭聲本淫, 而歌者又復抑揚宛轉.[8] By using a term from Confucian social criticism, "the lascivious music of the Zheng Kingdom" (*Zhengsheng yin* 鄭聲淫), to refer to the vocal style, Ye invokes Confucian norms, in which obscenity derives from excessiveness. Musically, this reference could mean excessive ornamentation and extra measures. What makes Ye's comment unusual is his emphasis on how the two singers' musical rendition made the sound particularly "cadenced and delicate" (*yiyang wanzhuan* 抑揚宛轉), beyond the normal level of eroticism brought about by excessive music. It seems that, on this occasion at least, the eroticism of the music itself outweighed the typically amorous content of the lyrics and the hint of a sexual relationship between the two singers.

We get a better sense of what constituted such musical excessiveness in

---

7. Lu Eting 陸萼庭, *Kunju yanchu shigao* 昆劇演出史稿 (Taipei: Guojia chubanshe, 2004), 77–81.

8. See Ye Shaoyuan, *Ye Tianliao nianpu bieji* 葉天寥年譜別記, in *Ye Tianliao sizhong* 葉天寥四種 (Shanghai: Beiye shanfang, 1936), 64. On the singer's genealogy, see Deng Changfeng 鄧長風, *Ming Qing xiqujia kaolüe* 明清戲曲家考略 (Shanghai: Shanghai guji chubanshe, 1994), 317–18.

Ling Mengchu's 凌濛初 (1580–1644) luxury songbook *Three Kinds of Southern Sounds* (*Nanyin sanlai* 南音三籟, ca. 1620s). Ling's editorial comments offer a technical assessment of professional singing and its contribution to the formation of musical traits associated specifically with the late Ming period. Ling condemns professional singers vehemently for their excessive music—the phenomenon of "gifted beats" (*zengban* 贈板, also written 增板, meaning "inserted beats," discussed in detail in chapter 2). Still, the technical details that Ling reveals are profound and worth quoting in full:[9]

> Yet in recent years, professional music teachers from the Suzhou area, good at nothing but showing off their voices with great pretensions to elegance, add numerous syllables to the original phrase or repeat the same syllable a few times so as to draw the listener into the charm of their singing skills. What they are ignorant of is that [by so doing] they are breaching the rules of music. Moreover, the inserted words naturally demand additional beats; once the additional beats are gradually accepted as the norm, the original form is distorted. The younger generation learns the distorted version and thoughtlessly models it when creating new lyrics. Cumulatively, there are mistakes so grave that nothing can be done to remedy them. Occasionally I correct such mistakes, to which singers respond that these [notes] are the heritage passed down from Huang Wenqin [黃問琴, the great descendant of Wei Liangfu]. They don't understand that Huang himself was the initiator of errors. This is why Shen Jing [沈璟, 1553–1610; *jinshi* 1574] claimed that he would plug his ears and flee whenever he heard the current fashion of "pure singing" in the Suzhou area.
>
> 而近來吳中教師，止欲弄喉取態，便于本句添出多字，或重疊其音，以見簸弄之妙，搶墊 [?] 之捷。而不知已戾本腔矣。況增添既多，便須增板，增板既久，便亂正板，後學因之，率爾填詞， 其病有不可救藥者。 偶一正之， 即云本王問琴所傳。 而不知作俑之為罪人。 沈伯英所謂聞今日吳中清唱， 即欲掩耳而避者也。

9. Ling Mengchu, "Fanli" 凡例, editor's preface in *Nanyin sanlai*, in *Shanben xiqu congkan*, 52:14. Note that Ling uses an incorrect surname for Huang Weiqin. The pronunciations of the two surnames, Wang 王 and Huang 黃, are the same in Ling's southern dialect. Perhaps Mr. Huang had such low social status that his employers did not respect him enough to get his surname straight, or perhaps the mistake occurred because the author was a generation younger than Mr. Huang.

Here, Ling Mengchu attacks an emerging and thriving tradition that is too strong for him to alter. To take the music teacher Ling mentions in the passage as an example, Huang Wenqin's career path connected him to both high and low strata of society—literati and courtesans. A first-generation follower of Wei Liangfu 魏良輔 (fl. sixteenth century), Huang taught the courtesan Wang Qingchi 王卿持,[10] worked in the household of Wang Ruqian 汪汝謙 (1577–1655), and served as a traveling companion and singer for Feng Mengzhen 馮夢禎 (1548–1606; *jinshi* 1577).[11]

The erotic sentiments evoked by the courtesan's "excessive" singing style were no less intense than her professional teacher's. In one *chuanqi* play, entitled *Tiger Hill in the Autumn* (*Qiu Huqiu* 秋虎丘), the vocal music of some "retainers singing popular songs" 唱時曲的清客 on the day of the singing festival wakes up a famous courtesan who had died of lovesickness and was buried in the Tiger Hill area several centuries earlier.[12] Her ghost joins the festival by singing alone in a pleasure boat. Her own singing, which laments her untimely demise and expresses her longing for love, turns out to be distinctively emotional and melancholic, outperforming the background human singing voices. The hero and his cohorts hear her voice and immediately sense the distinctiveness of her tone: "melancholy, sweet, soft and ethereal" 悽婉幽逸.[13] Two lines later in her song, everyone in the group concludes that the singer can only be a ghost. Notably, it is her vocal style that carries the dramatic intensity over to the moment when her true identity—a ghost in search of love—is disclosed. Shortly thereafter, the men leave the ghost singer and encounter a courtesan named Qiao, a historically famous courte-

10. Wang Xiaoyi 汪效漪, ed., *Pan Zhiheng quhua* 潘之恆曲話 (Beijing: Zhongguo xiju chubanshe, 1988), 118.

11. For Huang's teaching in Wang Ruqian's household and a growing circle of elite singers surrounding teachers such as Huang, see Wang, *Pan Zhiheng quhua*, 17. For his accompanying Feng Mengzhen on trips between 1599 and 1605, see Feng Mengzhen, *Kuaixuetang riji* 快雪堂日記, modern typeset edition edited by Ding Xiaoming 丁小明 (Nanjing: Fenghuang chubanshe, 2010), 149.

12. Wang Long 王鑨, *Qiu Huqiu*, 2 *juan*; no. 92 of *Guben xiqu congkan*, 3rd series 古本戲曲叢刊, 三集 (Beijing: Wenxue guji kanxingshe, 1957), scene 13, 59b–60a. For a discussion of the courtesan Wang Cuiqiao 王翠翹, the historical counterpart of the courtesan-ghost in the play, see Hua Wei 華瑋, "Nüxing, lishi yu xiqu: Qing chuanqi zhong Wang Cuiqiao gushi dui shizhuan yu xiaoshuo de gaixie jiqi yihan" 女性、歷史與戲曲: 清傳奇中王翠翹故事對史傳與小說的改寫及其意涵, in *Ming Qing xiqu zhong de nüxing shengyin yu lishi jiyi* 明清戲曲中的女性聲音與歷史記憶 (Taipei: Guojia chubanshe, 2013), 254–303.

13. Wang Long, *Qiu Huqiu*, scene 13, 60a.

san singer of *kunqu* and the main character of this scene, entitled "Encountering the Courtesan Qiao" (*Yu Qiao* 遇翹). Qiao begins a sentimental song about her lover (from whom she has long been separated), apparently rendered in the same "melancholy, sweet, soft, and ethereal" style as the ghost, thus leading the men to misidentify her as yet another female ghost. In a later scene, we are told that Qiao is the best courtesan singer in Suzhou. This *chuanqi* play is, of course, no more than an apocryphal story told by a Qing playwright with great nostalgia for the Ming golden age of singing, and yet it captures the signature vocal style of the late Ming *kunqu*—its amatory connotations, its popularity, and its necessity for courtesans.

Beyond improvised rich ornaments and long notes, another gendered and yet often ignored aspect of the courtesan's vocal production was a staccato quality associated with the entering tone in the Suzhou dialect. As we have seen in chapter 2, northern arias began to be adopted into the *kunqu* repertoire after master Wei Liangfu's intervention in the mid-sixteenth century. The new fad in the Yangtze delta—Suzhou, Songjiang (present-day Shanghai), Taicang, Hangzhou, Jiaxing, and Huzhou—rendered northern arias in southern dialects, which to conservative connoisseurs such as Shen Jing was problematic.[14] They insisted on adopting the Yuan rhyming system recorded in Zhou Deqing's 周德清 (fl. 1324) *Sounds and Rhymes from the Central Plain* (*Zhongyuan yinyun* 中原音韻, 1324) in the new fashion of *kunqu*—that is, applying to northern arias the four-tone system (without the fifth category of the entering tone) and the bilabial ending /m/ in a few rhyming categories. Shen even compiled a book entitled *Correcting the Suzhou Singers* (*Zheng Wu bian* 正吳編), part of which is now preserved in Shen Chongsui's 沈寵綏 (?–1645) *kunqu* thesis *What You Must Know About Singing* (*Duqu xuzhi* 度曲須知, 1639).[15] One essential "error" that had to be rectified was to keep the entering tone—a quintessential feature of the southern dialects in the areas where *kunqu* prevailed—in singing northern arias. Such southern characteristics, however, may have had some gendered charm or even erotic effects in courtesan singing—Ling Mengchu, Shen Jing, and Shen Chongsui may have hopelessly attacked a profitable domain in courtesan singing.

The best example we have of stereotypical courtesan singing is a poem entitled "Singing" (*Ge* 歌), found in Gu Zhengyi's 顧正誼 (fl. 1575–1600) printed collection of clichéd poems on late sixteenth-century vogues:[16] each

14. Qi Shenua 齊森華, Chen Duo 陳多, and Ye Changhai 葉長海, eds., *Zhongguo quxue da cidian* 中國曲學大辭典 (Hangzhou: Zhejiang jiaoyu chubanshe, 1997), 717.

15. Shen, *Duqu xuzhi*, in *Zhongguo gudian xiqu lunzhu jicheng* 中國古典戲曲論著集成 (Beijing: Zhongguo xiju chubanshe, 1959), 5:183–317.

16. Gu Zhengyi, *Baiyong tupu*, Beijing, National Library.

poem is carved in a calligraphic style and accompanied by an illustration on the opposite page (see fig. 11). In the present case, the illustration shows a banquet setting with men and women sitting at the same table—a seating convention signaling the soloist's identity as a courtesan. The courtesan-singer is clapping her hands to beat time for her own singing. What makes the poem on the opposite page interesting is its patchwork nature, as we identify various relevant clichés portraying the stereotypical diva at a midnight vocal concert, beginning with: "At midnight she sings a new song / Her delicate voice twitters like an oriole at dawn" 子夜發新聲，纖喉轉(囀)曙鶯. The solo begins at midnight and ends at dawn; the vocalization is soft and delicate. Midnight singing in the Wu/Suzhou style has its ultimate origins in the tradition of the "Midnight Ballads to the Local Tunes of the Wu Region" (*ziye Wuge* 子夜吳歌) in the Six Dynasties (roughly the third to the sixth century CE).[17] The original tunes, which had long been lost, later became a source of inspiration for poets. All the variations of this form involve a female persona who is longing for love. Perhaps because of the formal similarities between the Six Dynasties midnight singing and that of the late Ming, *ziye Wuge* became a commonplace allusion to midnight southern solos in late Ming poetry and songs. In 1627 Shen Defu 沈德符 (1578–1642) composed four poems in honor of the wedding of a friend and a courtesan, Miss Chen, which Shen hosted in his own household at Nanjing. One of these poems, concerning the vocal art of the bride, identifies the genre she was trained in as "the midnight songs of Jiangnan" 教出江南子夜歌 and her style as "light singing" (*weichang* 微唱).[18]

To reconstruct what a sixteenth-century oriole's cheeps sounded like is fraught with difficulty. The best we can do is dig up some clues so as to conceive of the courtesan's vocal production in a less intangible way than we previously imagined. One way to suggest specific vocal techniques associated

17. A few eleventh-century references, such as the *Xin Tangshu* 新唐書 and *Yuefu shiji* 樂府詩集, interpret *ziye* ("midnight") as the name of a woman who first created the tune, but this seems doubtful. By the eleventh century, the tune had long been appropriated by literati as a poetic form, perhaps the most salient examples being those of Li Bo 李白 (701–762). Meanwhile, the fact that *ziye* in Ming poetry refers also to boy singers' singing speaks to its contemporary usage simply as a classical allusion.

18. See Shen Defu, *Qingquantang ji* 清權堂集, 22 *juan* in vol. 1377 of XXSKQS, *juan* 5, 17b–18a, photo-reprint in the Hishi collection, Gest Library, Princeton University (hereafter Hishi collection), original in Naikaku Bunko. The title of the poem contains most of the background information: "Zhang Er'han Married Courtesan Miss Chen at My Household, Zhang Being a Yuezhou Native" 張爾含納陳校書于邸中, 張為越州人. The two lines read: "Well-trained in the midnight style of Jiangnan, / Her light singing in the hallway resonates with her gracious steps" 教出江南子夜歌，屧廊微唱響淩波.

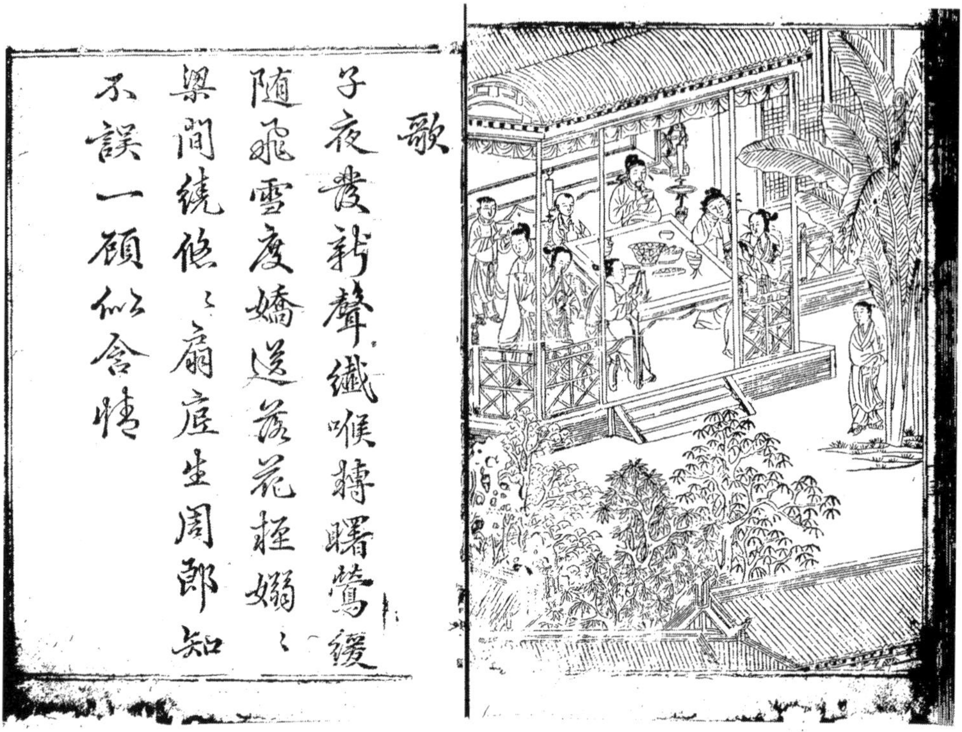

Fig. 11. "Singing," in Gu Zhengyi, *Illustrations of One Hundred Poems* (*Baiyong tupu*), 1596. (Courtesy National Library, Beijing.)

with this metaphor is to place it in its linguistic and dramatic settings. An onomatopoeia that often appears in the same setting with the oriole metaphor is *lik-lik* 嚦嚦, pronounced this way in the stage dialect of modern-day *kunqu* singing as well as in most late Ming southern dialects. An example is found in scene 10, "Startling Dream" (*Jingmeng* 驚夢), in Tang Xianzu's 湯顯祖 (1550–1616; *jinshi* 1583) *The Peony Pavilion* (*Mudan ting* 牡丹亭, 1598), that have become staples in the *kunqu* opera repertoire. The song from which the example is excerpted depicts the heroine's sexual awakening when strolling in an abandoned garden on a spring day. When the female lead sings of how the spring oriole sounds in her ears, the entire line in which *lik-lik* appears—嚦嚦鶯聲溜的圓—is translated by Stephen Owen as "from the warbling orioles comes a bright and liquid melody,"[19] and by Cyril Birch

19. Owen, *Anthology of Chinese Literature: Beginnings to 1911* (New York: Norton, 1996), 885.

as "liquid flows the trill of oriole."[20] The word "trill," which is defined as a rapid alternation of two adjacent tones, has a clear meaning in Western vocal training and brings out Birch's understanding of the *lik-lik* quality.

We all have our own projected ideas that could be blended into this complex sonic picture. In a remote way, the modern *kunqu* rendition of the onomatopoeia *lik-lik*, which is closely connected to the eighteenth-century singing master Ye Tang's 葉堂 1792 musical scores, can help us imagine its musical meaning in the sixteenth and seventeenth centuries: we have a repeated note with a momentary silence between the two syllables, followed immediately by the word "oriole" (*ying* 鶯) in a trill.[21] Because of the glottal stop (represented by "k") between the two syllables *lik-lik*, the onomatopoeia might bring to mind a tender, quasi-staccato quality of vocal production, with notes articulated in a detached form.

Certainly to the late Ming mind, the "oriole" analogy involved a much more complex texture of sound than a single line of modern operatic singing could possibly suggest. One example comes from a play (composed no later than the mid-1590s) elaborating on the love story of a courtesan, called "Spring of the Jade Hall" (*Yutang chun* 玉堂春), a tale that runs through several plays and stories. The courtesan sings a song about her own solo in the pleasure quarters: "My voice is mellow, just like the twittering sound of an oriole" 歌喉潤，恰便似嚦嚦鶯聲.[22] To return to the example from *The Peony Pavilion*, in 1598 Tang Xianzu may well have been aware of the increasingly close aesthetic association between female solo singing and the metaphoric lexicon of the "oriole" developing in the sixteenth century. On the surface, his heroine describes the oriole she hears in a deserted spring garden, but the "oriole" may actually be self-referential: the persona sings in exactly the same fashion as a twittering oriole, with a round, mellow timbre, just like the

---

20. Birch, trans., *The Peony Pavilion: Mudan ting*, 2nd ed. (Bloomington: Indiana University Press, 2002), 45.

21. For Ye Tang's "full" score of Tang Xianzu's *Peony Pavilion*, see *Nashuying simeng quanpu* 納書楹四夢全譜 (1792), photo reproduction in *Xuxiu siku quanshu*, vol. 1757. Ye's score gives no clue to the glottal stops; the signs for marking such vocal production were invented in later music printing. However, the notes he put down for lik-lik remain exactly the same in modern rendition. The best source for this live music example is an early twentieth-century gramophone recording of Yuan Anpu's 袁安圃 singing.

22. See the excerpted scene "Visiting the Pleasure Quarters Again" (*Fu ru yanhua* 復入煙花) from Ji Hongchuan's 記紅川 "Separating the Paired Hairpins" (*Fenchai ji* 分釵記), in *Qunyin leixuan* 群音類選, compiled by Hu Wenhuan 胡文煥 (fl. 1596) (photo rpt. of rare book in the Nanjing Library, Beijing: Zhonghua shuju, 1980), under the rubric "The Capital's Tune" (*Guanqiang lei* 官腔類), 21.1138.

courtesan Spring of the Jade Hall.[23] This is a double metaphor: the female lead and the oriole are one.

By the late sixteenth century, bird singing must have been established as an erotic object. In poetic diction referring to courtesan singing, it must thus have become a metaphor attached centrally to the courtesan's body. The first couplet of the following poem, written by Pan Zhiheng 潘之恆 (1556–1622) sometime between 1594 and 1596, describes in metaphor the performance given by a private female troupe during a party held in a certain retired Royal Censor Zhang's garden:[24]

> Swallows' chattering between rafters becomes more intimate;
> Young orioles' cheeps on the twigs are in tunes more fashionable than
> anything else.
> State- and city-toppling beauties compete for my gaze,
> But that's mostly because Maestro Zhou couldn't hear clearly.

> 燕子梁間語更親，
> 鶯雛枝上囀偏新。
> 傾國傾城爭相顧，
> 多為周郎聽未真。

"Maestro Zhou" is the historical figure Zhou Yu 周瑜 (175–210). A master player of the zither (and a legendary general of the Three Kingdoms state of Wu), he came to be considered the epitome of an elite connoisseur of music. Late Ming literati-singers possessed privileged musical knowledge because of their education in dramatic literature. Without exception, they were self-anointed maestros of vocal art. Here, in the last couplet, the poet indicates in a teasing tone that the special vocal quality and softness of the courtesans' voices created some difficulties for him in judging their performance.

The gendered basis for the oriole and swallow style of female singing is manifested clearly in the following two cases of personification. One is Shen

23. My understanding of the phrase *liudeyuan* 溜的圓 as referring to timbre or tone quality is different from its general translation as a kind of liquid flow of melody.

24. Pan Zhiheng, *Shejiang shi* 涉江詩, *juan* 5, 14–15b (Hishi collection). The same troupe is known to have performed for the playwright Mei Dingzuo 梅鼎祚 (1549–1615) in about 1598. See Mei Dingzuo, "A Letter to Lü Yusheng" *Yü Lü Yusheng* 與呂玉繩, in *Luqiu shishi ji* 鹿裘石室集, *juan* 6, 24b–26a. In the letter Mei describes the actresses as "very pretty and coquettish" 甚妖豔 but, like Pan, complains about the quality of the music. Censor Zhang's estate was located in present-day Hubei province, far from the Yangtze delta, the center of vocal art at the time.

Defu's 1633 poem entitled "The Early Oriole" (*Xinying* 新鶯).[25] Upon seeing the oriole preening itself, he thinks of female singers seen in moments of intimacy right after singing in a vocal concert; to him, butterflies resemble time-beating clappers, and willows evoke the garden setting (蝶能供拍板，柳為闢園亭). The other example is found in Fan Yunlin's 范允臨 (1558–1641; *jinshi* 1595) 1640 poem portraying two swallows nesting under the eaves of his Crystalizing Fragrance Pavilion.[26] He rolls up the pearly curtain so that he can watch them through the engraved window; to him, the new nest resembles a specialized concert hall for female singers (盡卷珠簾洞瑣窓，任教營壘鬱金堂). The Hall of *Yujin* (*Yujin tang* 鬱金堂) is a classical allusion to a beautiful woman's scented boudoir; it may also refer to a specific concert hall for a private female troupe that belonged to Fan Yunlin's little brother-in-law Xu Rong 徐溶 (better known for his style name Qingzhi 清之) (1597–after 1641), known for his extravagant life style before midlife.[27] Another Hall of Yujin near West Lake in Hangzhou was owned by Feng Mengzhen, the location for influential female singing competitions hosted by Feng.[28]

From a hybrid source, we have thus far gathered historical imaginings of what constituted an erotic singing style at the time. Given the intensity of the musical eroticism of *kunqu*, in many accounts of romantic Tiger Hill

25. See Shen Defu, *Qingquantang ji*, *juan* 11, 3b.

26. Fan Yunlin, "In the fifth month of the year 1580, over half of the summer has passed, a pair of swallows suddenly appeared and nested under my Crystalizing Fragrance Pavilion; after a full month of toil at it they finally completed it; I am writing these poems to reward them" 庚辰五月，夏已過半，忽有雙燕来余凝香閣下營巢，經營辛苦，匝月而成，作詩勞之, in *Shuliaoguan ji* 輸廖館集, 8 *juan*, facsimile reprint in *Siku jinhui shu congkan* 四庫禁毀書叢刊 (Beijing: Beijing chubanshe, 2000), vol. 101, 189–398, poem no. 2, *juan* 1, 79b–80a. Digital access: https://taiwanebook.ncl.edu.tw/en/book/NCL-9900012301/reader. In Fan Yunlin's poetic diction, however, oriole singing can sometimes refer to boy singers' vocal performance. See, for example, "Watching Plays" 觀劇, poems nos. 1 and 3, *juan* 1, 70b–71a.

27. Fan Yunlin, "Essay in Celebration of My Cousin Xu Qingzhi's Fortieth Birthday" 壽内弟徐清之四十初度序, states that Xu Qingzhi turned forty in the eighth month of the ninth year of the Chongzhen reign, that is, 1636. See *Shuliaoguan ji*, *juan* 3, 34a–37a. Shen Defu has a 1624 poem dedicated to Xu's private female troupe. See Shen Defu, *Qingquantang ji*, *juan* 2, 5b–6b.

28. Feng Mengzhen, "Essay on Building My Cottage near Mount Gu" (*Jielu Gushan ji* 結廬孤山記), in *Kuaixuetang ji* 快雪堂集, *Siku quanshu cunmu congshu* 四庫全書存目叢書 (Jinan: Qi Lu shushe, 2001), *jibu*, vol. 165, *juan* 28; Pan Zhiheng, "Talks on Singing" (*Xu qu* 敘曲), *Luanxiao xiaopin* 鸞嘯小品, *juan* 2, 1a–3a, (original copy in the Shanghai Library); Wang, *Pan Zhiheng quhua*, 8. Pan Zhiheng: "Since the singing competitions in the Hall of Yujin . . . the vocal art was slightly revived" 自鬱金堂之徵歌……音稍稍始振.

experiences, lyrical content is not mentioned at all; the romantic sentiments seem to derive directly from the music itself. Yet surely the high degree of eroticism in the courtesan's voices would have been reinforced by not only the social conditions of prostitution but also the romantic content of *chuanqi* plays. Creating erotic scenes and casting courtesans as female leads in them became a fad. Manifestations of this change in publication content include the songbook *A Hundred Brocades to Courtesan Singers* (*Chantou bailian* 纏頭百練) in which romantic scenes were extracted from various *chuanqi* plays and grouped into five sections. The first section, "Portrayals of Lovers' Secret Rendezvous" (*Youqi xiezhao* 幽期寫照), selects scenes that dramatize elopement, wedding nights, and other occasions of sexual intercourse. Ling Mengchu, author of the foreword, points out that the collection could easily incur criticism for being "excessive and obscene" 淫而蕩, but the main purpose of the audacious compiler, at least in Ling's rhetoric, was to cater to courtesan singers—to "buy one smile from them with one thousand taels of gold" 千金買一笑 and to promote the compiler as someone who uncompromisingly supported and understood their singing art (*zhiyinren* 知音人).[29]

II. The Intimate Formula and Soundscape

Singing style could be removed from its original acoustic setting, but some features intimately tied to specific sonic memories would not disappear; rather, it was the singing style that conveyed a sense of the place that was its typical setting. The connection between the singing voice and the ambient noise, between aesthetic choices and the physical conditions of performance, however, has been largely neglected in previous scholarship on Ming performance. This chapter uses the term "soundscape" to evoke a connection between space and sound, between physical conditions and performance, between the acoustic environment and singing.[30]

29. Ling Mengchu, "Chantou bailian xu" 纏頭百練序, in Chonghe jushi 冲和居士, *Yi chun jin* 怡春錦, 6 *ji* 集, in *Shanben xiqu congkan*, 19:6, 1. *Yichun jin* was another name for *Chantou bailian*.

30. For a seminal theoretical discussion of the notion of "soundscape," see R. Murray Schafer, *The Soundscape: Our Sonic Environment and the Tuning of the World* (Rochester, VT: Destiny Books, 1992). For a retrospection on the field's past and projection about its future, see Michele Hilmes, "Is There a Field Called Sound Culture Studies? And Does It Matter?" *American Quarterly* 57, no. 1 (2005): 249–59; also see Jay Beck and Tony Grajeda's response to Hilmes' article in "Introduction: The Future of Film Sound Studies," in *Lowering the Boom: Critical Studies in Film Sound,* ed. Beck and

Different kinds of evidence, including paintings and written accounts with or without illustrations, give information about the fashion of visiting courtesans' houses for overnight entertainment running from dusk to dawn. However, the events most richly commemorated by clients seem to have been nightlong ones, which were lengthy enough to allow demonstration of the courtesans' mastery in a variety of performance genres—and thus to involve the most prodigal expenditure by a chief client, accompanied by his cohort. There is no longer any extant documentation by means of which to fully reconstruct a courtesans' musical performance on one of those long, boozy nights, though we know that it could include some major genres, such as the percussive form of the "ten-instrument ensemble" (*shifangu* 十番鼓), which encouraged the guests to play any instruments they pleased along with the courtesan(s); the courtesans' choral rendition of northern songs (rendered in either the authentic *xiansuo* or the new *kunqu* style) to their own string accompaniment; southern solos (*nanqu* 南曲, mostly in the *kunqu* style) accompanied by either the mechanical beats (clappers or bare hands) or an orchestra with flutes and string instruments (*sanxian* 三弦 and *tiqin* 提琴); and team or solo dancing. Evidence suggests that *kunqu* solos took place at midnight or post-midnight moments and that they were rendered in a soft, pleasing-sounding voice. It was this midnight vocal music that provided the intimate performance model most suited to the "oriole/swallow" style of singing. Let us now turn to the sonic environment of the pleasure quarters in its relation to light singing.

Generally speaking, the late Ming pleasure quarters were allowed in noisy marketplaces and business centers filled with chariots, horses, and passersby during the daytime, rather than being confined to relatively quiet suburbs, as in Edo Japan.[31] A fair amount is known about the Old Compound

---

Grajeda (Urbana: Univ. of Illinois Press, 2008). For a discussion of "point of audition" in the context of American radio drama, see Neil Verma, *Theater of the Mind: Imagination, Aesthetics, and American Radio Drama* (Chicago: University of Chicago Press, 2012).

31. Timon Screech, "Going to the Courtesans: Transit to the Pleasure District of Edo Japan," in *The Courtesan's Arts: Cross-Cultural Perspectives*, ed. Martha Feldman and Bonnie Gordon (New York: Oxford University Press, 2006), 255–79. The premodern conception of "noise," however, focuses exclusively on sounds produced by mundane life in urban centers (as opposed to the pastoral ideal in rural areas), which the model figure of the literatus-hermit tradition, Tao Yuanming 陶淵明 (ca. 365–427), famously called the "populated environment" (*renjing* 人境). The first line of Tao Yuanming's famous fifth poem of the twenty-poem suite on "Drinking" (*Yinjiu* 飲酒) goes: "Among the haunts of men I build my cottage; / there's noise of wheels and hoofs, but I hear it not" 結廬在人境，而無車馬喧. This literati tradition of living

(*jiuyuan* 舊院, also known as *quzhong* 曲中) in Nanjing, which was located near the Confucius Temple, the Three-Mountain Street bookstores and the Examination Hall directly across the Qinhuai River, from the evidence in memoirs by Zhang Dai 張岱 (1597–ca.1684) and Yu Huai 余懷 (1616–1696), in woodblock-illustrated city guides such as Zhu Zhifan's 朱之蕃 (1558–1626; *jinshi* 1595) *Odes of Nanjing with Illustrations* (*Jinling tuyong* 金陵圖詠),[32] and in the catalogue of Nanjing courtesans *Seductive Women of Nanjing* (*Jinling baimei* 金陵百媚, preface 1618).[33] However, the relation of the inner space of the Old Compound to the musical activities of the neighborhood's inhabitants remains an underexplored question. Here I can only hope to suggest (1) a special sonic space for musical activities in the Nanjing pleasure quarters, which were marked by a dense population living in a cluster of buildings, and (2) a central garden in the brothel community for larger concerts starring courtesan-singers from different houses.

In the late Ming pleasure quarters the evening hours must have been boisterous, so that it became a symbol for "noisy space" in poetry, or what the theorist R. Murray Schafer terms a "keynote"—sonic features intimately tied to specific cultural memories.[34] Poets finding themselves in other crowded, tumultuous musical events, such as the annual Mid-Autumn Singing Festival, might recall their experience in the pleasure quarters and use the latter as a metaphor. For example, singing aficionado Zou Diguang wrote a poem entitled "Mid-autumn night, strolling in the Hui Mountain Temple; the moon a little obscure, but I was in high spirits; a poem with the rhyming word *zheng*" 中秋十五夜遊惠山寺，月色微明，而意興頗劇，得箏字.[35] In this poem Zou compares the Hui Mountain Temple, filled with the boisterous sound of singing, to the pleasure quarters (平林處處成伎館). Hui Mountain Temple was located in his hometown of Wuxi, which was about two days' travel by boat from Nanjing. Zou retired from office in 1593 and lived

in "seclusion" in *renjing*, however, may have added a poetic layer to the sonic environment of the Chinese pleasure quarters.

32. Si-yen Fei, *Negotiating Urban Space: Urbanization and Late Ming Nanjing* (Cambridge, MA: Harvard University Asia Center, 2009), 124–87, esp. 173. Also see Ōki Yasushi, *Chūgoku yūri kūkan: Min Shin shinwai gijo no sekai* 中國游里空間: 明清秦淮妓女の世界 (Tokyo: Seidosha, 2002), 125–35.

33. Weilinzi 為霖子 [Feng Menglong 馮夢龍 (1574–1646)], *Jinling baimei*, 2 vols. (n.p.: Changmen qian yiwu, ca. 1573–1644). Original in Naikaku Bunko, which released a microfilm version in 1966: I am grateful to the University of Chicago library for use of a printout. Digital access: https://www.shuge.org/view/jin_ling_bai_mei/

34. Schafer, *The Soundscape*, 272.

35. Zou Diguang, *Yuyilou ji* 鬱儀樓集 (prefaces by Zou Diguang and Feng Shike 馮時可 [ca. 1541–ca. 1620], 1604), *juan* 25, 7a.

the remainder of his life in a manner typical of late Ming hedonism, on a renowned estate called Yugong Valley 愚公谷 near the Hui Mountain. But he also spent many mid-autumn nights in Nanjing; by "the pleasure quarters" he may have had the Old Compound in mind.

In fact, the failure to produce such noise was considered an inauspicious sign of abnormality for the pleasure quarters. Sometime between 1593 and 1602, Zou Diguang visited Nanjing and recorded his observations of "the extreme misery of the pleasure quarters" 平康中零落殆甚 in a series of poems.[36] Zou passed by the entertainment district and missed its signature sound of high-volume noise mixed with communal laughter: "Occasionally the sound of singing and flutes issued from the [courtesans'] bowers / But it was not the same as before with guffaws and chatter" 偶然歌管樓中出，不是曩時笑語聲. In 1635 Shen Defu visited the Nanjing pleasure quarters and portrayed its decline from the same angle: "The most pathetic is the night with the moon and flowers; from ten compounds comes only one song accompanied by a reedpipe" 最憐花月夜，十院一笙歌.[37]

Such a cacophonous world would have given rise to certain conventions that led to the division of the night into two markedly different soundscapes. With this point of focus in mind, some familiar materials, such as the following quote from Yu Huai's memoir of the Nanjing pleasure quarters, *Miscellaneous Notes About the Long Bridge* (*Banqiao zaji* 板橋雜記, 1693), offer tangible details about the sequence of performances and their sound effects:[38]

36. Zou Diguang's poetry collection in *Yuyilou ji*, according to the author's preface, contains poems written between 1593 and 1602. See "Passing by the Long Bridge and Watching, I Composed Six Quatrains in Lament" 行經長板橋見，作六絕傷之, in Zou, *Yuyilou ji*, *juan* 28, 5b–6a. Zhang Fengyi's poem "The Nanjing Courtesans" 金陵妓 notes "the sudden silencing of singing and dancing" 一時歌舞忽銷沉 in the Nanjing pleasure quarters. Zhang offers further information in his own annotation to the poem: "At the time, the Director of the Board of Rites banned the pleasure quarters" 時大宗伯有平康之禁. See Zhang Fengyi, *Chushitang ji xuan* 處實堂集選, *juan* 6, 6b–7a. The Director of the Board of Rites may possibly refer to Shen Yiguan 沈一貫 (1531–1615; *jinshi* 1568), who assumed the position in 1594 and left for Beijing to accept a promotion in 1595. The ban must have not lasted long, for it left little trace in official histories.

37. Shen Defu, "Revisiting the Nanjing Pleasure Quarters, Noting Down My Thoughts, Two Poems" 重訪曲中志感二首, in *Qingquantang ji*, *juan* 12, 12a–b, poem no. 2.

38. Yu Huai, *Banqiao zaji*. Modern typeset edition, *Banqiao zaji jiaozhu (wai yizhong)* 板橋雜記校註外一種, edited by Li Jintang 李金堂 (Shanghai: Shanghai guji chubanshe, 1988), 8–9.

> Courtesans' houses joined together like the scales of a fish; they all lived next to each other. . . . When night fell, they blew flutes and thrummed zithers, or put on plays, the uproarious vibration resounded in the sky. . . . Whenever the night got cool and people grew quiet, as the breeze freshened and the moon brightened, . . . here one would hear the sound of the vertical flute, there someone would sing an elegant melody. All was quiet, but for the fish rising to the surface of the pond to listen.
>
> 妓家鱗次,比屋而居。. . . 入夜而擫笛搊箏,梨園搬演,聲徹九霄。. . . 每當夜涼人定,風清月朗, . . . 此吹洞簫,彼度妙曲,萬籟皆寂,游魚出聽。

Without modern technologies to facilitate the distillation of sound, or what Emily Thompson calls "the abstract sound" in modern concert halls, the courtesans' houses, and gardens, could not possibly have sealed off ambient noise and reverberation.[39] Rather, instrumental music and full-scale theatrical staging in one house must have added to the decibel level of the noise that guests in other houses endured until midnight. It made sense, acoustically, for the courtesan houses in densely populated neighborhoods to follow the custom of a program that reserved the peace and quiet of the hours after midnight, following the banquet, for salon-style entertainment.

The same sonic pattern is found in a first-person-narrative free-aria entitled "With Courtesans, Appreciating the Moon on the Long Bridge (on the Lantern Festival)" 攜妓長橋玩月, written by Hu Wenhuan (fl. 1596), a Hangzhou-based book merchant and compiler.[40] "All one can hear" when the night starts, the song goes, "is boisterous sounds of singing, loud wind instruments, and buzzing string instruments" 止聽得沸歌聲、喧管籥、雜絲弦. Against this sonic backdrop Hu's little dramatic encounter with his former courtesan girlfriend takes place; he follows her to her own house, and their romance resumes in the after-midnight quietude, when "they allow the jade water-clock on top of the watchtower to urge the silver arrow" 任樓頭玉漏催銀箭 and when only "sobbing-like vocal sounds" 歌聲咽 can be heard.

---

39. Emily Thompson, *The Soundscape of Modernity: Architectural Acoustics and the Culture of Listening in America, 1900–1933* (Cambridge, MA: MIT Press, 2002). Thompson observes a quintessentially modern suppression of ambient noise and reverberation to promote clarity in modern music halls; this is particularly inspiring for my reflection on sound in its relation to the two performance models in late Ming vocal concerts.

40. See Hu Wenhuan's collection of theatrical and nontheatrical arias, *Qunyin leixuan*, 4:2513–20.

Regrettably, when it comes to popular locations for late-night vocal concerts within the crowded courtesan community, very few accounts survive. Yu Huai's memoir hints at a garden setting, with ponds, bridges, and bannister rails, but offers no concrete details. Pan Zhiheng's commemorative essay, "The Long Bridge" (*Changbanqiao ji* 長板橋記), is to my knowledge the only direct account that expands our conception of the particular architectural and geographical design of the pleasure quarters.[41] Though written in a belletristic style rather than plain prose, it discloses to some extent the geographical layout of the courtesan community in its heyday—namely, the three decades beginning with the 1570s, when Pan frequented the Old Compound during his sojourn in Nanjing, and through to the end of the Wanli reign in 1620. This account not only contains historical names and facts that echo details in other sources, but it also retains some sense of chronological coherence. Given Pan's status as the most prolific late Ming music critic and biographer of several dozen courtesans, the highly ornate language does not detract from the historical value of this source.[42] The most detailed section of Pan's account brings out the significance of a certain central garden within the community. This was an enclosed space, not only walled (even locked at times), but also sandwiched between layers of courtesan dwellings:

> What I experienced in my youth and middle age I can still show and recount. The ruins of the desolate garden were spanned by two rainbow-shaped bridges. The space between neighboring houses was occupied by two stone gangways that connected them. Hundreds of lotus stalks sprang forth out of the filthy mud [in the pond], which made you stand and think of the lotus flowers in Western Paradise.[43]

41. Pan Zhiheng, "The Long Bridge," in *Luanxiao xiaopin, juan* 6, 27a–28b. The piece must have been published first in the 1610s, but for some reason Pan chose to revise it for another printing project in the last two years of his life (1621–1622). A few years later his son compiled his posthumous collection (1626) and included the version that we have in our hands today.

42. "Theater critics," meaning people who wrote about some aspects of music and theater, did not exist as an appellation in sixteenth- and seventeenth-century China. Those who wrote about music history usually had different theatrical and musical interests and focuses. Still, Pan's prolific writings make him our best source for music criticism, regarding especially the courtesans' vocal art.

43. The symbol of the lotus rising from the dirty mud was a conventional metaphor for the courtesan (related to the profession's worship of Guanyin or Bodhisattva Avalokiteśvara, the goddess of compassion). Thus, Mei Dingzuo's collection of biographies of courtesans is entitled *Lotuses from the Green Mud* (*Qingni lianhua ji* 青泥蓮花記).

> Double cushions on brocade cloths were spread on the ground, reminding you of the romantic way of life of the Six Dynasties. A flower-patterned lock opened the gate into the spacious courtyard, where a rug made a stage when the moon rose. Winding railings zigzagged along a ravine, kingfisher feathers [from women's hairpins] stirring in gentle breezes. To the east [of the garden] was Madame Ma Xianglan's garden; to the west was Madame Chu Qianying's pavilion.[44]
>
> 少壯所歷，今可指陳。蓋荒圃之墟，為雙垂虹所跨；芳鄰之隙，有兩石梁通之。百柱出於淤泥，佇想西方青蓮之勝；重茵鋪錦繡，依稀江左玉樹之標。葳蕤開瑣鑰於廣庭，氍毹月上；曲折轉闌干於邃谷，翡翠風輕。其前則馬湘蘭有園，其後則褚茜英有閣。

About Chu Qianying and her house we know very little. But the other dwelling mentioned, that of Ma Xianglan 馬湘蘭 (1548–1604), must have been one of the largest: by 1604 it housed Ma Xianglan, her three "daughters," and a troupe of no fewer than twelve actresses.[45] Ma Xianglan heads Pan Zhiheng's list of at least three generations of famous courtesans he had known in person. Of the youngest ones he speaks with a kind of everyday ease, disclosing further details about midnight entertainment within the garden:

> Often they lingered in the wind; together they turned to the moon to dance. At the Bower of Shadows I was with the two "Wen 文" sisters—Cui Jingwen and Cui Shuangwen. With their arms hooked they danced and sang from moonrise until past the fourth night watch. At the Pavilion of Beautiful Scenery, I invited the three "Ye 夜" girls—Chen Yeshu, Ma Yeyu, and Jiang Yelai. Standing by the pond, they looked at their reflections and freshened their makeup.
>
> 每淩風而徙倚，同向月以婆娑。幻景閣並攜二文(崔氏景文雙文)，聯臂踏歌，迎哉生而遲山吐；佳色亭特邀三夜(陳夜舒馬夜玉蔣夜來)，臨流顧影，印新額而黛殘眉。

44. Evidence shows that the locale known as the Old Compound was a stripe-shaped area, stretching from east to west. Yu Huai uses the same words *qian* 前 to refer to the east, and *hou* 後 for the west, in his *Banqiao zaji*.

45. Accounts of the Ma household in the Nanjing pleasure quarters can be found in various books, including Shen Defu's *Wanli yehuobian* 萬曆野獲編, Qian Qianyi's 錢謙益 (1582–1664), *Liechao shiji* 列朝詩集, and Feng Mengzhen's *Kuaixuetang riji* 快雪堂日記, to name a few.

It seems possible that the Pavilion of Beautiful Scenery (*Jiase ting* 佳色亭, where *jiase* is a double entendre that evokes both beautiful scenery and beautiful women) was a site of frequent musical activities within the central garden (see fig. 1 in the introduction). We may even infer from the evidence that the central garden was the main "public" venue inside the demimonde, where important guests such as Pan invited girls from different "families" for grander midnight programs. In his essay "Talks on Singing" (*Xuqu* 敍曲), Pan mentions in passing the "elegant gathering and performance at the Pavilion of Beautiful Scenery" 佳色亭雅集奏技, at which singing voices resounded until dawn 一聲而燭跋，再闋而雞號.[46] The purpose of the competition was, reportedly, to polish the still imperfect vocal art of the singers from the neighboring districts of Suzhou, which Pan believed comprise the "Central Plain" 中原 (meaning the genuine old school) of good singing. Beautiful participants, likely of both sexes, gathered together from all over the grand area of the Southeast 盡東南之美. It seems that singing competitions held in Nanjing did improve the courtesan-singers there, as by 1618 Pan acknowledged the superiority of Nanjing courtesan-soloists: "All the good [courtesan-]singers ultimately converged in Nanjing. Listening to them at midnight, how soft and supple the voices were!" 时善音皆集金陵。子夜闻之，靡靡耳.[47]

Another reference to the Pavilion of Beautiful Scenery has to do with its use as the venue for one of the earliest stagings of excerpts from Tang Xianzu's *The Peony Pavilion* sometime between 1602 and 1605.[48] The performance

46. Pan Zhiheng, *Luanxiao xiaopin*, *juan* 2, 1a–3a, "Talks on Singing"; also see Wang Xiaoyi, ed., *Pan Zhiheng quhua*, 8.

47. Pan Zhiheng, *Genshi* 亘史, *juan* 4, "Nostalgia Again [for the Nanjing Pleasure Quarters]" (*Yousi* 又思); *Luanxiao xiaopin*, *juan* 3, 13b; Wang Xiaoyi, ed., *Pan Zhiheng quhua*, 39–40. Pan Zhiheng, *Genshi* (1626), rpt. *Siku quanshu cunmu congshu*, vol. 193. Inner evidence suggests that Pan had finished compiling *Genshi waiji* in the 1610s, ten years before its posthumous publication by his sons.

48. Pan Zhiheng, "Zeng Wu Yishi" 贈吳亦史, in *Luanxiao xiaopin*, *juan* 3, 8b–9b; see also Wang, *Pan Zhiheng quhua*, 210. The date of the performance in the Pavilion of Beautiful Scenery was, as Pan puts it, "when *The Peony Pavilion* was first out" 湯臨川所撰還魂記初行. Present evidence supports the notion that the early circulation of the play in print occurred around the year 1605, although the manuscript had been completed in 1598 and circulated in the form of hand copies within a relatively small circle of friends before 1604. See Wu Shuyin 吳書蔭, "'Yumingtang simeng' zuizao de hekeben tansuo" 《玉茗堂四夢》最早的合刻本探索, *Xiqu yanjiu* 戲曲研究 1 (2007): 1–11; Xu Fuming 徐扶明, *Tang Xianzu yu Mudan ting* 湯顯祖與牡丹亭 (Shanghai: Shanghai guji chubanshe, 1993), 60–61. Pan mentions elsewhere in the same collection (*juan* 3, 5b–7b) that another staging of *The Peony Pavilion* at an unspecified venue, starring two boy actors belonging to Pan's friend Wu Yueshi 吳越石, took place

starred a boy actor from a private troupe as the hero; the audience included an assortment of famous poets, singers, and critics, including Pan Zhiheng, Wu Yunzhao 吳允兆 (fl. 1573–1610s), and Zang Maoxun 臧懋循 (1550–1620). This suggests that the pavilion may have been considered an ideal venue for small-scale theatrical performances given either by courtesans or by outside players, and that it could be borrowed or rented at a client's request.

To return to the sonic features of boozy night entertainment, the line may have been surprisingly clear between "banquet music" (string ensembles and choral singing, i.e. *xiansuo*, be it authentic or not) and "the after-midnight vocal concert" (solo singing, mostly *kunqu*), for they were two acoustically and aesthetically separate spheres of sound, as seen in the following record of an event that actually did not take place in Nanjing:[49]

> Several rounds of wine passed. There was an ensemble of courtesans making music. Guests were proceeding in an orderly manner. . . . [Instrumental] music was just about to stop and the mode of performance was about to change. All of a sudden [Chen] Yeshu emitted mournful tones, her look sorrowful and deeply sad.
>
> 酒數巡，妓樂協奏，賓筵秩如。. . . 奏甫欲闋而樂將更端。夜舒忽發悲吟，愀然愴懷。

The power of an individual talent became clear only in the solos which followed the choral singing that served as the background music for banquets. The soloist in this instance, Chen Yeshu 陳夜舒 (ca. 1580s–1610s), was perhaps the only Nanjing courtesan in the concert. Other courtesans who sang in the chorus were mostly local courtesans from Anhui province, including Hou Shuang 侯雙 (1589–?), a courtesan from the Shi family (*Shijia shu* 石家姝), Pei Biwu 裴碧梧, Sun Nanxia 孫赧霞, and Sun Xiangfeng 孫翔風.[50] The concert was actually Yeshu's farewell party on the first day of the

---

before this one, and that the two boys also learned another play of Tang's which was completed in 1602. It is therefore safe to deduce that the performance was put on between 1602 and 1605.

49. Pan Zhiheng, *Luanxiao xiaopin, juan* 2, 3a–5b, "Rainbow Terrace" (*Hongtai* 虹臺); also see Wang, *Pan Zhiheng quhua*, 64–66.

50. We know a bit about the courtesan Hou Shuang. When she was thirteen years old, Pan Zhiheng brought her to Suzhou and visited Zhang Xianyi 張獻翼 (1534–1604). Her gaiety and wit enchanted Zhang, who, after the autumn of 1603, when she lost her financial support in Suzhou and was sold into a Pei family in Jiangxi, wrote a poem entitled "Lantern Festivals, Accompanied by Ms. Lu I Visited Ms. Hu While

sixth month of the thirty-sixth year in the Wanli reign (February 16, 1608), just before her departure for Nanjing.[51] The location was a terrace in Pan Zhiheng's Garden of Dancing and Singing (*Posuo yuan* 婆娑園) in a small town in Anhui, very likely in the building that Pan renovated to house Chen Yeshu in 1607.

At the end of the concert at dawn, a rainbow suddenly rose over the terrace, which Pan Zhiheng the essayist considered to be a miraculous phenomenon evoked by the virtuosity of Yeshu. How her "mournful tones" sounded is a matter of conjecture, but there is little doubt that her style fitted the literati coterie's ideal for female singing. Pan reveals elsewhere in his essay that a group of literati-singers/critics frequently paid visits to and made contact with Yeshu in Nanjing, and that they played a central role in the cultivation of her virtuosity. Among them were Wu Yunzhao, Zang Maoxun, Cheng Jiasui 程嘉燧 (1565–1643), and Wu Tingyu 吳廷羽 (fl. 1580s–1610s).[52] Though Wu Tingyu (also known as Taining 太寧 or Zuoqian 左千) is better known as an outstanding Huizhou-school painter, disciple of the master Ding Yunpeng 丁雲鵬 (1547–1628), Pan reveals that he was also an excellent vertical flute player, even superior to the professional *kunqu* accompanists of Suzhou, and he may well have accompanied Chen Yeshu's *kunqu* singing

Missing Hou Shuang"; the poem is included in Qian Qianyi's *Liechao shiji*. Another acquaintance of Zhang's, Yu Wanlun 俞琬綸 (*jinshi* 1622), wrote that whenever he visited Zhang, he always saw Hou Shuang and other courtesans "surrounding him as he invited them to sing" 環膝徵歌; see Yu Wanlun, "Ten Songs Dedicated to Hou Xiaoshuang to the Tune of Languishingly Penciling the Eyebrows, with an Introduction" 侯小雙十調懶畫眉有序, in his song collection *For My Own Amusement* (*Ziyu ji* 自娛集), *juan* 9, quoted in Liu Zhizhong 劉致中, "Jiaoshan ji de zuozhe yu Zhang Xianyi zhi si" 蕉扇記的作者與張獻翼之死, in his *Ming Qing xiqu kaolun* 明清戲曲考論 (Taipei: Guojia chubanshe, 2009), 147. Pan purchased Hou Shuang back from the Pei family in the summer of 1604. See Pan, *Luanxiao xiaopin*, *juan* 1, 6a–8b, "[Writing] Instead of Grieving" 代慟. On another note, Pan clearly dates the death of Zhang Xianyi to the year of 1604, contradicting Shen Defu, who gives the date as 1601 in his *Wanli ye huo bian*.

51. The party ended with the melancholy mood of parting poems 分體理韻，致增離別之感. See Pan, *Luanxiao xiaopin*, *juan* 2, 3a–5b, "Rainbow Terrace"; also Wang, *Pan Zhiheng quhua*, 64–66.

52. See Pan, "Rainbow Terrace": "It is unknown how Yeshu's skills reached this high level. Maybe it was Yunzhao, Jinshu and Mengyang's appreciation and encouragement. How can their contribution be ignored? As for the combined help of Wenqin, Taining, Renshu, and Wuxiong, for sure she knew how to borrow what suits her" 不知夜舒技何以至是。抑允兆、晋叔、孟陽之賞激，功焉可誣。而問琴、太寧、訒叔、無雄之兼資，夫固知所取衷矣; also Wang, *Pan Zhiheng quhua*, 64.

with his instrument.[53] Evidence suggests that Yeshu's vocal style, which had won her fame in the 1606 singing festivals promoted by Pan and his coterie, did not help much with her business in Pan's hometown.[54] Before getting back to her Nanjing base she went to lodge at the house of a friend of Pan's in Wulin 武林 (i.e., Hangzhou), in the hope of regaining her popularity in a new location. In Pan's 1608 letter to this Wulin friend, who had witnessed Chen Yeshu's shining talent in the 1606 festivals, he discusses the principal aesthetic reason for her failure: her singing was "too elegant to please the vulgar taste" 第品太高，不能俗諧; "she could find no receptive audience for her style in the world, and could do nothing about it but sigh at her own loneliness" 世無知音，殊抱獨往之嘆.[55] Her vocal style, though much to Pan's liking, was too outside the mainstream to be profitable. The last time Chen Yeshu's name appears in Pan's writings is in 1619; and we are told that she has died long before.[56]

The case of Chen Yeshu's singing implies a special reception mode for the post-midnight solo performance: unlike the partial or sporadic attention accorded to a group of musicians plucking their instruments and singing in the background of a feast, literati paid undivided attention to soloists during a post-banquet concert. This is what I call an "intimacy formula" in courtesan solo performances in the midnight indoor concerts. For this kind of concert experience, the best source is an earlier figure painting, Wu Wei's 吳偉 (1459–1508) "Li Nunu's Singing and Dancing" 李奴奴歌舞圖, dated 1503

53. See Pan, *Luanxiao xiaopin*, *juan* 2, 11a–12a, "The Beginning Sound" (*Chuyin* 初音): "My friend Wu Taining had just started acquiring this skill, yet it already exhibited a world of difference from [the music of professional players such as] Mr. Qin and Mr. Xu from Suzhou" 吾友吳太寧始開此竅而金昌秦、許輩已覺霄壤. (For Pan's view on the professional flute players/accompanists, see "Talks on Singing" in the same volume, 1a–3a.) See also Wang, *Pan Zhiheng quhua*, 77–78. For Wu Tingyu's professional life as a painter, see Cai Xinquan 蔡鑫泉, "Ming Huizhou zhuming huajia Wu Tingyu Zuoqian shilue" 明徽州著名畫家吳廷羽左千事略, *Huizhou shehui kexue* 徽州社會科學 5 (2011): 44–48.

54. In 1606, Chen Yeshu was probably a teenager and the youngest participant in the singing festival. Her young age is also mentioned in Pan Zhiheng's letter to Zhang Ciqing 張次卿, in *Luanxiao xiaopin*, *juan* 12, 7b–8a. The 1606 festivals seem to have spurred many publications. In 1646, Tao Ting 陶珽 (*jinshi* 1610) reprinted Pan's writings in the same volume as those of the chief sponsor, Cao Dazhang, in *Shuofu xu* 說郛續, XXSKQS, vol. 1753, *juan* 46.

55. Pan, *Luanxiao xiaopin*, *juan* 12, 7b–8a, "A Letter to Zhang Ciqing."

56. Pan, *Luanxiao xiaopin*, *juan* 3, 9b–19b, "Summer Leisure" (*Xiaoxia* 消夏); also in Wang, *Pan Zhiheng quhua*, 36. In this 1619 essay Pan compares Chen Yeshu with an actor named Hao 郝 who specialized in female lead roles in Mao Yuanyi's 茅元儀 (1594–1640) private troupe: "Now Yeshu passed away long since, but Hao can compete with her" 今夜舒歿久，而郝賽之.

(see fig. 12).[57] This painting commemorates a private gathering in the Nanjing pleasure quarters to showcase then-ten-year-old courtesan Li Nunu's talent. The audience in the painting—four men accompanied by two adult courtesans—form a small circle tightly surrounding Li Nunu. In fact, the composition is a visual expression of the intimacy the audience may have felt rather than a mimetic rendering of a real situation, for such a seating arrangement would have severely restricted the space available to the performer for entrances, exits, and movement. More curious is the iconographic conceit of portraying Li Nunu with an exaggeratedly small, puppet-sized physique, in striking disproportion to the much larger figural group encircling her. Art historians have interpreted this as the painter's deliberate insertion of an unrealistic element into the "naturalistic" (*xieshi* 寫實) style, executed in the traditional mode of fine *gongbi* 工筆 brush-work. Beyond this focus on technique, some scholars follow the hermeneutic tradition in which a smaller physique suggests debasement, and accordingly read a political message into the body of the young sex worker—specifically, the social problem of prostituting teenage girls and the profligacy of late Ming erotic aesthetics.[58]

Both readings are possible. But I would emphasize again that, for sixteenth-century viewers, this peculiarity was more likely an effective visual expression of the concert experience associated with a familiar courtesan tradition of singing—a soft voice at low volume creating an intimate lure—that coincided with the increasing importance of solo songs in the repertoire throughout the century. In this sense, not only the close physical distance between performer and audience but also the singer's various means of expression, such as volume control, vocal color, and amorous glances, effectively generated the feeling of intimacy.

What the painter's intimacy scheme vividly captures are two types of audience: those who come to see (the dance) and those who come to hear (the singing). Two male figures to the left stretch forward to watch the girl dancing; in contrast, the other pair of male figures seems to respond to

57. The authenticity of the painting as well as that of the inscribed poems has not been questioned in recent art historical works and catalogues, except by the painter/connoisseur Huang Binhong 黃賓虹 (1865–1955), who expressed his style-based skepticism about the attribution. See Huang Binhong, "Gugong shenhua lu" 故宮審畫錄, in *Huang Binhong wenji* 黃賓虹文集 (Shanghai: Shanghai shuhua chubanshe, 1999), 89. In contrast to Huang's low opinion of the quality of both the painting and the calligraphy, recent reprints and catalogues generally praise the artistry of the painting and place it in a series of paintings of the same type attributed to Wu Wei, of which Huang does not seem to have been fully aware.

58. See, for instance, Liu Yingbei 劉英貝, "Wu Wei renwuhua fengge yanjiu" 吳偉人物畫風格研究 (master's thesis, Guoli Zhongyang daxue, Taipei, 2008), 53–56.

Fig. 12. Wu Wei, "Li Nunu's Singing and Dancing" (*Li Nunu gewutu*), 1503. (Original in Palace Museum, Beijing. Reprinted from Shan Guoqiang, *Yuanti Zhepai huihua* [Shanghai: Shanghai kexue jishu chubanshe, 2007].)

the singing without looking directly at the dancer. The man in the right foreground leans back on his right arm, his left hand placed on his lap, a typical gesture of beating time in the convention of southern solo music.[59] The prima donna, bowing toward her back (which is an acrobatic highlight in the repertory of a female role in traditional Chinese opera), successfully captivates both pairs by catering to the two sensory joys at once. It stands to reason that she is dancing while singing to the accompaniment of the clapper held by one of her "elder sisters," as indicated in the painting's title (obtained from Tang Yin's inscription). From the point of view of reception, it seems safe to conclude that Li Nunu offered everyone something to enjoy and remember, and that in the painting Wu Wei commemorates how people enjoyed the two sensory activities within an intimate atmosphere.

Traces of the audience's disposition toward singing can be further observed through what they wrote on the two-thirds-blank expanse of paper, where six explanatory inscription poems, written six years after the musical event, are exhibited chronologically.[60] All the poems point to the nighttime programming of the concert. They also provide a good basis for reconstructing the vocal dimension of Li Nunu's performance. Though a century apart from the case of Chen Yeshu, the story told by the inscription here seems to echo Yeshu's. In the third month of the lunar calendar, a lineup of Nanjing artists and advocates of courtesans' arts visited the pleasure quarters; among those we can identify were Tang Yin, Zhu Yunming 祝允明 (1460–1526), Chen Dasheng 陳大聲 (ca. 1488–1521), who signed his poem with his sobriquet "Lay Buddhist in Favor of the Seven Arts," *Qiyi jushi* 七一居士, Xie Chengju 謝承舉 (fl. ca. 1488–1566), who signed with his sobriquet "The Ninth Elder with a Thick Beard," Ran Jiuweng 髯九翁, and Wu Wei, the painter. The chief sponsor of the gathering, however, may have been a high official in the Nanjing system, a fervent connoisseur of vocal art or, as Chen Dasheng's verse puts it, a *shangyin* 賞音. It is speculative but not implausible

59. For a similar gesture, see the woodblock illustration portraying the courtesan Liang Xiaopian's 梁小翩 solo practicing in her garden in Wanyuzi's 宛瑜子 (Zhou Zhibiao 周之標) *Wuji baimei* 吳姬百媚 (Beijing: Beijing tushuguan chubanshe, 2002, rpt.), *juan* 2, 11a–b. Digital access: https://www.shuge.org/meet/topic/131344/

60. James Cahill has noticed "the absence of any setting" in Wu Wei's other genre painting of a female entertainer. I suspect that this could be a consistent emphasis that the painter was fully aware of, though the viewer can have a different feeling about the blankness when the subject changes. Whereas Cahill suggests that the blank setting in the portrait of a female lute-player indicates solitude, here the setting suggests to me the relatively quiet sonic space at a typical midnight vocal concert. See Cahill, *Parting at the Shore: Chinese Painting of the Early and Middle Ming Dynasty* (New York: Weatherhill, 1978), 105.

to identify one of the six poets, the "Lay Buddhist from Jinting" (*Jinting jushi* 金庭居士), as this *shangyin* official, for his poem dwells exclusively on Li Nunu's singing, rather than conveniently coupling singing with dancing in one inscription, as the others do. This poet attaches a footnote to declare his great passion for her voice (金庭居士甚愛李奴奴之音), and he adds: "The lingering sounds strive to rival my heart when breaking, they choke up as if the Qinhuai river refused to flow" 餘音欲與腸爭斷，咽住秦淮不肯流.

A clearer textual reference concerning how the singing sounded can be found in a poem added in 1508 by one "Lay Buddhist of Jiuhua" (*Jiuhua jushi* 九華居士), which comments on her vocal production and its expressivity: "The deeper the night falls, the softer the oriole's voice sounds" 鶯聲晚更幽. Li Nunu's voice must have been small and lacking in vocal strength. The next poem (1509) begins by complimenting her articulation of certain consonants: "From her lips burst out 'jade trees,' the phoenix's throat emitting fragrant notes" 唇噴玉樹鳳喉香. The first half of the line may also refer to the singer's forcible pronunciation of the plosives, a late Ming criterion of good singing, though the sputtering singer is not necessarily a pleasant image to our modern imagination.[61] Audible aural details (such as good articulation and accurate rhythm) may have provided the attentive listener with the grounds for vocal art connoisseurship. Hearing sensitivity could be exploited to such a full extent that "Maestro Zhous" sometimes considered their music criticism—or, their "finding fault" (*guwu* 顧誤), as Shen Defu put it in 1624—to provide an exhaustive service that "involved Maestro Zhou's ten thousands kinds of painstaking efforts" 役盡周郎萬種心.[62] Conceivably, given the lack of sound

61. In today's practice, Peking opera singers still put considerable emphasis on plosives, or *penkouyin* 噴口音 as they are called in opera teaching. One traditional method of training is to hold a piece of paper in front of one's mouth while singing; a good singer is supposed to completely dampen the paper with his or her saliva. As a practitioner of both Peking opera and *kunqu* opera in their classical styles, I can witness that this emphasis has faded in the *kunqu* singing tradition today. In the 1990s, when I frequented Peking opera performances in Beijing, I could see the conflict between the old aesthetic pursuit of clear, powerful plosives, and miked singing. Quite often the audience would hear an unpleasant explosive sound created by the combination of the old-fashioned pronunciation of words and the use of electro-acoustic devices onto which the singer tended to blow too hard. The new generation of Peking opera stars who rose in the 1990s has adapted to the new technological situation much better.

62. Shen Defu, "Xu Qingzhi, the Royal Librarian, Invited Me to Drink in His Garden and Presented His Private Female Troupe, Six Poems" 徐清之秘書園亭招飲家伎六首, in *Qingquantang ji*, *juan* 2, 6b, no. 6. The poem implies that the male connoisseurs' souls were touched precisely because they knew music well (色飛魂佚為知音).

amplifiers at the time and the possibility of soft singing, the poet needed to station himself intimately near the singer in a relatively quiet space, and had to strain his ears to catch this kind of vocal detail, in a posture not unlike that of the time-beating audience member in figure 12.

Another characteristic component of this intimacy formula—jealousy among competitor singers in the pleasure quarters—is not only hinted at in Tang Yin's inscription "Madame of the Qin State is her sister" 秦國夫人是阿姨 (an allusion to the rivalry between an imperial concubine and her sisters for the emperor's attention), but displayed visually. The older courtesan who is beating time with clappers shows no interest in the mesmerizing singing/dancing but modestly turns away from her party, which discloses her distance from the spotlight of the clients' attention. Such feigned ignorance and light rivalry construct a minidrama in its own right: at the midnight concert, there is something more in the air than mere intimate aesthetic appreciation.

Of great relevance to this psychological drama is the lute (*ruan* 阮) placed on the ground by the adult courtesan's feet. The painting's viewers in the sixteenth and seventeenth centuries would probably have associated it with the tradition of banquet choral singing accompanied by string instruments. They would have discerned in it the switch of performance mode from the prelude performance Li Nunu may have given in choral singing, joined by adult courtesan-singers, to the midnight solo concert where she shines alone. In this understanding, the lute codes time and signals the sequence of different performance modes during late-night entertainment. The lute and the elder courtesan together suggest the diminished amatory significance of choral singing, compared to the solo form, in the demimonde of the pleasure quarters.

III. The Evolution of Taste

To the evolution of taste, the flourishing of outdoor singing festivals starting in 1570 was a turning point. It is highly possible that the 1570 singing festival set out to promote a new ideal of the female solo other than the midnight "oriole" *kunqu* singing in the intimacy formula I have tried to illustrate. In different genres of literati accounts, we can see the male authors' fantasy of a woman singer who could execute fusion in style. Though far from becoming the mainstream practice, it remained largely how literati authors thought or wished the female singer should sing.

In the early autumn of 1570, an elite-sponsored music festival of courtesans took place in Nanjing, with the fancy name "The Gathering of Immortals on the Water Lily Terrace" (*liantai xianhui* 蓮臺仙會). The event was doubtless a novelty and sensation, and the prototype for a series of similar events—in 1606, for instance, six or seven such festivals took place in the Qinhuai River area.[63] It must also have made a deep impression on the young Pan Zhiheng, then a fifteen-year-old sojourner in Nanjing, for about forty years later he collected and published a number of documents commemorating the event.[64]

A mental picture in accord with the unusually rich documentation on "The Gathering" would include the seductive yet free performance of the courtesans pulling in many passersby on the banks of the Qinhuai River, the wealthier patrons of courtesan art steering their boats to get better angled toward the terrace, the front-row seats on the terrace facing the river being as usual reserved for the judges, who consisted of the chief sponsor's artistic cohort of self-anointed "immortals," among them the top *kunqu* singing connoisseur and dramatist Liang Chenyu 梁辰魚 (1519–1591), also the protagonist of the next chapter. Liang was an influential singing master who developed his own *kunqu* style and taught it late in life when he became less financially independent. Besides Liang Chenyu, Cao Dazhang 曹大章 (1521–1575; *jinshi* 1559), and Wu Qin 吳欽 (more commonly known as Wu Kunlu 吳崑麓) were among the most avid advocates of the legendary singing master Wei Liangfu's vocal art.[65] In particular, the chief sponsor of singing contests, Cao Dazhang, leveled criticism at the multiple standards that his eleventh-century predecessors had established in ranking courtesans—namely, temperament 情興, artistic talent 才技, and sexual charm 豐姿—seeing the first and last categories as hotbeds of dishonesty and unfairness that his contest would abandon completely. By leaving art as the only component, the 1570 contest claimed to be a revolutionary corrective. Though Cao's announce-

63. Pan Zhiheng, *Luanxiao xiaopin*, *juan* 2, 3a–5b; also see Wang, *Pan Zhiheng quhua* (Beijing: Zhongguo xiju chubanshe, 1988), 64. According to Yu Huai's memoir *Banqiao zaji*, a Mr. Shen Yuruo 沈雨若, a Jiaxing native, spent 1,000 taels of silver to hold courtesan competitions and publicize the rankings (費千金定花案). See Yu Huai, *Banqiao zaji*, modern typeset edition edited by Li Jintang, *Banqiao zaji jiaozhu* (*wai yizhong*), 54. Shen Yuruo may or may not be the painter and garden-design expert Shen Chunze 沈春澤 (fl. 1573–1622), a Suzhou native.

64. Pan Zhiheng, *Genshi*, 522–29.

65. See Cao Dazhang, *Qinhuai shinü biao* 秦淮士女表, in Tao Ting, *Shuofu xu*, *juan* 44. For a counterargument that reverses the hierarchical order and places sexual charm on top, see Ye Yikui 葉一夔, "Editorial Principles" (*fanli* 凡例) to *Jinling baimei*, which depicts various cultural activities and leisure moments enjoyed with courtesans.

ment is less likely a truthful report of reality than an indication of his self-anointment as an impartial singing connoisseur, it is undeniable that, in comparison to their predecessors, the mental composition of these judges did demonstrate seriousness toward art, and that they did attempt to distinguish between the courtesan's two identities—sex worker, and singer.

The 1570 search for such a paragon narrowed to one contestant. Out of fourteen courtesans who made the final list in the singing festival, a girl named Chen Yuying 陳玉英 alone merited a line of comment about her singing, particularly relating to her voice:[66]

> Her name fragrant,[67] her beauty endures in spring.
> Her tunes elegant, her precious voice flies into the sky.
>
> 芳英春駐色,
> 雅調玉飛聲。

The rest of the group did sing, but their performances have slipped from vocal history without leaving a trace.[68] This sort of account centers mostly on the final ranking, home address, and charm of each winning courtesan. Rarely do we run across any mention of these top courtesans' musical talents. Indeed, most of those who participated failed to arouse enough musical interest. To be sure, the background noise in such an outdoor concert (and in many more festivals and contests to follow in the next decades) did not make things easy: those produced by the need for food delivery and toileting, the slap of the water against the sides of small boats, the prattling (and flirting) between neighboring boats, the chatting, the cheering or hissing, and perhaps the occasional brawling.[69] These sounds may well have gen-

66. Pan Zhiheng, *Genshi*, *juan* 3, 4b.

67. The courtesan's name, Ying (Flower), is built into the pun.

68. That the male judges focused more on the attendees' sexual appeal and commercial potential than on their vocal art sounds like a reasonable explanation, yet their almost complete silence in terms of music criticism—of which there is even less than in the openly eros-driven boy-lovers' manuals (*huapu* 花譜) of the eighteenth century—remains a question begging other answers. For a discussion of the later "flower register" or *huapu* literature, see Andrea Goldman, *Opera and the City: The Politics of Culture in Beijing, 1770–1900* (Stanford: Stanford University Press, 2012), 9–11, 17–60.

69. For a fictional description of noisemaking, including the sound of boisterous bravos (*qi sheng hecai* 齊聲喝彩), in a late Ming competition of boy singers that lasted from early evening to daybreak, see Yang Hsien-yi and Gladys Yang, trans., *The Scholars* (New York: Columbia University Press, 1992), 385–86.

erated the need for high-effort singing that could compete with the noise. It would have been intolerable to sit through a long concert—fourteen courtesans made the final list, so the audience and judges must have listened to dozens of singers—without the interruptions and distractions. Such was the concert experience in late Ming China—the exact opposite of the quiet, awestruck listening often depicted in the sources of nineteenth-century Western romanticism.

This new form of entertainment—elite-sponsored music festivals featuring courtesans—may also have spurred another popular form of urban entertainment in the late sixteenth- and early seventeenth-century Jiangnan region, that is, small-scale concerts featuring singers of the opposite sex—in particular, a literatus singer and a courtesan. Catalogues of courtesans such as *Seductive Women of Suzhou* (*Wuji baimei*) and *Seductive Women of Nanjing* (*Jinling baimei*) exhibit a distinctive narrative mode that recounts a literatus lover's first meeting with a courtesan in a boat, in which he listens to her singing or sings with her.[70] The concerts were open to everyone, admission free. Audiences drawn by a courtesan's singing voice seem to have been an indispensable element of such concerts; typically, people gathered around the courtesan and expressed their admiration for her singing. But to avoid being too fanciful we should also imagine the background noises—the sound of people eating and drinking, going to the toilet, chatting, cheering or hissing, and so forth—that no doubt competed with the singers' voices. After all, audience behavior in public performances would have remained quite stable regardless of the audience size.

Historians of European operatic singing have noticed that the recognition of new vocal techniques coincided with the emergence of virtuoso solo singing in the late sixteenth century, a transitional period in music history between the late Renaissance and the Baroque era. Based on vocal tutors' treatises and manuals of singing, they conclude that it was these new vocal techniques, including coloratura through throat articulation and firm phonation or strong glottal closure, that distinguished virtuoso soloists from choral singers.[71] Primary sources for studying the Chinese tradition, however, are too scarce to allow a similar observation. However, there is no doubt that the post-1570 decades saw the increasing visibility of courtesan-singers

70. See, for example, Zhou Zhibiao's 周之標 (fl. 1610–1647) first encounter with courtesan Jin Jingluo 金驚洛 in *Wuji baimei*, vol. 1, 57a; and Li Yunxiang's 李雲翔 first meetings with courtesans Gu Mei 顧媚 and Gu Junxian 顧筠仙 in *Jinling baimei*, vol. 1, 64b and vol. 2, 5b, respectively. For Gu Mei's biography, see Yu Huai, *Banqiao zaji*, modern typeset edition edited by Li Jintang.

71. James Stark, *Bel Canto: A History of Vocal Pedagogy* (Toronto: University of Toronto Press, 1999), xvi, 31, 34–36, 154, 190.

in the history of cultivated *kunqu* soloists—partly thanks to the singing festivals that promoted the literati ideal of stylistic combination—such as Chen Yeshu, Chen Yuying, Wang Qingchi,[72] Li Renzhi 李紉之,[73] and Liang Xiaopian,[74] to name just a few. Accordingly, this may have been a time when clearer standards for courtesan solo performance were taking shape and put into wider practice. Such is the hypothesis I propose to help explain my second type of evidence, which comes largely from early seventeenth-century literati writings about courtesans capable of the sonorous singing style.

One common feature they share is their early musical education in the *xiansuo* style and later adoption of *kunqu* in their repertoire. In the literati accounts, their *kunqu* singing surpassed their peers' due to their vigorous style. First, the tradition of sonorous singing seems to have been more popular among those who were born into courtesan families, hence with early education in *xiansuo*. One of the "Original Songs from the Flower-Register" (*Hua'an yuanqu* 花案原曲) included in *Seductive Women of Suzhou*, the catalogue of Suzhou courtesans, describes this type of courtesan-singer:[75]

> A pleasure-quarters-born courtesan she is. Ordinary beauties are not comparable to her. Truly [her singing is a high art] comparable to [the ancient elegant tunes of] "Bright Spring" or "White Snow"; so sonorous her voice is, piercing the clouds. Each song from her deserves a present.
>
> 家世秦樓。不比尋常仕/士女流。真個是陽春白雪，響遏行雲，一曲纏頭。

On the surface, the song is dedicated to the courtesan Feng Youbai 馮幼白, whose natural mother Feng Xi 馮喜, Elder Aunt Feng Xianghuang 馮湘皇, and Younger Aunt Feng Tianran 馮天然 all rank high in the same cata-

72. Pan Zhiheng, *Genshi, juan* 6, 563–64. Wang Qingchi was a student of Huang Wenqin and excelled at *kunqu* singing. Pan records that he met Qingchi in Yangzhou in 1611 and listened to her.

73. Pan Zhiheng, *Genshi, juan* 4, and *Luanxiao xiaopin, juan* 3; also see Wang, *Pan Zhiheng quhua*, 26–28 and 131. Li Renzhi was a student of the professional singing teacher Chu Yangxin 褚養心. After having established his name in the singing-art world in his thirties, Chu took up teaching *kunqu* singing in his hometown, in the Wuxi 無錫 area. In his fifties, he met Li and accepted her as one of his disciples. Li, though only a young woman at the time, was the only student Chu ever acknowledged as a "qualified successor of his singing art" (*siyinren* 嗣音人) during the more than twenty years of his teaching career.

74. *Wuji baimei, juan* 2, 11a–b.

75. *Wuji baimei, juan* 1, 37a–b.

logue.[76] However, the song was also copied almost verbatim into another catalogue of the same nature, *Seductive Women of Nanjing*, dedicated to a Nanjing courtesan.[77] That the song could be attached to two different courtesans speaks to its stereotypical nature. There is probably more truth in its sense of the contemporary typology of courtesans than in the faithful characterization of any particular woman. What we can gather from the song, therefore, are not facts about those two individual courtesans but the stylistic features of a courtesan-singer born into a courtesan family and able to sing in a sonorous style.

The song may also reflect the terms in which courtesans with this family background chose to express their pride as singers capable of a style unconventional in the courtesan world. When the heroine of the *chuanqi* play *The Western Bower* (*Xilou ji* 西樓記, completed before 1622) first introduces herself to the audience, she speaks proudly of "being born in the pleasure quarters" 教坊出身.[78] Audiences familiar with late Ming vocal history would have quickly grasped the implications of this introductory line: her familial background suggests her solid early musical education in *xiansuo*, a dying art at the time of the play, and perhaps also outstanding singing skills in the vigorous style. As the plot unfolds, she does indeed distinguish herself among her courtesan peers for her expertise in setting *kunqu* music to new songs written by the hero, a lyric writer of high caliber.

Such fusion of *kunqu* melodies and *xiansuo* vocal delivery evidently had some special appeal for and was promoted by elite audiences. In contrast, the mainstream practice of courtesan singing remained conventional. At least if Pan Zhiheng is telling the truth in the remark from his posthumous notes: "I've seen quite a bit courtesan singing; . . . rarely do I see anyone whose voice can roll up around the rafters" 吾嘗觀妓樂矣 . . . 其曼聲繞梁者鮮矣.[79] Pan uses an allusion originating in a Daoist text, the "Tangwen" 湯問 chapter in *Liezi* 列子. The power of Han E's 韓娥 singing is such that it can

76. The Feng family, dwelling in the Golden Gate area of Suzhou, also adopted courtesans from other families, such as Feng Pianhong 馮翩鴻 and Feng Nan'ge 馮南哥; but certainly only Feng Youbai qualified as "a pleasure-quarter-born courtesan" and deserved this song.

77. Weilinzi, *Jinling baimei*, *juan* 1, 66a.

78. The completion of the *Xilou ji* is dated no later than 1624 by Meng Sen 孟森; see "*Xilou ji* niandai kao" 西樓記年代考, in Meng, *Xinshi congkan* 心史叢刊 (Shanghai: Dadong shuju, 1935; rpt. Hong Kong: Zhongguo guji zhenben gonyingshe, 1963), 2:121–53. A close study of the performance history of the play may push its completion date back to no later than 1622.

79. Pan Zhiheng, *Genshi*, *juan* 6, 12b.

change the mood of an entire village that she happens to pass by. Implicit in the story is the strident sonority of her singing, which can reach everyone, old or young, in the village. The same impression of the Suzhou courtesan singing during the famous Tiger Hill festival of 1629 was found in Shen Defu's poem: "Slight beats on an autumn fan, musical phrases lightly sung /. . . . The recent fashion of singing among Wu people favors a delicate voice; / all one can hear is the sound of flutes and woodwinds" 秋扇微敲樂句輕. . . . 吳儂近日歌喉細，但聽簫聲與管聲.[80]

In 1641, Mao Xiang 冒襄 (1611–1693) first heard the famous courtesan-singer Chen Yuanyuan 陳圓圓 (ca. 1620s–1680s), and fell in love with her because her aesthetically perfect singing (despite its "vulgar" 俗 musical style, *Yiyang qiang*) made him feel "as though he were going to reach transcendence or to expire" 令人欲仙欲死.[81] We might recall diarist Li Rihua's depiction of the erotic effect of the *kunqu* virtuoso monk's midnight solo—"At each juncture he sang with full seductive energy, I shall expire [with pleasure]"—quoted earlier at the opening of this chapter. The amorous allure of the singer seems not to have dwelled on one particular music genre but depended on some aspects of the vocal art. One of the two metaphors Mao Xiang used to describe Chen's vocal art was "clouds coming out of a mountain peak" 如雲出岫, suggesting that her solo voice must have been in the uppermost register. This counterintuitive connection between the vigorous style and amatory sentiment is reinforced by the atypical context in which this anecdote appears—Mao Xiang's book-length memoir of his beloved concubine Dong Xiaowan 董小宛 (1624–1651), which curiously contains no mention of Dong's vocal art at all, though another source reveals that she was good at *kunqu* singing. Evidently the aesthetics of singing weighed supreme in Mao's judgment; and in extreme cases in the history of taste, a style that the majority of women singers adopted may have become tiresome.

Coda

Post-Ming *chuanqi* dramas look at these two traditions nostalgically—the courtesan's role as a serious theater artist diminished drastically when scholar-officials were banned from visiting brothels, and when urban commercial theaters featuring all-male troupes emerged as the main venue. The

80. Shen Defu, "My Impression of the Suzhou Courtesans Singing" (*Wuzhong ting ji yougan* 吳中聽伎有感), in *Qingquan tang ji*, *juan* 7, 40b–41a.

81. Mao Xiang, *Yingmei'an yiyu* 影梅庵憶語, *juan* 1. See Ōki Yasushi, *Mao Xiang he Yingmei'an yiyu* 冒襄和影梅庵憶語 (Taipei: Liren shuju, 2013), 179.

fusion-style appears in the *chuanqi* play *Palace of Lasting Life* (*Changsheng dian* 長生殿, completed in 1688), which presents the heroine as a diva of style and execution whose versatility operates across a wide spectrum of styles. After her tragic death, an aria assigned to a musician nostalgically enumerates various mental images that her virtuosic singing was able to project, two of which are precise representations of the aesthetic poles of intimacy (i.e., the oriole and swallow 恰便似鶯與燕弄關關) and seclusion (i.e, the crane 恰便似緱嶺上鶴唳高寒). These are perhaps the best metaphors that capture the contrasting sound images evoked by the two styles are that of a twittering oriole and swallow and that of the legendary cry of a crane atop a freezing peak visited by a Daoist immortal.

The midnight "oriole" solo singing in the intimacy formula is fully reproduced in Kong Shangren's 孔尚任 (1648–1718) historical drama *The Peach Blossom Fan*, completed half a century after the collapse of the Ming dynasty (1699). I suspect that Kong was actually using the typical late Ming "boozy-night" form in the pleasure quarters as a model to sequence the different forms of musical performance presented in a scene entitled "Auditioning the Courtesans" (*Xuanji* 選伎). In this way, the sequence of musical events creates in itself an aura of reminiscence. The scene begins with a little "theater-within-the-theater" scene, a rehearsal of the villain's new play script, in which the best courtesans from the Nanjing pleasure quarters gather in the Nanjing palace upon the request of the emperor. The audience is the emperor, a drinking man looking at his musicians. His eros-driven radar quickly locks onto the heroine Li Xiangjun 李香君, a fledgling courtesan, not because of her histrionic skills (she has been viciously cast in the clown role) but because of her beauty. She is brought to stand very close to him; at this very spot, she is about to be urged to sing an aria taken from the only play she knows, *The Peony Pavilion*. In terms of how she performs her solo, the playwright does nothing more than copy Tang Xianzu's lyrics verbatim. The dramatic energy focuses instead on the moment before the singing begins: the female lead acts far too coy (羞不唱介); and seeing her "cheeks turning rosy, apparently too shy [to sing]" 粉面發紅, 好像是靦腆, the emperor considerately calls for a peach-blossom palace fan. This is a symbolic gesture that turns the "audition" into a midnight oriole's vocal concert. As one of the commentators points out, "This is a fan used in vocal concerts, a real-life peach-blossom fan" 歌場之扇，真桃花扇也.[82]

Evidence that I have pieced together suggests that around the 1570s,

82. See the Lanxue tang 蘭雪堂 edition (1895) of *Taohua shan chuanqi* 桃花扇傳奇, *juan* 3, scene 25, 35a.

the literatus-singer's musical ideal for a female soloist became the combination of these two distinct performance models in the courtesan's vocal tradition—intimate midnight light singing and vigorous big voice, associated with the courtesan's *kunqu* and *xiansuo* traditions, respectively. In some literati accounts, musical eroticism that once boosted *kunqu* in the pleasure quarters seems to have transferred to other music genres that encouraged sonorous singing reminiscent of the "authentic" *xiansuo* style. The long boozy night concerts featuring female chorus, solos, and dances were the sine qua non of late Ming brothel entertainments, toward which Qing literati felt nostalgic.

CHAPTER 4

The Courtesan and Two Great *Kunqu* Plays

Thus far I have presented various types of evidence to remedy the lack of a recognized history of courtesans and theatrical performance in late Ming China. In the last three decades of the sixteenth century, the well-established tradition of female performance manifested itself in many new dramatic compositions (see appendix). The two plays I have chosen for this last chapter—Liang Chenyu's 梁辰魚 (1519–1591) *Washing Gauze* (*Huansha ji* 浣紗記; ca. 1570) and Sun You's 孫柚 (1540–ca. 1613) *The Zither and Lust* (*Qinxin ji* 琴心記; ca. 1586)—provide further evidence of how theatrical conditions and writing styles shifted to accommodate the visual and vocal spectacles of courtesan performances.

As pointed out in the Introduction, the courtesans' theatrical performances in the southern genres such as *kunqu* were conceived as amateur participation (the signature term is *chuan* 串). A fuller cast often involved their professional teachers, brothel hangers-on, and other male amateurs to play some of the supporting roles. But this complex new institution, with its unique gender composition, altered the theatrical landscape in terms of writing for the stage. On this change, our best evidence is Pan Zhiheng's 潘之恆 (1556–1622) assessment of the prolific Suzhou dramatist Zhang Fengyi's 張鳳翼 (1527–1613) literary productivity in its relation to Peng the Tenth 彭十 and Bai the Sixth 白六, who in all likelihood were brothel performers:[1]

1. Pan Zhiheng, *Luanxiao xiaopin* 鸞嘯小品, *juan* 2, 24b (original copy in the Shanghai Library); Wang Xiaoyi 汪效漪, *Pan Zhiheng quhua* 潘之恆曲話 (Beijing: Zhongguo xiju chubanshe, 1988), 56.

> The first time I visited the Suzhou area was between 1579 and 1582, and I immediately befriended Zhang Fengyi and Wang Zhideng (1535–1612). At the time, most popular in the theater were [Wang Daokun's (1526–1593; *jinshi* 1547) four *zaju* plays from] *The Great Elegance Hall* and Zhang Fengyi's four *chuanqi* plays entitled *Ms. Red Whisk*, *Stealing the Commander's Tally*, *The Tiger Tally*, and *Becoming a Buddhist Monk*. Excellent amateur performers included Peng the Tenth and Bai the Sixth; they all enjoyed good names. . . . Afterward, however, Ms. Peng died and Ms. Bai got married. Mr. Zhang thereupon lost all interest in playwriting. Yet another few years passed, and Ni the Third started off in acting, which rekindled his interest. He thence wrote new plays such as *Burning the Wooden Latch*.
>
> 余初遊吳，在己卯壬午之間，即與張伯起王百谷善。其時《大雅堂》、《紅拂》《窃符》《虎符》《祝髮》四部甚傳。串演者彭十、白六諸俊，皆有令名。……其後，彭生死而白娘嫁，張公之興為索然。又數年，倪三出，復大振，有《扊扅》諸記。

Rarely do we encounter such a straightforward statement about brothel performances as an engine of literary creativity after the 1570s, and about the emergence of female agency in a theatrical context. In chapter 3, we saw that the 1570 music festival of courtesans entitled "The Gathering of Immortals on the Water Lily Terrace" (*liantai xianhui* 蓮臺仙會) in Nanjing marked the rise of courtesans as serious operatic singers. In addition to its significance in terms of female agency in theater, 1570 saw completion of the *chuanqi* play *Washing Gauze* by Liang Chenyu, a towering *kunqu* master and one of the main judges for the 1570 festival.[2] Standard historiography has painted *Washing Gauze* as a milestone in Chinese music/theater history because it was the first *chuanqi* work to follow the special rules of *kunqu* prosody so strictly that other "vulgar" southern musical theaters could not possibly stage the play, hence the very first full-scale staging of *kunqu* in history.[3] Although I do not

2. For scholarly debates on the dating of the play, see Li Guotao 黎國韜 and Zhou Peiwen 周佩文, *Liang Chenyu yanjiu* 梁辰魚研究 (Guangzhou: Zhongshan daxue chubanshe, 2007), 174–81; Xu Shuofang 徐朔方, *Wan Ming qujia nianpu* 晚明曲家年譜, 3 vols. (Hangzhou: Zhejiang guji chubanshe, 1993), 1:137–38.

3. Zhou Yibai 周貽白, *Zhongguo xiqu fazhanshi gangyao* 中國戲曲發展史綱要 (Shanghai: Shanghai guji chubanshe, 1979), 262. Grant Guangren Shen, *Elite Theatre in Ming China, 1368–1644* (London: Routledge, 2005), 9; William Dolby, *A History of Chinese Drama*, 1976, 90–92; Aoki Masaru, *Shina kinsei gikyokushi*, 1st ed. 1930 in Japanese; Chinese translation by Wang Gulu 王古魯, 1936, rpt. 2010, 152; Olivia

deny the possibility of Liang Chenyu writing the play with a *kunqu* rendition in mind, the same could have been true of any *chuanqi* playwright who favored *kunqu* music over other southern genres. Instead of treating *Washing Gauze* as a radical break, this chapter sees it as an organic part of a gradual evolution that witnessed a series of new *chuanqi* works that were sympathetic toward female performance, including our second case, *The Zither and Lust*. In contrast to *Washing Gauze*, with its unique position in music/theater history, *The Zither and Lust* has drawn little scholarly attention to date. But this chapter will prove it to be particularly significant in our revised history that emphasizes female agency in this period.

I. The Representation of a Courtesan's Life in *Washing Gauze*

The playwright Liang Chenyu was a literatus-singer with a permanent niche in the vocal history of *kunqu*, second only to that of the legendary godfather of *kunqu*, Wei Liangfu 魏良輔 (fl. sixteenth century). This is the only reason for the prevailing view of *Washing Gauze* as a sublime work of art in which the playwright was attempting to nationalize his favorite music genre. However, I have long considered Liang's literary inventions to be a response both to the emergence of courtesans as participants with agency in the theatrical world and to the new dynamics of performance that they brought with them into *kunqu*. By situating this play within the context of brothel entertainments, I propose a reading that is entirely different than the prevailing view.

Liang Chenyu reportedly taught singing in the demimonde of late sixteenth-century brothels. In his heyday in Nanjing's upscale brothels, he wrote love songs on behalf of both courtesans and their lovers as a profitable hobby. On one occasion, he may have received twenty taels of silver for ghostwriting a song addressed to a specific lover of his courtesan client.[4] Nineteen of these songs were included in two of his libretti collections, published in 1556 and 1575, respectively.[5] Liang's connections to the courtesans'

Milburn, "The Silent Beauty: Changing Portrayals of Xi Shi, from *Zhiguai* and Poetry to Ming Fiction and Drama," *Asia Major* 26, no. 1 (2013): 23.

4. Wang Duanshu 王端淑 (1621–ca. 1706), comp., *Mingyuan shiwei chubian* 名媛詩緯初編, Qingyintang edition, 1667, *juan* 23, 24.6b. Digitalized facsimile copy available at https://digital.library.mcgill.ca/mingqing/search/details-poem.php?poemID=40069&language=ch

5. Wu Shuyin 吳書蔭 feels that the first collection was published after 1556 and the second in the Wanli 萬曆 reign (1573–1620). See Wu Shuyin's *Foreword* to his compilation of Liang Chenyu's complete works, *Liang Chenyu ji* 梁辰魚集 (Shanghai:

world were undeniably stronger than those of any other literatus in his time. In the popular imagination of the seventeenth century, he was the singing master of numerous courtesan students. As one late Ming literatus-singer famously put it, "Singing boys and dancing girls would consider themselves to be ill-omened if they stopped seeing Liang Chenyu" 歌兒舞女，不見伯龍，自以為不祥也.[6]

Washing Gauze was produced during Liang's sojourn in Nanjing between 1570 and 1571, a period that witnessed an increase in the courtesan's passion for the theatrical performance of southern dramas. It tells several parallel stories that center on the interlocking stratagems that the King of Yue adopts, mostly from his strategist Fan Li 范蠡, to avenge himself on the King of Wu. The most important stratagem portrayed in the play is that of finding China's "Helen of Troy" so as to seduce the King of Wu with the pleasures of the flesh to such an extent that he loses political potency. Most critics find this narrative static, jammed with information unnecessary to the development of characters and plot, which is a prime factor in the play's loose structure.[7] But as I show below, this main line of plot is nevertheless a coherent literary representation of Nanjing's brothel life. My main approach is close reading. There are some characters, subplots, and milieux, I argue, that are constructed around the heroine's transformation from a country lass into a seductive courtesan—with Fan Li, her first lover, as the talent scout, the Queen of the Yue Kingdom as the brothel's female teacher, and the King of the Wu Kingdom as her patron.

To my knowledge, the loss of sexual innocence of a girl in the sex enterprise had never been a central plot in any other southern dramas. Whorehouses appear in *Embroidered Cushion* (*Xiuru ji* 繡襦記; 1493), *The Jade Pendants* (*Yuhuan ji* 玉環記; undated), and another play with a similar title in

---

Shanghai guji chubanshe, 1998), 4. My estimation of the publication dates is based on inner evidence. For example, the latest poem in the second collection mentions in its title the year of composition to be 1575. For other scholars' dating that agrees with mine, see Peng Fei 彭非, ed., *Jiangdong baizhu* 江東白紵 (Shanghai: Shanghai guji chubanshe, 1989), 1–3; Li and Zhou, *Liang Chenyu yanjiu*, appendix 4, 259–65.

6. Xu Youling 徐又陵, *Woting zading* 蝸亭雜訂, quoted in Jiao Xun 焦循 (1763–1820), *Jushuo* 劇說, *juan* 2, *Zhongguo gudian xiqu lunzhu jicheng* 中國古典戲曲論著集成 (Beijing: Zhongguo xiju chubanshe, 1959, rpt. 1980), 8:117.

7. Guo Yingde 郭英德, *Ming Qing chuanqi zonglu* 明清傳奇綜錄 (Shijiazhuang: Hebei jiaoyu chubanshe, 1997), 59; Guo Yingde, *Ming Qing chuanqi shi* 明清傳奇史 (Nanjing: Jiangsu guji chubanshe, 1999), 123. Liang's contemporaneous critics who shared such comments include Wang Shizhen 王世貞 (1526–1590; *jinshi* 1547), Xu Fuzuo 徐復祚 (1560–after 1629), Lü Tiancheng 呂天成 (1580–1618), and Ling Mengchu 凌濛初 (1580–1644).

English, *The Jade Pendant* (*Yujue ji* 玉玦記; 1577) merely as the social setting in a flesh trade ruled by heartless, greedy urban bawds.[8] In these plays, the courtesans enter the stage as mature sex workers whose pre-prostitute identity is not addressed openly. The same is true even in a 1584 *chuanqi* drama that established the courtesan as a serious literary figure, Mei Dingzuo's 梅鼎祚 (1549–1615) *The Courtesan* (*Zhangtai liu* 章臺柳; also known as *The Jade Box*, or *Yuhe ji* 玉合記; 1584).[9] In these plays and other examples we can cite, the narrative force derives not from the sexuality of the heroine but rather from her chastity—understandably, defending one's chastity in prostitution is much more difficult and interesting than in a normal situation. *Washing Gauze*, in contrast, treats us to a detailed depiction both of the heroine's necessary musical education and of her sex life in the palace in Suzhou, celebrating her sensual nature and cultural sophistication over her chastity. Under the name of the legendary patriotic beauty Xi Shi 西施, we witness a country girl coming to the capital of the Yue Kingdom and setting up as a courtesan.

The initial presentation of Xi Shi emphasizes in her own words her humble origins. She cannot afford a mirror or hair oil but has to use basin water for both (scene 2).[10] She wears coarse fabrics and thorn hairpins. She gets paid for her needlework and for weaving hemp. For her night work she has to borrow lamps from her neighbors. On sunny days her main daytime labor is to wash gauze in a stream nearby. After the sweat and toil, she is "unaware of the tilt of her hair knot" 不覺髻兒斜.[11] When Fan Li, the hero, stunned by her innocent beauty, proposes marriage, her answer cannot be humbler: "My talent as low as a thatch roof, my status no more than a village girl. Yet you the nobleman did not discard wild herbs despite their worthlessness but ask for my hand in marriage" 蓬茅陋質,田野村姑,蒙君子不遺葑菲之微,實賤妾得荷絲蘿之托.[12] Even though Fan Li mentions in passing obtaining Xi Shi's parents' permission for the marriage, we are not to see them until twenty-one scenes later, on Fan's second visit to the village, and even then they do not appear onstage—the father is away from home, and the sick mother hides in her own chamber (scene 23).[13] In scene 11, when

---

8. For the dating of these two plays, see Cheng Huaping 程華平, *Ming Qing chuanqi biannian shigao* 明清傳奇編年史稿 (Jinan: Qilu shushe, 2008), 13, 74–75.

9. I follow Guo Yingde's dating rather than two other hypotheses, 1586 and 1583. See Guo, *Ming Qing chuanqi zonglu*, 167.

10. Zhang Chenshi 張忱石, ed., *Huansha ji jiaozhu* 浣紗記校注 (Beijing: Zhonghua shuju, 1994), 5.

11. Zhang, *Huansha ji jiaozhu*, 5.

12. Zhang, *Huansha ji jiaozhu*, 6.

13. Zhang, *Huansha ji jiaozhu*, 128.

Fan proposes escorting Xi Shi to the Wu Kingdom as part of their "beauty stratagem," he describes her as "a virgin living by herself in the mountains" 有一處女，獨居山中.[14] We are reminded of her parents' existence in scene 34, when Xi Shi misses home and worries about their health.[15] Finally, in scene 45, we learn from Fan Li that the parents will soon be picked up from Xi Shi's hometown to join the newlyweds on their trip to another kingdom.[16] In retrospect, we can say that destitute families provided no grounds for practicing the Confucian norms of marriage—namely, following parents' orders and deploying a matchmaker—and that ignorable parents are a requisite condition for prostitution.

In the dialogues between the two lovers in their first reunion, there is perhaps the strongest evidence that earlier critics cite to defend a reading of "the pattern of patriotic self-sacrifice that provides the central meaning of the play."[17] In my reading of the dialogue, however, there are more concerns about prostituting Xi Shi's body and adequately equipping her with the artistic skills of a courtesan than there are patriotic sentiments (scene 23):[18]

Fan Li (played by male lead): . . . We have searched throughout the land without finding the right person. It then occurred to me that you alone possess supreme beauty. It so happened that I spoke my mind and praised you, and my Lord thus conceived the desire to seek your help. You have never granted me your assent, and so I presume to visit you in your stately home and humbly inquire whether or not you would be willing. Lady, what is your view?

Xi Shi (played by female lead): I am just a simple village woman, dressed in a coarse skirt and wearing a thorn hairpin. How is it that I should go to the houses of courtesans? Since I don't know anything about singing pearl-smooth notes and dancing with kingfisher-feather hairpins, . . . I am afraid that I cannot switch from one man to another.

生：......尋遍國內，再無其人。我想起來，只有小娘子儀容絕世，傾國傾城，偶爾稱揚，主公遂有訪求之心。小娘子尚無見許之意，故敢特造高居，奉問可否，小娘子意下何如？

旦：賤妾不過是田姑村婦，裙布荊釵，豈宜到楚館秦樓？現不諳珠歌翠舞。......賤妾為身，恐難移彼易此。

14. Zhang, *Huansha ji jiaozhu*, 119.

15. Zhang, *Huansha ji jiaozhu*, 199.

16. Zhang, *Huansha ji jiaozhu*, 249.

17. Cyril Birch, *Scenes for Mandarins: The Elite Theater of the Ming* (New York: Columbia University Press, 1995), 70.

18. Zhang, *Huansha ji jiaozhu*, 129.

Xi Shi's dilemma is similar to that of a courtesan-to-be who is unfortunately in love with a man who cannot afford her virginity. Yet her concerns about her womanly virtue soon go away when Fan Li throws in the following reason: "If you could quietly go there, then not only would the country be safe, but I would be safe. Eventual reunion would be possible. If you insist on not going, then the country will perish, and I will die, too" 若能飄然一往，則國既可存，我身亦可保。後會有期，未可知也。若執而不行，則國將遂滅，我身亦旋亡. Fan Li's life is at Xi Shi's mercy now; to achieve the final reunion—the conventional happy ending that southern drama demands structurally—she has no other choice but to go to the bed of a lecherous old king. This girl, with her village obscurity and simplicity, agrees to leave for the capital to be trained as a seductive consort because she is motivated to protect her lover (or his body in the Chinese original) and because of the possibility of a second marriage with him. We thus need to recognize the challenge to the conventional reading of her patriotic sentiments within this dialogue.

Moreover, a piece of semantic evidence can be found in Xi Shi's argument against the idea of bringing her to the Yue capital. She exclaims, "How is it that I should go to the *qinlou chuguan*?" 豈宜到秦樓楚館. Chinese dictionaries clearly define the term *qinlou chuguan* 秦樓楚館 as meaning "pleasure quarters."[19] We quickly discover, just one scene later, that the courtesan's signature skills she claims she lacks—finery, etiquette, song, and dance—are acquirable with a good teacher and diligence.

There is another instance in the play where the capital of the Yue Kingdom is explicitly referred to as *qinlou chuguan*. At the juncture of the King and Queen of Yue's departure for the Wu Kingdom to be hostages, the King of Yue warns his queen not to wear palace makeup 盡收拾宮妝 and not to mistake their destination (the Wu palace) for home, which is *qinlou chuguan* 你休還認在秦樓楚館 (scene 10).[20] In the rhetoric of both cases, the capital of Yue and the houses of courtesans are one. In fact, Xi Shi is not the only courtesan whom Yue has sent to Wu. Earlier in the play two women are sent as bribes to a treacherous villain, a courtier of the Wu Kingdom. They are dressed in the contemporary high fashion of courtesans—"tall 'cloud' coiffure" 雲鬟高髻 and "weightless dancing costumes with embroidered

---

19. For Yuan-Ming-Qing usage of this phrase referring to brothels, see dictionary definitions such as that in *Hanyu dacidian* 漢語大詞典, 2nd ed., ed. Luo Zhufeng 羅竹風 et al., 12 vols. (2001; rpt., Shanghai cishu chubanshe, 2008), 3:382; *Gu hanyu dacidian* 古漢語大詞典, ed. Wang Jianyin 王劍引 et al. (Shanghai cishu chubanshe, 2001), 2193.

20. Zhang, *Huansha ji jiaozhu*, 56.

lovebirds" 繡鴛鴦翩躚舞衣 (scene 7).[21] Upon seeing them, the courtier's concubine starts cursing them: "You prostitutes appearing from nowhere! You came here to steal my business" 那處娼根，到來奪我買賣. In a radical reading, this line would likely have teased the brothel audience into laughter because it carried some truth.

Fan Li is most outspoken in stating the mission of Xi Shi: "to satiate the King of Wu's cravings for sex and generate more" 以逞其慾 (scene 23).[22] By this time Xi Shi is no longer a healthy country lass who is enduring financial pressures; rather, she has suffered from lovesickness and developed a peculiar disease called "heartache" that only adds to her sexual appeal (scene 17). Her seductiveness is further heightened after she is fully trained in the ways of a courtesan in the palace of the Yue Kingdom. This is how she conceives her mission when she departs for the Wu Kingdom: "Seduce the King day and night. . . . Whether [the entire scheme] succeeds or fails, I will have to try my best to act in love [with him]" 迷君不論昏晝......成共否，要竭力將無作有 (scene 27).[23]

To "act in love," the theatricality of seduction in brothels, was a way of life. As Sanjay Gautam comments in the Indian context, "The narrative of love, true love, is deployed as a means to produce pleasure as an end. That is the reason the distinction between the real and the artificial does not make any sense in the theater of pleasure, because the logic of the real and the artificial, truth and appearance, is put in the service of pleasure."[24] It is the theatricality of emotion and the fragility of sex that distinguish Xi Shi from the rest of the lovesick heroines found in southern romances. Her pain is the pain of a courtesan who deals with elusive brothel love. Similarly, the King of Wu's failure to see through Xi Shi's "love acting" seems to have happened so often in the world of prostitution. When the King of Wu's courtier reveals Xi Shi's true identity as a village girl and the fiancée of Fan Li, rather than a younger sister of the King of Yue, as has been claimed, the King of Wu holds on to his belief in Xi Shi's love and says: "She loves me heart and soul.

21. Zhang, *Huansha ji jiaozhu*, 40.

22. Zhang, *Huansha ji jiaozhu*, 129.

23. Zhang, *Huansha ji jiaozhu*, 158.

24. Sanjay K. Gautam, *Foucault and the Kamasutra: The Courtesan, the Dandy, and the Birth of "Ars Erotica" as Theater in India* (Chicago: University of Chicago Press, 2016), 103. On theatricality of brothel culture as represented in late Ming fiction and visual culture, see Keith McMahon, *Saying All That Can Be Said: The Art of Describing Sex in the "Jin Ping Mei"* (Cambridge, MA: Harvard University Asia Center, 2023), 95; Peng Xu, "The Courtesan's 'Role Portrait': Brothel Performances and the Qiu Ying Models in Late Ming Suzhou," *Ars Orientalis* (55) (forthcoming, 2025).

No more such nonsense!" 娘娘與我是一心一意的人，再無此說話 (scene 42).[25] At the very moment of his suicide in front of the Yue army, the King of Wu sings about his eternal passion for Xi Shi, her company, her "pure songs and vivacious dances" 清歌妙舞, and, importantly, her care for him while he was intoxicated.[26] The patron's fetish for a courtesan's "love" is given an ironic twist here because it is Xi Shi who has convinced him to flee to a mountain and who then signaled the Yue army to besiege it (scene 41).[27]

Xi Shi's "acting in love" leads directly to a moment of high arousal in scene 30, "Picking Lotus" 採蓮, a popular extracted scene in the late Ming performance history. This is a rare instance in which Xi Shi acts fully as though she is a tenderhearted woman in love, an important characteristic that embellishes her supposed love for the King. One can imagine that this is a typical day in their love life: she sings folk songs from her hometown; he compliments her after each song, both in words and by drinking heavily to the point of becoming drunk. Then come her words that impassion him: "My lord, the wind hits the shore and returns, the sun is setting against the top of the mountains, the water is getting colder. . . . Shall we sail back home?" 大王，浦口風回，山頭日落，水面涼生……回船去罷. To this he responds: "What a trustworthy and kindhearted beauty! She cares for me so much" 好知心腹趣的美人，恁的般顧愛我.[28]

It is this conversation that leads into one of the most revealing references in the play to the great physical costs of being a prostitute:[29]

To the tune of *Ancient Bügür County*:

. . .

(The Painted Face, or the King:) For tonight's ecstasy, I fumble my way to the silk bed-curtains. Underneath the covers, the two of us are like a pair of frolicking lovebirds. How to make this time together last forever? A night to abandon myself in sensual love. [Acting being drunk. Extras assist him in walking.]

(Female Lead, or Xi Shi:) A fading petal, a broken jade, a smashed rouge, many ruined kingfisher feathers. I can enjoy nothing but have to force myself to do it.

[古輪臺]

……

25. Zhang, *Huansha ji jiaozhu*, 231.
26. Zhang, *Huansha ji jiaozhu*, 232.
27. Zhang, *Huansha ji jiaozhu*, 229.
28. Zhang, *Huansha ji jiaozhu*, 173.
29. Zhang, *Huansha ji jiaozhu*, 174.

(淨)今夜歡娛，忙投羅帳，看雙雙被底效鸞凰。肯教輕放，趁良宵
　　恣意顛狂。(作醉，眾扶科。)
(旦)殘香破玉，蹂紅踐翠，只得支吾勉強。

The imagery of damaged goods that is projected onto the sexual experience of the heroine suggests a typical understanding of the withering health conditions of sex workers at the time. In a song prior to this one, Xi Shi compares her vagina to the seedpod of a lotus suffering from cold dewdrops 風露冷，怎奈摧頹蓮房, echoing the King's claim of having had intercourse with her more than a thousand times over the course of several days 不多日算不得盡了上千遭雲雨之情.[30] The idea that excessive sex damages a woman's health is reiterated by Xi Shi's palace retinue: "Very likely, day and night, her body has been used and weakened by our lord" 想被大王爺日夜弄壞了 (scene 34).[31] The comic effect and eroticism of this statement are transparent, but they may also entice audience/reader sympathy. What else would have propelled the playwright to put his heroine in a familiar life situation, other than his strong emotional bonds with his courtesan audience/readers?

Liang Chenyu's presentation of Xi Shi as a sad, unfortunate woman, a fallen angel, ends in the final scene of the play with a beautiful completion. The textual variations of the scene help deepen our understanding of the characterization of Xi Shi in the aftermath of the "beauty stratagem" and the defeat of the enemy army. All the extant editions agree on the basic plot, in which she and her just-married husband, Fan Li, flee the Yue Kingdom on a boat trip; they also share the basic musical structure: a complete suite of songs, with northern and southern tunes alternating and assigned to the male lead (Fan Li) and female lead (Xi Shi), respectively.[32] However, two

30. Zhang, *Huansha ji jiaozhu*, 171.

31. Zhang, *Huansha ji jiaozhu*, 199.

32. Extant Ming editions include (1) *Yangchuntang* edition 陽春堂 (preface 1608), published by Yangchuntang [Studio of the Sunny Spring] in Hangzhou; original in the Central Library in Taipei, microfilm in the National Library (Beijing) and the Library of Congress (Washington, DC); (2) *Wu Yue chunqiu yuefu* 吳越春秋樂府 [*Opera Based on the Spring and Autumn Annals of the Wu and Yue Kingdoms*], publishing house unknown, with illustrations in the Huizhou style, approximately from the Wanli reign (1573–1620); original in the National Library (Beijing); (3) *Wenlinge* edition 文林閣, published by Wenlinge ["Woods of Texts" Pavilion] in Nanjing; original in the National Library (Beijing), approximately from the Wanli reign; (4) *Jizhizhai* edition 繼志齋, published by Jizhizhai [Studio of Inherited Wills] in Nanjing; original in the National Library (Beijing); (5) *Li Zhuowu xiansheng piping Huansha ji* 李卓吾先生批評浣紗記 [*Washing Gauze, with Commentaries by Mr. Li Zhuowu*]; original in the National Library (Beijing); (6) *Yiyunge* edition 怡雲閣, published by Yiyunge [Pavil-

different textual renditions give us different images of Xi Shi—one clings to the belief in a "happy ever after" scenario, whereas the other evokes transcendental, if not religious, thoughts that recall the religious practices in late Ming pleasure quarters.[33] In the former rendition, Xi Shi displays no complex feelings but only her absolute faith in and longing for Fan Li's love. She speaks to Fan Li first about her loyalty to him despite the material enjoyments the Wu palace has offered her: "As I recall my earlier times spent in the Wu palace, we had carnivals every morning and night. But I always responded and served reluctantly. All that I could think of was you, my darling" 想當日，妾在吳宮，雖是朝朝上巳，夜夜元宵，總只是勉強應承，一心兒掛著君子 (scene 46).[34] She also declares her resolution to give up a well-off urban life for the sake of their new conjugal life 賤妾寧可戀穠華而忘伉儷.[35] In her last solo, she reenacts her routine in the Wu palace—serving wine, but this time to her new husband. Even though she is on a boat sailing to a deserted island, the action of serving wine symbolizes the continuation of a secular life with secular joys—sex, wine, singing, and dance. We thus see a Xi Shi who embraces her future conjugal life spiritedly as the continuation of her former status.

In contrast to the spiritually simplified version of Xi Shi, another Xi Shi appears to be less naïve about departing for an unknown land. This more spiritually mature woman narrates her life in retrospect in her opening solos—how she regrets not having been able to restrain her amorous feelings for her fiancé Fan Li and having hastily promised to wed 芳心不自持……急忙裏便許成佳配 (scene 45);[36] how she has been lovesick in her three years of waiting for him; how she has been forced to leave her hometown for the Wu palace (unfortunately, by her fiancé); how grateful she is to the King of Yue, who has urged Fan Li to marry her. In an aria responding to Fan Li's memory of his own dangerous military experience, she tells the audience that the Yue victory has led her to reach a point of transcendence. Abruptly, she points to her dwelling in the Wu palace as they are sailing by it and says: "Look, that's the Palace for Keeping the Beauty, covered by weeds and

ion of Beautiful Clouds], approximately from the Chongzhen reign (1628–1644); (7) Jiguge edition 汲古閣, included in the compendium called *Sixty Plays* (*Liushi zhong qu* 六十種曲).

33. Yuhang Li, *Becoming Guanyin: Artistic Devotion of Buddhist Women in Late Imperial China* (New York: Columbia University Press, 2020).

34. Zhang, *Huansha ji jiaozhu*, 254.

35. Zhang, *Huansha ji jiaozhu*, 255.

36. Zhang, *Huansha ji jiaozhu*, 250.

shrubs" 你看館娃宮荊榛蔽.[37] This is particularly intriguing when we recall that at the beginning of the scene, the poem she chants conveys an opposite sentiment: "If we are to sail our boat on the lake, it would be appropriate not to pass by the Palace for Keeping the Beauty" 若泛扁舟湖上去，不宜重過館娃宮.[38] Before the boat sails out to the lake, she has mundane, social concerns about woman's virtues; her change of attitude toward the palace is therefore a moment of detachment from such concerns. It seems that the heroine's perspective on her personal history, and on life in general, ascends to a different realm. It is this perspective that gives the play a lingering tone of tragedy, a unique flavor that can be achieved only by having a courtesan as the prototype for Xi Shi. As such, this ending deviates from the master plot of reunion or "happy ending" adopted by most southern dramas, with a few exceptions, such as the much later play *The Peach Blossom Fan* (*Taohua shan* 桃花扇; 1699).[39]

There are resonances of the image of a detached courtesan in Beata Grant's studies of late Ming women's religious beliefs and practices, and in Ma Xianglan's 馬湘蘭 (1548–1604) admiration for the Daoist heroine in her preface to Liang Chenyu's *zaju* play we discussed in detail in the Introduction.[40] The full spectrum of the courtesans' lifestyle was supported by the two poles of religious transcendence and luxurious tastes. In this sense, the ending of *Washing Gauze* is bound to incorporate the spiritual dimension of a courtesan if it indeed intends to unfold the entire picture of contemporary brothel life. This speculation may lead us to recall the portrayal of the physical and emotional sufferings that Xi Shi endures in the Wu palace, which would end naturally with detachment from the mundane world.

My last piece of evidence for Liang's contemporary courtesan friends being the prototype for Xi Shi springs from biographical investigation: in my view, the 1569 death of Liang's beloved courtesan-cum-consort Xu Yunfang 胥雲房 motivated him to dramatize the story of Xi Shi. Xu Yunfang is the title character in two suites included in the collection of Liang's song suites, *Sequel to White Hemp from the South* (*Xu Jiangdong baizhu* 續江東白苧).[41] Her life and their love story are sketched as follows: They first met

37. Zhang, *Huansha ji jiaozhu*, 251.

38. Zhang, *Huansha ji jiaozhu*, 249.

39. Wai-yee Li, "The Representation of History in the *Peach Blossom Fan*," *Journal of the American Oriental Society* 115, no. 3 (1995): 421–33.

40. Beata Grant, "Through the Empty Gate: The Poetry of Buddhist Nuns in Late Imperial China," in *Cultural Intersections in Later Chinese Buddhism*, ed. Marsha Weidner (University of Hawai'i, 2001), 73–86.

41. Liang Chenyu, *Xu Jiangdong baizhu* in *Liang Chenyu ji*, ed. Wu Shuyin, 397–98.

briefly around 1554, when Xu was a courtesan, but were separated for the next decade due to some misunderstandings or misfortunes. They wrote letters in the first years but then were out of touch with each other. In a moment of despair, they encountered each other again. Here we have a lively depiction of the encounter in a song, in which Liang compares Xu Yunfang to Xi Shi:

> To the tune *River Water*:
> A glimpse of you in the deep alley, at an open gate
> I was wondering why, when you were about to turn away, stopped, stood there and stared at me
> At first, I thought you were the beauty Xi Shi from the western village
> Then I recognized you, the girl I had admired for years
> In an elegant skirt made of white hemp
> You stood alone against the wind
> Gazing at me as if we had known each other

> [江兒水]
> 瞥見深深巷，款款扉。緣何欲避還凝佇？初疑施氏西村女，原來宋玉東鄰姝。雅淡裙衫白苧，小立迎風，注目似曾相識。

This song was written in 1563, the year of their second encounter, and perhaps their marriage as well. In 1569, a year before the completion of *Washing Gauze*, Xu Yunfang died of an unknown disease. Liang Chenyu was fifty-one years old. He had already lost all his political ambitions and sunk deeply into the courtesan's world. His economic status was declining as well, after his return from trips to the inner regions of China.[42] At the same time, he had become an influential singing master, developed his own style, and taught it in the pleasure quarters. In both the opening and ending poem of *Washing Gauze*, he gives a hint of his sense of self-identity: he refers to himself as a poor local man from the Wu Kingdom, selling firewood in the market 負薪吳市. I am certainly not suggesting that Xu Yunfang was the only woman who inspired *Washing Gauze*. Rather, Liang's life trajectory suggests that the play was itself a commodity, subject to the needs of the pleasure quarters. But this line of female sponsorship has never been acknowledged as in the rare case of his other play, *Ms. Red Silk* (*Hongxian nü* 紅線女).

42. Li and Zhou, *Liang Chenyu yanjiu.*

II. The Representation of a Courtesan's Training in *Washing Gauze*

Xi Shi's training in scene 25, "Imparting the Skills," belongs entirely to the discourse of courtesan arts. Judith Zeitlin correctly singles out the scene as an "imaginative representation" of courtesans' training sessions—a scene that initiated the vogue of incorporating such scenes as "stock components" in operas.[43] But I would point out that this dramatization of Xi Shi's singing lesson should be distinguished from the one for the courtesan-to-be in *The Peach Blossom Fan* discussed in chapter 3, because it is the representation of an ideal rather than of reality. In a way it intersects with the category of "pedagogical literature." As Daphene Lei's study of another female character Wang Zhaojun 王昭君 suggests, the female plot can be shaped by performance convention and "the attempt to locate the agency of the *feminine* despite the compelling violence against her."[44] By putting words in the mouths of the Queen of the Yue Kingdom and her disciple Xi Shi, Liang presents a treatise full of ideas representative of the new connoisseurship of the courtesan arts made by Cao Dazhang 曹大章 (1521–1575; *jinshi* 1547) and his cohorts, including Liang Chenyu, through the 1570 singing festival in Nanjing.

Here we shall recall from chapter 3 how Cao goes to extremes to get his point across: that *his* contest would abandon unfair and dishonest standards in judging those courtesan participants but leave *art* as the only component.[45] We have reason to believe that in the last three decades of the sixteenth century, there was a time when public opinion considered courtesans' artistic talents to be an important factor in their commercial success. At that

43. Zeitlin, "'Notes of Flesh' and the Courtesan's Song in Seventeenth-Century China," in *The Courtesan's Arts: Cross-Cultural Perspectives*, ed. Martha Feldman and Bonnie Gordon (Chicago: University of Chicago Press, 2006), 92.

44. Daphne Lei, *Uncrossing the Borders: Performing Chinese in Gendered (Trans) Nationalism* (Ann Arbor: University of Michigan Press, 2019), 29.

45. See Cao Dazhang, *Qinhuai shinü biao* 秦淮仕女表, in Tao Ting 陶珽, *Shuofu xu* 說郛續, *juan* 44 (rpt. XXSKQS, vol. 1753). The search for serious artists among courtesans was a cultural phenomenon in the last three decades of the sixteenth century. In early seventeenth-century publications on the same subject, we find an opposing voice. Though Ye Yikui 葉一夔 does not explicitly address Cao's essay in his 1618 preface to a guidebook on upscale Nanjing brothels, *Seductive Women in Nanjing* (*Jinling baimei* 金陵百媚), clearly he endeavors to reverse the trend by emphasizing sexual charm alone as his criterion in ranking courtesans included in his catalogue. See Ye Yikui, "Editorial Principles" (*fanli* 凡例) to *Jinling baimei*. *Jinling baimei* depicts various cultural activities and leisure moments enjoyed with courtesans, without an emphasis on musical entertainment.

time, brothels in urban centers were not only places of luxury and pleasure but venues for the debuts and early performances of many plays.

The scene begins by announcing the significance of singing and dancing in the overall art of seduction—a beauty without these two skills would be considered to be tasteless. Liang Chenyu's dramatic presentation of this argument begins with Xi Shi's uninformed comment that downplays the importance of singing and dance before her lesson with the Queen of Yue begins: "It just occurred to me that even my looks, beautiful enough to infatuate the whole city, may not work, not to speak of dancing and singing well. What's the good of learning them?" 我想起來，傾城的容貌尚不足恃，就是十分歌舞得好，也要他何用?[46] This underestimating of the significance of artistic skills to the art of seduction, of course, is soon to be corrected by Xi Shi's music teacher, the Queen, who lectures her new student as follows:

> To be called a "peerless beauty" [a woman needed to meet three standards] in ancient times: one, a pretty face, two, [talents in] singing and dancing, and three, proper mien [during singing and dancing]. Even with a pretty face, she cannot be deemed remarkable if she doesn't understand [the art of] singing and dancing. Even with a general comprehension of [the art of] singing and dancing, she cannot be deemed stunning if her mien is not perfect. . . . Singing has its special mien. So does dancing. Only by demonstrating elegance and gentility, with a delicate gait, can she touch his heart.
>
> 古稱絕色：第一容貌，第二歌舞，第三體態。若是容貌雖好，歌舞未諳，不足為奇，歌舞雖通，體態未善，不足為妙。……歌有歌體，舞有舞態，須要態度悠閒，行步嫋娜，方能動人。

This synopsis of the best qualities of a brothel artist, with a clear emphasis on the skills of singing and dancing, echoes the trend of taking the courtesan's arts seriously.

At Xi Shi's request, the Queen lists songs and dances popular among ancient people (*guren* 古人) and "today" (*jin* 今). Cyril Birch identifies all the songs and dances on the Queen's lists as erotic ones from medieval times, which thus may function to remind us of the classical setting of the story.[47] But given that the setting of the drama in the Warring States period (sixth century BCE) actually predates most of the medieval songs and dances, we

46. Zhang, *Huansha ji jiaozhu*, 142.
47. Cyril Birch, *Scenes for Mandarins*, 78.

may also seek their contemporaneous associations in the popular culture instead of returning to *loci classici*. One reference that should not be omitted is Liang Chenyu's two collections of free-arias (*sanqu* 散曲), both with "White Hemp" (*baizhu* 白苧) in their titles, published in 1556 and 1575.[48] The 1575 collection includes more songs devoted to courtesans of Nanjing, where he sojourned after 1566. So when the Queen comments on the popularity of "White Hemp" songs in "today's wondrous southern land" 即今江南佳麗之地，多用白苧、採蓮, Liang may be bragging about his own literary/music achievement.[49]

The Queen makes two sets of lists, each set containing two parallel lists, one denoted as in vogue "today," and the other favored by "ancient people." To assess what the Queen means by "today"—namely, the late sixteenth century, when Liang wrote *Washing Gauze*, or the sixth century BCE, when the story is set—we need to recognize the contemporaneity of the female dance/singing lesson in Liang's play, which this book as a whole strives to illuminate. The prototype of this pedagogical scene is not the glamorous entertainment of an ancient court but, rather, an imaginative representation of courtesans' training sessions designed to show the dramatist's own aesthetics, to borrow Cyril Birch's words, "in the manner of Hamlet's instructions to the players."[50] Through the person of Xi Shi, Liang applauds the power of courtesan arts that transform a peasant woman into a real beauty.

The Queen then elaborates on how to sing a solo well, in phrases that strike us as a compilation of clichés from Wei Liangfu's treatise on singing.[51] This treatise appears, with textual variations, under different titles in five seventeenth-century printed texts, including the two excerpted in table 5: (1) the foreword (dated 1616) to Zhou Zhibiao's 周之標 (fl. 1610–1647) *A Selection of Refined Songs from Suzhou* (*Wuyu cuiya* 吳歈萃雅); and (2) the fore-

48. Peng Fei, ed., *Jiangdong baizhu*. White hemp is a local cloth product.

49. Evidence for the popularity of Liang Chenyu's lyrics abound in his friends' poetry. For example, Liang's admirer Pan Zhiheng confirmed the popularity of Liang's operatic librettos and free-arias in a poem: "Your lyrics compositions have been sung by thousands of people" 填詞贏得萬人傳. See Wang Xiaoyi, ed., *Pan Zhiheng quhua*, 236.

50. Cyril Birch, *Scenes for Mandarins*, 77.

51. The manuscript *Nanci yinzheng* 南詞引正 itself, said to have been written in 1547 by the hand of a famous calligrapher, is in fact lost but was transcribed and published with annotations by Qian Nanyang 錢南揚 and first published as Qian Nanyang, "Nanci yinzheng jiaozhu" 南詞引正校注, *Xiju bao* 戲劇報 7, no. 8 (1961): 58–66; a slightly revised edition appears in Qian Nanyang, *Han shang huan wen-cun: Liang Zhu xiju jicun* 漢上宧文存: 梁祝戲劇輯存 (Beijing: Zhonghua shuju, 2009), 81–100.

word to Xu Yu's 許宇 *Beautiful Sounds from the Forest of Songs* (*Cilin yixiang* 詞林逸響, 1623 edition).[52] For a solo to contain clichéd "dos and don'ts" of vocal art is a rare occurrence in the entire collection of southern dramas of all times. In this sense, the Queen's aria can be seen as a musical rendition of a piece of pedagogical literature:

> To the tune of *My Fair Lady*:
> At the feasts your voice must be [powerful enough] to make the dust arise and stop floating clouds;
> Speaking of melodies, you must decorate them with twists and turns, your tones mellow and full;
> Never swing your head, close your eyes, twitch your mouth or curl your lips;
> (Refrain:) Retain your charm, [and] as you enter the inner quarters of a splendid hall at midnight
> You will surely light up the entire banquet and intoxicate [the men].
>
> [好姐姐] 當筵要飛塵遏雲,論音調又須紆徐淹潤,切忌搖頭合眼歪口及撮唇。(合)須風韻,華堂深處中宵進,管取一座春風醉酒樽。

A point of controversy here is the line "Never swing your head, close your eyes, twitch your mouth or curl your lips." A typical default practice, adopted mostly by professional actors and professional singing tutors (vis-à-vis "ama-

52. The five texts are (1) "Qulü" 曲律 is the foreword (dated 1616) to Zhou Zhibiao, comp., *Wuyu cuiya*, 4 *juan* in vols. 12–13 of *Shanben xiqu congkan*, 12:23–32; (2) "Kunqiang yuanshi" 崑腔原始 is the foreword to Xu Yu, *Cilin yixiang* (1623 edition), 4 *juan* in vols. 17–18 of *Shanben xiqu congkan*, 17:13–20; (3) "Qutiao" 曲條 is the foreword to *Yuefu mingci* 樂府名詞. The text of the foreword (Wei's treatise) is transcribed in Wu Xinlei, "Ming keben *Yuefu hongshan* he *Yuefu mingci* zhong de Wei Liangfu qulun" 明刻本《樂府红珊》和《樂府名詞》中的魏良輔曲論, *Nanjing shifan daxue wenxueyuan xuebao* 南京師範大學文學院學報 1 (2005): 133. The songbook is a late Ming imprint; according to *Beijing tushuguan shanben shumu* 北京圖書館善本書目, 8 vols. (Beijing: Zhonghua shuju, 1959), 4:3112, it was published by a commercial publisher named Zhou Jingwu 周敬吾; (4) "Fanli ershitiao" 凡例二十條 (1602) is the foreword to Qinhuai Moke 秦淮墨客, *Yuefu hongshan* 樂府紅珊 (imprint of 1800), 16 *juan* in vols. 10–11 of *Shanben xiqu congkan,* ed. Wang Qiugui 王秋桂 (Taipei: Taiwan xuesheng shuju, 1984), v. 10, 7–13; (5) "Wei Liangfu qulü" 魏良輔曲律 [the 1637 text] is the foreword to the 1637 (combined) edition of *Wusao hebian* 吳騷合編. This entire work is reprinted in *Juyi tang ji* 居易堂集, ed. Xu Fang 徐枋, vol. 49 of *Sibu congkan guangbian* 四部叢刊廣編 (Taipei: Taiwan shangwu yinshuguan, 1981), 15–16.

Table 5. Discrepancies in the Descriptions of Singing Practice in Two of the Five Woodblock Print Versions of Wei Liangfu's *Treatise on Singing*

Zhou Zhibiao, *A Selection of Refined Songs from Suzhou*	Xu Yu, *Beautiful Sounds from the Forest of Songs*
(*Wuyu cuiya*, 1616)	(*Cilin yixiang*, 1623)
The face reddening, blue veins appearing on the neck, the head swinging and the feet stamping [to the rhythm], [as though] sitting on the edge of his seat. . . . Yet only if you reach that phase can your singing be called perfect.	The face reddening, blue veins appearing on the neck, the head swinging and the feet stamping [to the rhythm], [as though] sitting on the edge of his seat. . . . [Looking like this] is surely a debasement; even if the singing sounds excellent [this way], why bother?
面上發紅，喉間筋露，搖頭擺足，起立不常 ......然能成此，方為盡善	面上發紅，喉間筋露，搖頭擺足，起立不常 ......則賤矣，曲雖工，亦奚以為?

teur" performers in brothels), was for the singer to do exactly the opposite: swing their head, close their eyes, and twitch their mouth or curl their lips.

We have two pieces of evidence of the "swing your head" version being common practice in the professional world. One comes from textual comparisons among the five versions of Wei Liangfu's treatise on singing (see table 5). I have argued elsewhere that the 1616 text was a treatise representing the professional singing tutor's views.[53] The other evidence is found in the preface to one of the thirteen late Ming editions of *The Lute* (*Pipa ji* 琵琶記), entitled *The Story of Bojie, Definitive Edition* (*Bojie dingben* 伯喈定本), published in the early 1620s.[54] It first imagines a voice representing an uniniti-

53. Peng Xu, "The Music Teacher: The Professionalization of Singing and the Development of Erotic Vocal Style During Late Ming China," *Harvard Journal of Asiatic Studies* 75, no. 2 (2015): 270–73.

54. There are four copies extant: a woodblock imprint in the rare books collection of the National Library and three transcripts of a nonextant late Ming imprint of *Bojie dingben*, which contains rich prefatory materials (sixty-eight pages in total) missing from the Beijing imprint. I was able to read, at the University of Tokyo, one of the three Japanese apographs. But Chinese scholar Huang Shizhong informed me in private conversations that a Chinese rare book dealer has discovered a second woodblock imprint of *Bojie dingben* that has all the prefatory materials found in the Japanese transcripts. The preface quoted here, entitled "Gai Pipa dingyi" 改琵琶定義, belongs to the Japanese transcripts. For the identification of the editor as an otherwise obscure literatus Lu Mingfu 陸明輔 (1544–1590) and dating of the completion of the book to the 1580s rather than the publication year of the extant woodblock edition in Beijing, see Peng Xu, "Editing *Pipa ji* for Late Ming Popular Theater: The Identity of the 'Sing-

ated reader who believes the professional theater practitioners (*Liyuan* 梨園) to be "good enough to delight the eye" 亦堪悅目矣. But the editor, writing under a pseudonym—the Singing Hermit—replies to this as follows: "As for professional actors' methods of performance, entering the stage they swing their heads [while singing] . . . all of which contributed to cultivation of a corrupt Way" . . . 梨園家 . . . 至其作法,登壇搖首,皆成惡道.[55]

In late Ming pedagogical literature on singing, professionals had always been a problematic entity, and criticism of professional soloists seems to have tipped the balance of power, at least rhetorically, from the professional to the amateur (e.g., literati singers and courtesan students). As we have seen in table 5, even Wei Liangfu's treatise holds bifurcated attitudes toward them. Neither the "debasement" 賤 in the 1623 singing treatise nor the "corrupt Way" 惡道 in the late sixteenth-century preface to *The Lute* did justice to the "show mode" of ornate singing pursued by professional soloists. But it is obviously this collective sentiment against such a popular "show mode" that led Liang Chenyu to reframe the pedagogical language into an aria assigned to his heroine.

The next aria, in which Xi Shi describes her own singing, is another example of "pedagogical literature" unique to this period of the rise of courtesans as serious artists. Liang Chenyu creates a near-ideal female soloist who successfully combines the two extreme styles discussed in chapter 3, representing the aesthetic poles of intimacy and seclusion, femininity and masculinity. He has the heroine sing about how her own singing sounds, and thereby fleshes out his aesthetics of courtesan solo singing:

To the tune of the Second Variation of *River Water*:
My fragrant voice, so pure, so pretty
Listen to my fragrant voice, so pure, so pretty, as if from afar
Like pearls rolling on a plate
There at the Houses of Pleasures, feasts of delicacies, luxurious cushions
The oriole's singing is getting faster and faster with the wind
How delicate—the fragrant dust arises
How delicate—the fragrant dust arises
How sinuous—the rosy clouds stop floating
. . .

[二犯江兒水]

ing Hermit' and His Editorial Work," *Late Imperial China* 41, no. 1 (2020): 159–201.

55. Tokyo transcript of *Bojie dingben*, *juan* 1, 6a–b.

香喉清俊，聽縹緲香喉清俊，似珍珠盤內滾，向秦樓楚館綺席華茵，見鶯聲風外緊
裊裊起芳塵，裊裊起芳塵，亭亭住綵雲……

Here we again see an explicit reference to the pleasure quarters (*qinlou chuguan*). The heroine's vocal performance was sometimes a dimly discernible voice, comparable to the sound of an oriole singing, and sometimes a voice of sonority and high range, with a vibrating power that can shake dust (i.e., from the rafters) and exert a hypnotic power on the floating clouds—both classic allusions highlighting the effect of virtuosic singing. Clearly, this was the male connoisseur's ideal of the female voice—a combination of sonority in a high range and a hyperfeminine tone quality that evoked the mental image of a lithe female body, a circling round pearl, a singing oriole, and even the sense of the singing body's fragrance.

Liang's admirer Mei Dingzuo stands out as holding almost the same views on courtesan singing. Mei's heroine in *The Courtesan* has the ideal qualities of a "pure" (*qing* 清) and "coquettish" (*qiao* 俏) voice, delivers the sound-imagery of an oriole singing 似啼鶯, and at the same time exhibits the virtuoso power of "making dust on the beams disappear" and "setting the woods and river banks aquiver" 梁塵暗消, 聲振林皋. These "pedagogical scenes" offer insights into the vocal quality sought after by late Ming male connoisseurs. They liked the sound-imagery of an "oriole singing" with its small, thin voice, as though it were blown in by a wind from afar, but at the same time, they also preferred the obvious effects attained through loud, high notes, comparable to the famous ancient singer's magic virtuoso power. Turning solos into a piece of "pedagogical literature," these playwrights shared certain basic ideas about how a female singer should sing, already elaborated on in chapter 3.

On the formal level, our reading of the song as a vehicle for the connoisseurship of courtesan solo singing finds musical evidence in the unconventional composition of the suite—more precisely, this northern song (to the northern tune of "Second Variation to *River Water*") is set within the frame of a southern song suite, which was considered by the music theorist Shen Jing 沈璟 (1553–1610; *jinshi* 1574) to be a violation.[56] The modern *kunqu* connoisseur Wang Jilie points out that the northern tune of "Second Variation to *River Water*" is particularly suitable for singing while stage-walking

56. For Shen Jing's remarks, see *Nan jiugong shisandiao qupu* 南九宮十三調曲譜 (Beijing: Beijing daxue chubanbu, 1921, photo-reprint), *juan* 20.

最宜於且行且唱.[57] The heroine in Zhang Fengyi's *Ms. Red Whisk* (*Hongfu ji* 紅拂記; 1545) sings her two arias written to this same northern tune when eloping from her former patron's mansion. And Mei Dingzuo's Miss Liu in *The Courtesan* uses this tune while instructing her maidservant how to sing well.[58] By abruptly switching musical mode—a deliberate decision, as I understand it—Liang reminds the listener of the uniqueness of this particular song and dubs his own narrative voice into the heroine's real-time performance.

The last example from this scene, the Queen's solo to the tune of *My Fair Lady*, sets the standard for the most fashionable female dancing:

> To the tune of "My Fair Lady" (*hao jiejie* 好姐姐):
>
> Onstage you must stand out with exceeding gracefulness. Speaking of gestures and mien, you must spiral swiftly and lightly. [Let them] see no dust arising during your movements, be it stretching, bending down, facing upward, or twirling.
>
> 當場要娉婷出群,論體態又須盤旋輕迅。看縱橫俯仰迴身不動塵.

---

57. Wang Jilie 王季烈, *Yinlu qutan* 螾廬曲談 (Shanghai: Shangwu yinshuguan, 1934), 31b–32a. Wang included the extracted scene, entitled *Runaway* (*siben* 私奔), in the *kunqu* music scores he compiled and published in 1925 through the Commercial Press, *Jicheng qupu* 集成曲譜. Unfortunately, this scene is no longer part of the living repertoire of contemporary professional *kunqu* troupes.

58. Mei Dingzuo even inherited Liang Chenyu's unconventional usage of song structure—inserting the northern tune "Second Variation of 'River Water'" into a southern suite. The modern scholar Cheng Yun 程芸 traces the use of the tune in the late Ming and suggests that Tang Xianzu 湯顯祖 (1550–1616; *jinshi* 1583)—who also opted for the tune's northern version, like the two *kunqu* masters Liang Chenyu and Zhang Fengyi—was deeply influenced by the *kunqu* singing tradition. Thus Cheng questions the famous claim of Xu Shuofang 徐朔方 that Tang wrote specifically for his local troupes specializing in a certain local opera, as opposed to the more elite *kunqu*. See Cheng Yun, *Tang Xianzu yu wan Ming xiqu de shanbian* 湯顯祖與晚明戲曲的嬗變 (Beijing: Zhonghua shuju, 2006), 154–66. Cheng's book contributes to our understanding of the significance of the tune per se, but we should nevertheless notice that Tang used it (no matter whether it was a northern or southern tune) in a northern suite, whereas Liang and Zhang used it in a southern suite. A close look at the dramaturgical function of the northern tune when appearing in a southern suite allows us to see how it can be totally different from Tang's insertion of it in military scenes: this tune offers adequate performance contexts for the female lead to present some manual gestures and stage movements while singing.

I have not found examples in pedagogical literature that echo the Queen's prescriptive language for dancing as I have done with the vocal pedagogy. But as a remedy to the dry, technical language of pedagogy, Liang Chenyu immediately arranged another aria to the northern tune of the Second Variation of *River Water* sung by Xi Shi, in which she displays to us the actual sensual aesthetics of this dance: she is aware of the moment of high arousal when she changes costume. With the dance, she needs to "gently and slowly shed the silk cape" 軟款款羅衣寬褪 and expose her "tiny waistline" 一捻小腰身. Her gait is vivacious and seductive: "I suddenly get closer to show my affection; I hesitate when stepping back" 乍進殷勤，欲退逡巡. Wind blows open her skirt and brings with it her body fragrance 香馥馥風開繡裙. The overall impression she makes is that of a cloud, soft, delicate, and gentle; in the Chinese amorous literature, that cloud is permanently associated with lovemaking 軟迷離似陽臺一片雲. Xi Shi is both a created and a self-creating sex object during the typical courtesan's solo, despite her character as a legendary ancient beauty. According to Pan Zhiheng's review of dance scenes in the history of *chuanqi* theater, Liang Chenyu's "Xi Shi dance" was one of the earliest scenes that began the tradition of what he calls "*chuanqi* dance" (dance of the southern drama) 傳奇之舞 (see fig. 13).[59] My reading of this particular "*chuanqi* dance" highlights Liang Chenyu's strong investment in lyrical eroticism entangled with brothel entertainment. This new form of "solo dance within a play" reprises our opening caveats concerning the neglect of gender factors in the linear conception of music/theater history.

III. Traces of Female Performances in *The Zither and Lust*

The second play examined here, Sun You's *The Zither and Lust*, has never been taken seriously as a landmark work in *chuanqi* history, even though it presents various sensual experiences true to its time and was one of the most influential plays in theater of the 1580s. It dramatizes the most famous elopement in early Chinese history, the same subject matter as *Soaring the Sky* (*Lingyun ji* 凌雲記), discussed in detail in chapter 1. It tells of the poor but eminent scholar Sima Xiangru 司馬相如, who seduces a young, rich widow, Zhuo Wenjun 卓文君, into eloping with him to his hometown, where the new couple makes a living by selling wine. This story was so popular that it was told in at least eight Ming dramas—one *zaju* play and seven *chuanqi* plays. Of these, three are extant, including *The Zither and Lust*. Due to its

59. Wang Xiaoyi, ed., *Pan Zhiheng quhua*, 90.

Fig. 13. Illustration to "Teaching Singing and Dancing" (scene 25) from *Washing Gauze* (*Huansha ji*). (Courtesy National Palace Museum, Taipei.)

complex texture and everyday nature, this play is worth a book-length analysis. Here I confine myself to a single line of inquiry, about the traces of brothel performances in this play.

Drama historians have never offered strong evidence for dating the play: Xu Shuofang speculates that it was completed in 1569 or slightly earlier; Cheng Huaping dates it to the 1540s (which is impossible because its author Sun You was born in 1540).[60] My suggestion of 1586 or slightly later for the completion is premised on the synchronizing relationship between Sun You's garden, named the Gorge of Vines (*Tengxi yuan* 籐溪園), on

60. See Cheng Huaping 程華平, *Ming Qing chuanqi biannian shigao* 明清傳奇編年史稿 (Jinan: Qi Lu shushe, 2008), 35. See Xu Shuofang, *Wan Ming qujia nianpu*, 1:256.

Mount Yu in Changshu County, and his literary creation—a relationship not previously noted in modern scholarship. At the closing moment of the play (scene 44), a character comments: "Scholar Sun, no matter how disheartened and impoverished, his heart will never sink" 落魄孫生萬古心.[61] This self-referential comment suggests that the play was finished during or after Sun You's financial troubles—a victim of usury, he lost ownership of his aesthetic garden in early 1586.[62] The garden was built in a mountainous area of roughly 1.65 acres in 1581.[63] Until his bankruptcy in 1586, Sun must have been able to enjoy an affluent life, with the Gorge of Vines as the site of his cohort's numerous gatherings to enjoy poetry, wine, and operatic entertainments. Banqueting scenes abound in *The Zither and Lust*; lavish details portray a "realistic" garden setting that the careful reader can reconstruct on a map. Evidence also suggests that Sun's network included eminent cultural celebrities such as Gu Zhengyi 顧正誼 (fl. 1575–1600), Mo Shilong 莫是龍 (1537–1587), Sun Qizheng 孫七政 (1528–1600; Sun You's uncle), and Liang Chenyu.[64]

Another uncharted area of study is *The Zither and Lust*'s undeniable role as a source of inspiration for Tang Xianzu's *The Peony Pavilion* (*Mudan ting* 牡丹亭, 1598). Not only are there similarities in the poetic lexicons of the two

61. According to the 1687 Changshu county gazetteer, Sun You wrote another play, no longer extant, possibly a *zaju* drama, called *Zhaoguan* or *The Zhao Pass* 昭關. Gao Shiyi 高士鸃 et al. comp., *Changshu Xianzhi* 常熟縣誌, in *Zhongguo difangzhi Jiangsu fuxianzhi ji* 中國地方誌集成江蘇府縣誌輯 (Nanjing: Jiangsu guji chubanshe, 1991), *juan* 20, 29a.

62. Sun You, "The last of the winter months of the year of Yiyou (early 1586), in utter destitution we lacked food; I entrusted my Gorge of Vines to several warmhearted people; when the spring blossoms covered the gorges and mountains again in the following year, I revisited here and composed [the following] poems" 乙酉冬暮，家貧絕食，以籐谿屬諸好事者，明年春花滿山谷，再游谿上成歌, in Sun You, *Tengxi shi* 籐谿詩, 1 *juan*, photo-reprint of a Qing manuscript in *Siku weishou shu jikan* 四庫未收書輯刊 (Beijing: Beijing chubanshe, 2007), 21:658. Su You describes that the two main forces that drove him into poverty were (1) the government officials requested tax payments delayed by several years; and (2) rich moneylenders wanted high usurious interest 官長要索積年逋，富家欲益子母利. For more details about the history of the garden, see Sun You's preface to *Tengxi shi*, "Tengxi ji" 籐谿記, 652–55.

63. Chen Jiru 陳繼儒, ed., *Pan'e ji* 槃阿集, "Tengxi ji" 籐谿記, 4:15b–19a; this piece is also incorporated in Sun You's *Tengxi shi*, 660–61.

64. For a detailed discussion of this particular cohort of theater connoisseurs centering on three gardens in Suzhou (Zhang Fengyi's garden), Huating (Gu Zhengyi's garden in present-day Shanghai) and Yushan (Sun You's garden), see Peng Xu, "Editing *Pipa ji* for the Late Ming Popular Theater: The Identity of the 'Singing Hermit' and His Editorial Work," *Late Imperial China* 41, no. 1 (2020): 188–89.

Table 6. Textual Example of the Influence of Sun You's Stage Poetry in *The Zither and Lust* on Tang Xianzu's *The Peony Pavilion*

Sun You, *The Zither and Lust* (ca. 1586)	Tang Xianzu, *The Peony Pavilion* (1598)
Scene 29, "A Drinking Party in the Morning of the Flowers" (*Huazhao jushang* 花朝舉觴)	Scene 10, "Startled Dream" (also known as "Strolling in the Garden," or *Youyuan* 遊園, in the *kunqu* repertoire)
Fair season, fine scene—laughing together. We find true pleasure in our own garden that is better than the immortals'. 向良辰美景同歡笑, 眞樂事勝蓬島	Fair season, fine scene—overwhelming weather. Where and in whose garden shall we find pleasure and the heart's delight? 良辰美景奈何天, 賞心樂事誰家院

plays, but there is also a site called the Peony Pavilion in the large garden space delineated in *The Zither and Lust*.[65] In one extreme example, we can see Tang Xianzu's marvelous rephrasing of Sun You's lyrics in the famous scene 10 of *The Peony Pavilion*, "Startled Dream" 驚夢. It is a wondrous transformation from a rather banal, "realistic" portrayal of a banquet into the most celebrated and cited scene in any *chuanqi* play up to the present day (table 6).

In a way, Tang converted Sun's "realistic" portrayal of his suburban garden into a profoundly deep, philosophical question. Although it is beyond the scope of this book, it is worth mentioning that, as table 6 shows, *The Zither and Lust* nourished quite a few later *chuanqi* plays, including ones that demonstrated tremendous staying power in the *kunqu* living repertoire. But its own name withered quickly, somehow falling into obscurity in modern times. The primary reason for this, I contend, is *The Zither*'s proclivity for female performances, which declined in popularity in the last decade or so of the Ming dynasty.

Both a close reading of the text per se and textual comparisons between different editions argue for the play's significance in the history of female performance in *chuanqi* drama. As in the case of *Washing Gauze*, the strongest evidence for the truly characteristic response to the convention of female performance in *The Zither and Lust* lies in its outspoken identification of the heroine as a courtesan. The most conspicuous reference to the pleasure quarters (*qinlou chuguan*) is put into the mouth of the rich widow Zhuo Wenjun in her opening aria portraying the scenery in scene 6—"No clouds above the House of Courtesans, how small the moon is" 楚館雲空, 秦樓月小. Another term that Sun employs is *beili* 北里, or the "northern quar-

65. Scene 10, "Eloping to Chengdu" (*Ye wang Chengdu* 夜亡成都). The Peony Pavilion is where the maidservant stores luggage she has prepared for the heroine.

ters," which refers to Tang-dynasty brothel areas but is used in the ending couplet of scene 9, "Waiting for Her by the Gorge" 臨流守約. The first line of the couplet indicates the time, location, and soundscape of the scene: "In the pleasure quarters, the reedpipes carry the late autumn moon by wind" 北里笙吹秋後月. A third term is *yanhua* 煙花, which means "prostitutes" and which appears in the hero Sima Xiangru's aria in scene 7, "Plucking at Her Spring Heartstring" 挑動琴心. He enters with his prop zither and sings: "If I wish to be entangled in a love affair in a brothel, I have to rely on my zither" 欲了煙花債,全仗絲桐在.

In performance, the most colorful spectacle in the play must be scene 23, "Lamentations in the Lonely Boudoir" 空閨永嘆. This scene clearly pays homage to *The Lute*, the fourteenth-century canonical southern drama that became a bible for *kunqu* singers in the sixteenth century. The heroines of both plays are lovesick women separated from their husbands, singing an introductory aria followed by a set of four arias to the tune of *Sichaoyuan* 四朝元. Despite the similarities in musical structure, *The Zither* differs from *The Lute* in its unabashed references to contemporary brothel musical life. After each of the heroine's first three arias, Sun You inserts a song in a minor genre popular in the late Ming brothels that is sung by two watchmen played by clowns. These popular songs by minor figures create a soundscape typical of the pleasure quarters after midnight. One song, in the *Wuge* 吳歌 style, is as follows:

> Lotus leaves are round yet withering in the autumn.
> The moon is round yet buried in the clouds.
> The mirror is round; into it there is only me looking.
> Plums are round yet in their hearts are crooked seeds.
>
> 荷葉團團秋裏衰。亮月團團雲裏埋。鏡子團團奴房裏照。梅子團團心裏歪。

Upon hearing the song, the heroine ponders its lyrics and rephrases them in the much more refined, lyrical *kunqu* style, reinterpreting the watchmen's song as a faithful portrayal of her own emotional core—the eternal female desire for reunion and the lamentable loneliness of a long autumn night. She sings: "Listen carefully to the local Wu song again; they say 'withered leaves in the residue of autumn; the bright moon being shadowed by half; the blueish bronze mirror with no trace of mundane dust; the plum with only one seed inside'; [these are all] things joyful only on the surface" 把吳歈再審,他道敗葉秋殘, 皓魄陰生, 靑鏡塵空, 梅花子另, 虛卻團圞景.

Scene 23 of *The Zither* is Sun You's playful parody of both the canonical play *The Lute* and the everyday musical experiences in the pleasure quarters, an interesting interaction between fiction and fact in this period. In theatrical performances of the 1580s, weaving the local popular songs into the texture of a dramatic scene was most likely a new fad, a feature of the Jiangnan area's courtesan performances. Similarly, Xu Wei's 徐渭 (1521–1593) *zaju* play, closely studied by Yuming He, includes a lesser-known minor musical genre performed by a female ensemble.[66] Doing so was to become a conventional literary device within a few decades, so common in the 1610s that even Zang Maoxun's 臧懋循 (1550–1616; *jinshi* 1580) *Selection of One Hundred Yuan Plays* (*Yuanren baizhong qu* 元人百種曲, 1615, 1616) integrated lesser-known musical genres into the "Yuan" dramas. In *kunqu* music, in particular, *Wuge* could be seamlessly merged because, as Shen Chongsui's 沈寵綏 1639 singing treatise puts it, "the regional tunes of the Wu area are nowadays sung to the accompaniment of string instruments (*xiansuo*)" 即如今之以吳歌配絃索, and *kunqu* since the reform in the mid-sixteenth century had long harbored *xiansuo* instruments in its music (see chapter 2).[67]

While the original version of *The Zither and Lust* was intended for female performance, its textual variants reveal how later editions tended to erase earlier traces of courtesan performances. This play has three editions: the first released by the Fuchun Hall (*Fuchun tang* 富春堂) bookshop in Nanjing in the Wanli reign (1573–1620); the second by Mao Jin's 毛晉 (1599–1659) Drawing from Antiquity Pavilion (*Jigu ge* 汲古阁) publishing house during the Chongzhen reign (1628–1644); and the third as later incorporated into Mao Jin's large *chuanqi* collection, *Sixty Plays* (*Liushi zhong qu* 六十種曲), also during the Chongzhen reign.[68] We find erotic imagery in the stage poetry of the Wanli edition being eliminated in the two Chongzhen editions. One example is an aria to the tune *Jade Twigs* (*Yujiaozhi* 玉交枝) that is assigned

66. He, "Difficulties of Performance: The Musical Career of Xu Wei's 'The Mad Drummer,'" *Harvard Journal of Asiatic Studies* 68, no. 2 (2008): 93–99. The author suggests that the *wubei* lyrics 烏悲詞 performed by a female chorus in Xu Wei's play was more likely to be Xu Wei's fabrication than folk songs being integrated into a "serious" dramatic work. It remains a matter of conjecture but I lean toward the folk-song hypothesis.

67. Shen Chongsui, "Xianlü cunwang," in *Duqu xuzhi* 度曲須知, *Zhongguo gudian xiqu lunzhu jicheng*, 5:239–41.

68. The *Fuchun tang* edition, entitled *Xinke chuxiang yinzhu Sima Xiangru Qinxin ji* 新刻出像音注司馬相如琴心記, is reprinted in the *Budengdaya wenku zhenben xiqu congkan* 不登大雅文庫珍本戲曲叢刊 (Beijing: Beijing daxue tushuguan, 2003), 9:77–295. The *Jigu ge* edition is reprinted in *Guben xiqu congkan* 古本戲曲叢刊, 2nd series. One distinguishing feature of this attitude, for example, manifests itself in the Chongzhen editions' change of the heroine's status from a young widow returning to her parent's home 芳年受寡 to a virgin "widow" whose fiancé dies 未字而寡 (scene 3).

Table 7. Textual Variants in the Stage Poem in Scene 7, "Plucking at Her Spring Heartstring," in Three Editions of Sun You's *The Zither and Lust* (ca. 1586)

The Original Wanli Edition	The Two Later Chongzhen Editions
(released by Fuchun Hall bookshop in Nanjing in the Wanli reign era, 1573–1620)	(released by Mao Jin's publishing house, and later included in his *chuanqi* collection *Sixty Plays*, both during the Chongzhen reign era, 1628–1644)
Sleepy seagulls and egrets are content to be idle;	A white egret creates ripples, looking playful.
眠鸥宿鹭能無賴	衝波白鷺能無賴
On the Princess-Feather Islet they enjoy gentle caresses.	It flies toward us from the Princess-Feather Islet.
蓼花汀上相捱	蓼花汀上飛來

to the young male role at the banquet in scene 7 (table 7). The lyrics in the Wanli edition exhibit tangible connections to courtesan performances by portraying an amorous atmosphere in which pairs of seagulls and egrets—symbols of sexual happiness—rest languorously on the Princess-Feather Islet at dusk. In the Chongzhen editions this intimate, quiet scene is turned into a heightened, kinesthetic one in which a single white egret swoops by the Islet, creating ripples in the water.

Conclusion

About two decades after Sun You's death, the drama critic Xu Fuzuo 徐復祚 (1560–after 1629) created a list of plays featuring abundant excellent stage poetry but chaotic structures and excessively large casts that harmed the integrity of the *chuanqi* genre and posed a great challenge to staging 極有佳句，第頭腦太亂，腳色太多，大傷體裁，不便於登場.[69] Unsurprisingly, the list includes, in descending order of literary merit in Xu Fuzuo's judgment, Liang Chenyu's *Washing Gauze* (ca. 1570), Sun You's *The Zither and Lust* (ca. 1586), Tang Xianzu's *The Purple Flute* (ca. 1578) and *The Purple Hairpin* (ca. 1587), and Mei Dingzuo's *The Courtesan*. It seems that from about 1570 to the mid-1580s, a type of mentality and literary taste evolved which led to the features in common that Xu Fuzuo identified. Writing in the post-1630

69. Xu Fuzuo, *Sanjia cunlao qutan* 三家村老曲談, in *Lidai quhua huibian: Mingdai bian* 歷代曲話彙編明代編, ed. Yu Weimin 俞為民 and Sun Rongrong 孫蓉蓉 (Hefei: Huangshan chubanshem, 2009), 2:268–69.

era, however, Xu Fuzuo had lost a sense of the courtesan performances as the context for playwriting five decades before. He had probably never seen these plays in full-fledged courtesan performances, as their playwrights had, and thus could not possibly register the emotions appropriate to their dramaturgy and plots. Standards of literary merit had changed in the ensuing half century, along with other developments in theatrical conditions—so that the marks the courtesan had made on the literary landscape of late Ming drama were now cast in a negative light. This view, inherited by modern drama scholars, is rectified in the present volume.

In conclusion, by around the 1600s, stage poetry was a product of the land of pleasure, and this context largely shaped many features unfavored by later critics and scholars. The impetus behind Liang Chenyu's literary creation was more the wish to cater to "theater women" and the desire for courtesan performances than the wish to promote *kunqu* from concert to operatic music. If this is true, then we must rethink what standard historiography tells us about the rise of *chuanqi* drama being an outgrowth of a single music genre, *kunqu*, during the sixteenth century.

Coda

Imagine a summer night in the late sixteenth century when lunar coronae were observed during a long drinking party in the garden of a mountain estate. In fond memory of that spectacle on that intoxicating night, a dramatist composed a stage verse and assigned it to a young male character in his play to sing. The play he wrote has been passed down to us in two versions. In the earlier version, produced by a bookshop near the renowned high-end brothel area in Nanjing, we are presented with the descriptive phrase *fenggao ying mai* 鳳膏影埋, whereas in the version released several decades later, the phrase has become *qingguang man huai* 清光滿懷. Anyone with basic education in Classical Chinese would need no dictionary to understand that *qingguang man huai* means "(the lunar coronae) give me an armful of pure moonlight." In contrast to this lyrical but simple diction, *fenggao ying mai* is a resounding rejection of linguistic clarity and stage articulation. *Fenggao* (literally, "phoenix fat") is an obscure way to denote "expensive colorful candles"—in this case, tapers whose shadows (*ying*) are shrinking (*mai*) due to the increasing brightness of the moon's coronae. This highly literary expression would take us a moment to comprehend and savor, referring as it does to the real space, real color, and real lighting conditions characteristic of late Ming outdoor nighttime entertainments. Paradoxically, it would be interesting to—and could be savored by—only those who had themselves attended such opulent late-night garden theaters; to others, it might seem simply an example of bad stage poetry employing unfamiliar diction.

Readers of chapter 4 may have already guessed that these two phrases are from the Wanli and the Chongzhen editions, respectively, of Sun You's (1540–ca. 1613) 孫柚 play *The Zither and Lust* (*Qinxin ji* 琴心記, ca. 1586).

The archetypal garden is in all likelihood modeled on Sun You's own garden, the Gorge of Vines (*Tengxi yuan* 藤溪園), on Mount Yu in Jiangsu Province. From our temporal distance in the twenty-first century, it is difficult to judge which of the two phrases is a faithful representation of Sun's original intention, and from the perspective of print culture, neither of them is (since authorial intentions were always lost in the medium of printing). Nevertheless, it is the kind of language represented by *qingguang man huai* that is conventionally labeled in drama criticism as being "emotionally genuine" or having "true color" (*bense* 本色). My point is that we need to recognize the deep, often hidden relationship of "bad" stage poetry (such as the phrase *fenggao ying mai*) to a gendered performance culture. This relationship was characteristic of literary endeavors to better serve the courtesan performances delineated throughout this volume. It seems worth asking whether the label of non-*bense*, or failed dramatic literature, is not too limiting, and whether we should reconsider the gendered foundation of the *chuanqi* and *zaju* plays created in this period. I hope that the historical investigation of the courtesan's memory and voice in this book has provided a preliminary theoretical framework for rethinking literary criticism and history.

In the preceding chapters, I explored the connections between the decline of the "authentic" *xiansuo* performance as the legacy of early Ming imperial music offices in which courtesans had been registered; the rise of *kunqu* along with the Wei Liangfu 魏良輔 (fl. sixteenth century) musical reform; the boom of *zaju* publications; and the flowering of *chuanqi* drama with references to courtesans' lives and arts. These historical phenomena, I suggested earlier, may be located in courtesans' choices that were influenced by some aspects of their musical training, such as their memory habits and vocal preferences. As a way to close this book, I offer one more gendered interpretation of the problematics of a characteristic textual variation, as seen in *"The Western Wing" in Its Southern Version* (*Nan Xixiang* 南西廂, hereafter the Southern Version), adapted around the 1530s for operas sung in southern dialects.[1] The Southern Version was popular in the late Ming theater, and at some point its *kunqu* rendition replaced the fourteenth-century *"The Western Wing" in Its Northern Version* (*Bei Xixiang* 北西廂, hereafter the *Northern Version*) in the regular repertoire of brothel performances. The musical achieve-

1. The first bibliographical record in which this play appears is *Baichuan shizhi* 百川書志 compiled by Gao Ru 高儒 (fl. 1522–1572) in 1540. It claims that the Southern Version was completed first by Cui Shipei 崔時佩 and later augmented by Li Rihua 李日華. But most other Ming drama critics believed Li Rihua to be the single author. Another Li Rihua (1565–1635; *jinshi* 1592) was mistakenly credited as the adaptor.

ments of the *kunqu* rendition not only earned recognition in the Ming and Qing dynasties but are believed to have sustained the extended stage life of *The Western Wing* in the much smaller *kunqu* repertoire today.[2] According to Li Yu 李漁 (1611–1680), seventeenth-century *kunqu* theatergoers elevated the Southern Version to the level of the canonical southern play *The Lute* (*Pipa ji* 琵琶記), and worshipped them both 令家尸戶祝，居然配饗琵琶.[3]

A brief discussion of the Southern Version will bring the present study to a sense of full closure because this play represents a small group of *chuanqi* works—that is, southern adaptations of earlier *zaju* drama, as identified by Ming and modern drama critics—which haven't been analyzed in this book. Such works include the anonymous southern play *Praying to the Moon* (*Baiyue ting* 拜月亭),[4] Tong Yangzhong's 童養中 *The Rouge* (*Yanzhi ji* 胭脂記),[5] the anonymous *The Jade Pendants* (*Yuhuan ji* 玉環記),[6] and Zhang Qi's 張琦 *Inscribing the Pagoda* (*Tita ji* 題塔記),[7] to name a few. In literary criticism, there is the tendency to portray southern adaptations as a degradation in the level of stage poetry compared to that of their northern counterparts, and hence as achieving their musical conveniences at the expense of literary quality. It is

2. Zhang Qi 張琦, *Hengqu zhutan* 衡曲塵談, in *Zhongguo gudian xiqu lunzhu jicheng* 中國古典戲曲論著集成 (Beijing: Zhongguo xiju chubanshe, 1959, rpt. 1980), 10 vols., 4:265–76, and the item for *Nan Xixiang* in Huang Wenyang 黃文暘 (b. 1736) ed., *Quhai zongmu tiyao* 曲海總目提要 (Hong Kong: Dadong shuju 大東書局, 1930), *juan* 7, 3a–b.

3. See Li Yu, *Xianqing ouji* 閒情偶寄, in *Zhongguo gudian xiqu lunzhu jicheng*, vol. 7, *juan* 3, 34.

4. Similarly, Wang Guowei 王國維 feels that part of the southern *Baiyue ting* 拜月亭 is derived from Guan Hanqing's 関漢卿 *zaju* version. See Wang Guowei, *Song Yuan xiqu shi* 宋元戲曲史 (Nanjing: Fenghuang chubanshe, 2010), 143–50.

5. Qi Biaojia, *Yuanshantang qupin* 遠山堂曲品 in *Zhongguo gudian xiqu lunzhu jicheng*, 6:129, 119. Digital access: Chinese Text Project, http://ctext.org/wiki.pl?if=en&chapter=716601

6. Zhou Yibai 周貽白 believes that *Yuhuan ji* is adapted from the Yuan author Qiao Ji's 喬吉 (ca. 1280–1345) *zaju* play *Yuxiaonü liangshi yinyuan* 玉簫女兩世姻緣. See Zhou Yibai, *Zhongguo xijushi changbian* 中國戲劇史長編 (Beijing: Renmin wenxue chubanshe, 1960), 300.

7. This southern play was an adaptation of Feng Weimin's 馮惟敏 (1511–1580) *zaju* drama, *Bu fulao* 不伏老. Wu Mei 吳梅 thinks that it is a southern adaptation of Feng's northern drama but is "ten times better than *'The Western Wing' in Its Southern Version*" (*Guqu zhutan* 顧曲塵談). Another adaptation of the same drama, also entitled *Tita ji*, was written by Xu Fuzuo 徐復祚 (1560–after 1629). The whole play is lost; unlike Zhang Qi's work, which can be found in a few late Ming drama miscellanies such as *Xuanxue pu* 玄雪譜 (reprint in *Shanben xiqu congkan* 善本戲曲叢刊, 977–86), Xu Fuzuo's work leaves no traces.

hard to fathom how female performances in the institution of brothel theater could have participated in this "lowering" of southern adaptations.

In the case of the Southern Version, however, we are privileged to have at least seven editions printed in the post-1570 era (although this is a small number compared to the more than sixty late Ming woodblock imprints of the Northern Version), which was a time of prodigious musical and dramatic creativity associated with the thriving of brothel performances. We thus have enough data to understand how the supposed "lowering" in the literary quality of stage poetry took place after courtesan-actresses entered the enterprise of southern theater as contributors with active agency. Among these seven editions of the Southern Version, the romantic encounter scene in the Fuchun Hall edition (no. 1 in the list below), which is labeled "with new additions" (*xinzeng* 新增), provides a rare glimpse of the excessive mode of romantic enchantment in a way that echoes my analysis of the traces of brothel performances in the two great *kunqu* plays spotlighted in chapter 4. Below is the list of the late Ming editions of the Southern Version, all from the post-1570 era:

1. "Xinke chuxiang yinzhu hualan Nandiao *Xixiang ji*" 新刻出像音注花欄南調西廂記 (*Newly engraved, illustrated, decorated with flowery patterns, southern music,* "The Story of the Western Wing") published by the Fuchun Hall 富春堂 in the Wanli reign[8]
2. "Xinkan hebing Li Rihua *Xixiang ji*" 新刊合併李日華西廂記 (*Newly engraved, combined edition, Li Rihua's* The Story of the Western Wing), edited by Zhou Juyi 周居易, published in the Wanli reign[9]
3. "Qiuchi dongtian Li Xixiang cangben" 仇池洞天李西廂藏本 (*Collection of Mr. Qiuchi dongtian* [Liang Chenyu], *Li's* The Western Wing), preface attributed to Liang Chenyu[10]
4. "*Nan Xixiang ji,*" late Ming edition, 34 scenes[11]
5. "*Xixiang ji,*" No. 1 in the third series of *Sixty Plays Engraved with Illustrations* (*Xiuke yanju liushi zhong* 繡刻演劇六十種), published by Mao Jin's 毛晉 (1599–1659) Jiguge Pavilion publishing house 汲古閣 in the Chongzhen reign

8. Reprinted in *Guben xiqu congkan* 古本戲曲叢刊, 1st series.

9. Rare edition in the library of Chinese Academy of Arts 中國藝術研究院.

10. Rare edition in Nanjing Library. The preface attributed to Liang Chenyu is included in Wu Shuyin, ed., *Liang Chenyu ji* 梁辰魚集 (Shanghai: Shanghai guji chubanshe, 1998).

11. Rare edition in the National Library in Beijing.

6. "*Xixiang ji*," No. 11 in *Sixty Plays* (*Liushi zhong qu* 六十種曲), published by Mao Jin in the Chongzhen reign
7. "Li Rihua *Nan Xixiang ji*" 李日華南西廂記, in the *Six Illusions of Meeting Oriole* (*Huizhen liu huan* 會真六幻) collection, compiled by Min Yuwu 閔寓五, dated to 1640[12]

The encounter of the lovers takes place in the last suite of the first act in the Northern Version (where the musical evidence discussed in detail in chapter 2 comes from), and in scene five of all seven editions of the Southern Version. The lovers' very first encounter in the Fuchun Hall edition is missing from all other six editions of the Southern Version. In it, Scholar Zhang is given a tour of a temple by a monk just before the heroine Lady Oriole and her maidservant enter it, and Zhang is enthralled with Oriole at first glance. The "with new additions" label appears on the title page of the scene in the Fuchun Hall edition, probably meant to increase the book's market value. The second encounter—the only encounter in all other six editions—occurs when the two female characters return to the stage, sing, and dance to a few more arias, while the scholar is again enamored by what he sees. The length of the scene in the Fuchun Hall edition is precisely double that in the other six editions because it lets the two lovers meet twice. Textual comparison shows that the Fuchun Hall scene contains ten more arias (see table 8).

As shown in table 8, the Fuchun Hall edition includes four songs to the tune title *Ganzhou Song*, five arias to the tune title "Sobering Up After a Three-Day Drunk," and a coda, all of which are missing from the other six southern editions. Each of the two encounters within the Fuchun Hall scene consists of a stand-alone song suite with its own coda. Even some key lines are repetitive, which incurs unavoidable logical mistakes. For this reason, Zhang Shuying, the editor of the modern typeset edition of the Southern Version, considers the Fuchun Hall edition to be the least worthy of all the seven editions: "The narrative goes that Scholar Zhang sees Oriole in the Buddhist temple, admires her delicate beauty, sighs and sings: 'So touching, her coy glance at me before she departed, that it is unbearable to me,' and then remarks that 'I thought she's the manifestation of Guanyin Bodhisattva

12. The date is provided by the modern typeset edition of *Nan Xixiang*. Zhang Shuying 張樹英, ed., *Mingzhu ji, Nan Xixiang ji* 明珠記南西廂記 (Beijing: Zhonghua shuju, 2000). Because the compiler's notes mention his intentional avoidance of using the taboo word of Emperor Jiajing's reign name, Yao Hua 姚華 believes that this edition was a reprint of an earlier edition published in the Jiajing reign (1522–1566). See Yao Hua, *Luyishi quhua* 菉漪室曲話, in *Xin quyuan* 新曲苑, ed. Re Zhongmin 任中敏 (Taipei: Zhonghua shuju, 1970, rpt. of 1913), 603.

Table 8. Aria-Structure Comparison between the Romantic Encounter Scene in the Fuchun Hall Edition and the Six Other Editions of *"The Western Wing" in Its Southern Version* (*Nan Xixiang*, adapted ca. 1530s) Printed in the Post-1570 Era

	The Fuchun Hall Edition		Other Six Editions
Tune Pattern	Singing Role	Important Stage Directions and Key lines	
Ganzhou Song 1 (*Ganzhou ge* 甘州歌)	Scholar Zhang		No
Ganzhou Song 2	Scholar Zhang		No
Ganzhou Song 3	Scholar Zhang	Female lead and secondary female role enter, walk, exit. 旦紅上，遊，下	No
Ganzhou Song 4	Scholar Zhang		No
Sobering up after a Three-Day Drunk 1 (*Jie san cheng* 解三酲)	Scholar Zhang	"So touching, her coy glance at me before she departed, that it is unbearable to me!" 怎當他臨去秋波那一轉!	No
Sobering up after a Three-Day Drunk 2	Scholar Zhang		No
Sobering up after a Three-Day Drunk 3	Scholar Zhang		No
Sobering up after a Three-Day Drunk 4	Scholar Zhang	"The door blocks pear blossoms from being seen, deep in the small courtyard. The white wall is tall, as if touching the azure sky" 門掩梨花深小院，粉牆兒高似青天	No
Sobering up after a Three-Day Drunk 5	The Monk		No
Coda (*Wei* 尾)	Scholar Zhang		No
Tete Song (*Tete ling* 忒忒令)	Scholar Zhang	Female lead enters 旦上	Yes
The Beautiful Garden (*Yuanlin hao* 園林好) 1	Oriole	Female lead and secondary female role enter 旦紅上	Yes

The Beautiful Garden 2	Scholar Zhang	Female lead and secondary female role enter	Yes
Black Silk Robe (*Zaoluo pao* 皂羅袍) 1	Oriole and Maidservant		Yes
River Water (江兒水 *Jianger shui*)	Scholar Zhang		Yes
Black Silk Robe 2	Oriole	(missing stage direction: Female lead and secondary female role enter) Female lead and secondary female role exit [at the end of the aria]	Yes
Paddling an Oar in a River (*Chuan bo zhao*) 1	Scholar Zhang		Yes
Paddling an Oar in a River 2	Scholar Zhang	"The door blocks pear blossoms from being seen, deep in the small courtyard. The white wall is tall, as if touching the azure sky. . . . So touching, her coy glance at me before she departed, that it is unbearable to me!" 門掩著梨花小院，粉牆兒高似青天……怎當他臨去秋波那一轉	Yes
Coda (*Weisheng* 尾聲)	Scholar Zhang		Yes

of the South Sea, but it turns out that she's actually a member of the prime minister's family' 我道是南海水月觀音現，誰料是相公家宅眷; then he passes the worshipper's hall, where he runs into Oriole once again, is startled by her beauty again, and learns again from Monk Facong that Oriole is the daughter of the minister."[13] Zhang thus chooses Mao Jin's Chongzhen edition (no. 5 in the list above) as the "basic text" (*diben* 底本), so as to bypass the unruly textual repetitions in the Fuchun Hall edition. That the hero discovers the

13. Zhang Shuying, ed., *Mingzhu ji, Nan Xixiang ji*, 3.

heroine's identity twice is indeed intolerable according to modern editorial rules that have persisted for some time. Yet this may not have been a concern for readers in the culturally efflorescent post-1570 era, to whom the label "with new additions" was probably a commercial draw—since the repetition was a desirably excessive mode of theater. I see the repetition as a sign of the intervention of brothel theater, where an excessive dose of sensuality was favored at the expense of logic.

The Fuchun Hall edition's addition within the romantic encounter scene also brings us back to the recurring theme of a courtesan archetype that we have identified in the figures of Xi Shi 西施 and Zhuo Wenjun 卓文君 in chapter 4. For a girl of Lady Oriole's social status, the culturally proper choice is to return to where she lives and shut the gate once she becomes aware that male strangers are present. That is exactly how Oriole behaves in the Northern Version. In the Fuchun Hall edition, however, she enters the courtyard, orders her maidservant to shut the door, but then immediately returns for the second encounter. At the moment of her return, her maidservant reminds her that someone is coming close to them, so, for the second time, Oriole turns away from him 只索自回旋.[14] But in fact, she still lingers onstage: as revealed by her next aria, she "breaks a flowering twig and, smiling, holds it" with her fingers 笑折花枝自撚, and even begins to flap at butterflies with her round silk fan 幾番慾待展齊紈，飛向錦香叢裏，教人尋不見.[15] Not only is this an activity representative of a woman's sexual charm in Chinese visual culture, but a round fan was a signature prop for courtesan *kunqu* singing in the late Ming (see chapter 2). This aria is sung by both the heroine and her maidservant, whereas all other editions seem to be uncomfortable with this rather bold image of the heroine and instead assign it to her maid alone.

The hero has no difficulty catching sight of Oriole's dance. He actually stays very close to her and observes what her waist, her face, and even her eyebrows look like 宜嗔宜喜春風面，弓樣眉兒新月偃.[16] He comments on the singing voice of the female lead after hearing her earlier aria: "Just like the sound of an oriole twittering beyond the flowers" 卻便似嚦嚦鶯聲花外囀.[17] The whole phrase is borrowed from the Northern Version and appears in its earliest extant edition (1498), in which, following the conventions of northern *zaju* drama, Oriole does not sing but instead speaks to her maidservant, so that Zhang comments on her speaking (rather than

14. Fuchun Hall edition, *juan* 1, 8b.
15. Fuchun Hall edition, *juan* 1, 8b.
16. Fuchun Hall edition, *juan* 1, 9a.
17. Fuchun Hall edition, *juan* 1, 9a.

singing) voice. In the context of female performance in the post-1570 era, however, this earlier usage of characterizing a woman's speaking voice had been extended to describe a singing style typical of the courtesan's vocal delivery (see chapter 3).

Oriole stays well within the bounds of the hero's visual field while singing her third aria:

Female lead sings in the tune of *Black Silk Robe*:

Idly walk across the court where grow green phoenix trees.
Walking on mosses for too long, my golden lotuses are soaked.
Numerous red and purple flowers compete for their beauty.
Pairs of sparrows are strolling on roofs as if reading over their writing desks.
Swallows hold in their mouths the elapsing spring;
But I will restrain my feelings of youth.
I am just afraid that, following the flowers, I will become old before being seen and loved by somebody.
With a little thin silk fan, I cover my shy face.

旦唱:[皂羅袍]
閑步碧梧庭院. 步蒼苔已久濕透金蓮◦紛紛紅紫鬥爭◦雙雙瓦雀行書案◦燕啣春去,芳心自斂◦只怕人隨花老無人見憐◦輕羅小扇遮羞臉◦

Even though this song, with the oft-seen theme of a young woman's sadness in seeing things emerge in springtime, also appears in other full editions, its Fuchun Hall version is unique in presenting translucent connotations of seduction, because only in this text is the heroine fully aware that the scholar is walking nearby and watching her movements. She is aware of both her own beauty and of its being an object of his gaze; everything in the spring scene—flowers, sparrows, swallows—is now saturated with amorous undertones. When she leaves the stage, as the last line tells us, she expresses her bashfulness by hiding her face behind a fan—not only because of her own awakening sexual desire, triggered by the scholar's fervent gaze, but because of her consciousness of being admired by him. The stage direction in the nineteenth-century *kunqu* performance handbook *Notes for Understanding the Voice and Appreciating Canons* (*Shenyin jiangu lu* 審音鑒古錄, 1834) gives a precise description of how the female lead should act before singing this line: "The young female role and the young scholar role bump into each other face to face. The former immediately uses the fan to cover 'her' face but, in the hope of ogling 'him,' turns back, with the left tiptoe hooking [and the heel] tapping the ground, [and] ogles 'him.' Then [she] turns around, walks, and sings" 小旦與小生睹面，即將扇遮，欲盼，紐身，用左腳尖勾踏，作眼傳情，又轉行介，唱.[18] Only in the Fuchun Hall edition is the encounter by nature a flirtation between a young couple, for the erotic color is clearly washed off in the six other editions.

The expanded encounter scene in the Fuchun Hall edition became a staple in the eighteenth- and nineteenth-century *kunqu* repertoires, renamed "Touring the Temple" (*Youdian* 游殿) in drama anthologies such as *Notes for Understanding the Voice and Appreciating Canons* (1834) and *A White Patchwork Fur* (*Zhuibaiqiu* 綴白裘, 1770). The connections between the living performance tradition and the Fuchun Hall edition are unquestionable. For example, *Sobering Up After a Three-Day Drunk*, which is omitted from the six other editions of the Southern Version, remains in these eighteenth- and nineteenth-century anthologies. In these performance-oriented texts, the lovers encounter each other three times for an increased density of romance. Although the resemblances of the Fuchun Hall edition to the performance tradition make it stand out from the six other late Ming editions, our modern bias in favor of coherence can nevertheless lead to devaluing the significance of the Fuchun Hall edition in the performance history of plays with a hidden female origin.

The omission of the very first encounter in the other six late Ming editions of the Southern Version changes Oriole's image from that of a brave girl actively seeking to encounter her potential lover for the second time, similar to the heroine in Tang Xianzu's 湯顯祖 (1550–1616; *jinshi* 1583) *The Peony Pavilion* (*Mudan ting* 牡丹亭), to a much more reserved lady, free of lovesickness. In the temple scene in the other six editions, Oriole is never allowed to see the scholar. At the end of the scene, her maid says: "There are people in the Buddhist hall. We must go now." To this Oriole agrees, and chants her final two lines before leaving the stage: "The secluded Buddhist temple seldom has visitors. The mosses that cover the steps serve as a foil to scarlet fallen petals" 寂寂僧房人不到, 滿階苔襯落花紅.[19] This couplet, copied from the Northern Version, further reinforces our impression of the heroine's innocence and virtue, despite the impending love affair. Moreover, Scholar Zhang is always kept at a distance when observing her, while she seems never to detect his presence. When Oriole sings her third aria, par-

18. *Shenyin jiangu lu*, reprinted in *Shanben xiqu congkan*, ed. Wang Qiugui (Taipei: Xuesheng shuju, 1983–1987), vols. 73–74, 632.

19. Zhang Shuying, ed., *Mingzhu ji, Nan Xixiang ji*, 10.

Fig. 14. Illustration of scene 5 in *Newly engraved, illustrated, decorated with flowery patterns, southern music, "The Story of the Western Wing,"* Fuchun Hall edition. (Reprinted from *Guben xiqu congkan*, 1st ser. [Beijing: Wenxue guji kanxingshe, 1957].)

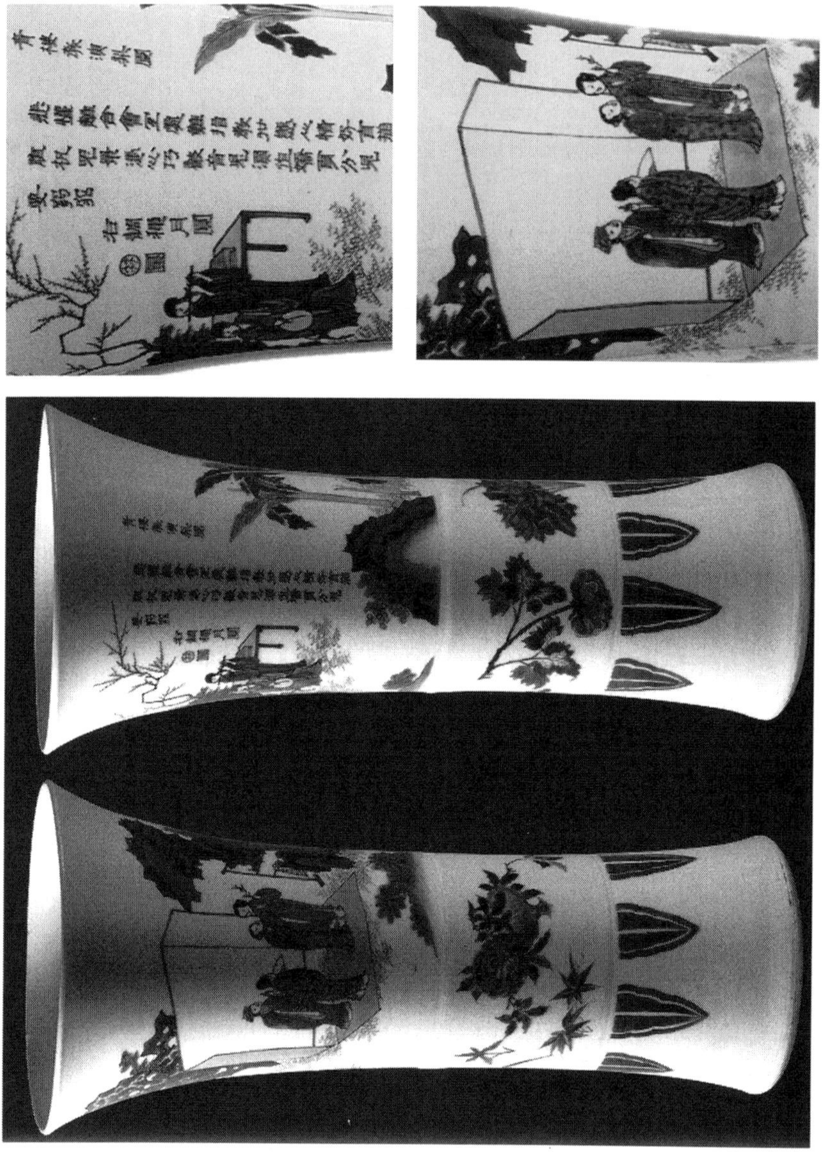

Fig. 15. Gu vase with courtesans rehearsing *The Story of the Western Wing*, Shunzhi reign (ca. 1645–1655). (Photograph © The Butler Collection.)

ticularly the last line—"With a little thin silk fan, I cover my shy face," not only does hiding her face appear pointless (why should she do so, if unaware of the male gaze?), but it also becomes impossible for the hero and heroine to enact the nineteenth-century stage direction to "bump into each other face to face" because Scholar Zhang and Oriole are *not* standing close to each other. Reading heavily edited editions can thus lead to ignorance of such details that are rich in the flavor of courtesan performances. For instance, C. T. Hsia observes that "in the southern version of the drama known as *Nan Xixiang ji*," the authorial attempt to defend "the honor and chastity" of Oriole becomes more than transparent; and that compared with the Oriole in the Northern Version, the southern Oriole is culturally proper in her behavior.[20] Such an impression might come from reading editions other than the Fuchun Hall edition.[21]

The Fuchun-Hall Oriole also better matches the description of Oriole's behavior in a later scene that recaps what has happened in the encounter scene from the perspective of two servants who witnessed it. Scholar Zhang's pageboy compares Oriole's gesture to his master with the wriggles of a silkworm—a joke which reveals the truth that she does turn and ogle him on the stage. Modern editors might tend to see the Fuchun Hall edition as the "culprit" in fusing two separate song suites together, creating unnecessary incoherence in the dramatic narrative. But the evidence presented here suggests otherwise: it is highly possible, instead, that late Ming editors who wished to maintain the innocent, noble image of the heroine cleansed the six other editions of the Southern Version of some erotic traces of the courtesan performance that remain in the Fuchun Hall edition.

It makes perfect sense, therefore, that courtesans would enact the Fuchun Hall version of Oriole rather than the reserved lady version of other editions. The second encounter of the lovers, as portrayed in the illustration of the Fuchun Hall edition (fig. 14), is also displayed in "[the courtesans] training and rehearsing in the pleasure quarters" 青樓教演梨園 scene on an early Qing (ca. 1645–1655) vase (fig. 15). The side-blown flute and the way the drum is held in figure 15 indicate the musical genre as being *kunqu*. The most outstanding feature of figure 15, however, is Oriole's physical response to Scholar

20. "An Introduction to *The Romance of the Western Chamber*," in *C. T. Hsia on Chinese Literature* (Columbia University Press, 2004), 98.

21. The most accessible editions of the Southern Version in the twentieth century are perhaps (1) the two of Mao Jin's editions; (2) the Nuanhongshi 暖紅室 edition published by Liu Shiheng 劉世珩 in the early Republican time. The latter takes the Min Yuwu edition as basic text (*diben*). For a discussion of Mao's edition and a story of how Liu got the Min Yuwu edition, see Yao Hua, *Luyishi quhua*.

Zhang's presence: her slightly twisted body, captured in the moment frozen on the vase, matches the seductive image described in the Fuchun Hall edition and echoes the nineteenth-century stage directions. The inscription on the vase (a rough counterpart to the stage directions in a playtext) reads: "[Actresses] should adapt themselves to any setting as needed, skillfully improvising with voices melodious and touching and gestures graceful and charming" 隨機兒景憑心巧, 聲音兒須作嬌, 身分兒要窈窕.[22]

The varying nuances of the heroine Oriole's demeanor in the Fuchun Hall edition versus the six other editions of the Southern Version demonstrate both the complexity of the response that courtesan performances encouraged and the erasure of a female genealogy by the patriarchal ideology that annihilates unruliness. This book intervenes in this process by redirecting our attention to a late Ming phenomenon of women and theater that cannot easily be seen in patriarchal terms. Yet the late Ming phenomenon is only a tiny portion of a much larger tapestry of early modern and modern Chinese gender history—namely, that of the arrival of actresses on the stage and their impact on printed literature. For the case of the Southern Version and many other analyses provided in the book, I do not expect gendered interpretation to become the single line of argument that dominates. But I am certain that the neat, linear history that has excluded female performances should be deeply revised.

22. My translation is based on Michael Butler's translation in *Shanghai bowuguan yu Yingguo Batele jiazu suo cang shiqi shiji Jingdezhen ciqi* 上海博物館與英國巴特勒家族所藏十七世紀景德鎮瓷器 (Shanghai: Shanghai Museum, 2005), 152.

Appendix

New Chuanqi *Plays from the Era, 1570–1600*

Plays are arranged by date or approximate date. All the datings are my own judgment.[1] Some vary from existing dating.[2]

Huansha ji (*Washing Gauze* 浣紗記; ca. 1570) by Liang Chenyu 梁辰魚 (1519–1591)
Mingfeng ji (*Singing Phoenixes* 鳴鳳記; 1567–93), attributed to Wang Shizhen 王世貞 (1526–1590)
Zixiao ji (*The Purple Flute* 紫簫記; ca. 1578) by Tang Xianzu 湯顯祖 (1550–1616)
Guanyuan ji (*Watering Gardens* 灌園記; before 1579) by Zhang Fengyi 張鳳翼 (1527–1613)
Qiefu ji (*Stealing the Commander's Tally* 竊符記; ca. 1579–1582) by Zhang Fengyi

1. For an example of how I dated *Tanhua ji* (ca. 1594 in this list), see my Chinese essay "*Tanhua ji* chuanqi xiezuo shijian kao"《曇花記》傳奇寫作時間考 [When Was the *Chuanqi* Play *Udumbara Blossoms* (*Tanhua ji*) Written?], *Xiqu yu suwenxue yanjiu* 戲曲與俗文學研究 (Beijing: Social Science Academic Press, 2018), 6:77–91. I do not offer explanatory notes for dating in this appendix but will likely publish these notes in the future.

2. The three major published chronicles of *chuanqi* drama are Xu Shuofang 徐朔方, *Wan Ming qujia nianpu* 晚明曲家年譜 (Hangzhou: Zhejiang guji chubanshe, 1993); Cheng Huaping 程華平, *Ming Qing chuanqi biannian shigao* 明清傳奇編年史稿 (Jinan: Qilu shushe, 2008); and Wu Xinlei 吳新雷, *Chatuben kunqu shishi biannian* 插圖本崑曲史事編年 (Shanghai: Shanghai guji chubanshe, 2015).

Hufu ji (*The Tiger Tally* 虎符記; ca. 1579–82) by Zhang Fengyi
Zhufa ji (*Becoming a Buddhist Monk* 祝髮記; 1582 or 1583) by Zhang Fengyi
Qingpao ji (*The Blue Robe* 青袍記; ca. 1583–97), a.k.a. *Zhegui ji* (*Plucking the Cassia Twig* 折桂記), attributed to Wang Qianzhang 王乾章 (1527–1599; *jinshi* 1562)
Yuhe ji (*The Jade Box* 玉合記; 1584) a.k.a. *Zhangtai liu* (*The Courtesan* 章臺柳) by Mei Dingzuo 梅鼎祚 (1549–1615)
Guandeng ji (*Visiting the Lantern Fair* 觀燈記; 1586) by Lin Zhang 林章 (1551–1599)
Qinxin ji (*The Zither and Lust* 琴心記; ca. 1586) by Sun You 孫柚 (1540–ca. 1613)
Yanyi ji (*Burning the Wooden Latch* 扊扅記; ca. 1586) by Zhang Fengyi
Zichai ji (*The Purple Hairpin* 紫釵記; ca. 1587) by Tang Xianzu
Yuzan ji (*The Jade Hairpin* 玉簪記; before 1591) by Gao Lian 高濂 (1528–1602)
Jiexiao ji (*Chastity and Filial Piety* 節孝記; before 1593) by Gao Lian
Hongqu ji (*The Red Lotus Flowers* 紅蕖記; ca. 1589) by Shen Jing 沈璟 (1553–1610)
Jinghong ji (*The Startled Swan Dance* 驚鴻記; before 1590) attributed to Wu Shimei 吳世美 (fl. 1570s)
Qingshan ji (*The Blue Robe* 青衫記; 1592) by Gu Dadian 顧大典 (1541–1596)
Geyi ji (*The Hemp Shirt* 葛衣記; 1592 or 1593) by Gu Dadian
Jianchai ji (*The Lovebird Hairpin* 鶼釵記; 1593) by Shi Pan 史槃 (ca. 1533–1630)
Taohua ji (*The Peach Blossoms* 桃花記; before 1593) by Jin Huaiyu 金懷玉 (fl. 1590s–1640s)
Wangyun ji (*Gazing into the Clouds* 望雲記; before 1593) by Jin Huaiyu
Tanhua ji (*The Dharma Blossoms* 曇花記; ca. 1594) by Tu Long 屠隆 (1544–1605)
Caihao ji (*The Lustrous Brush* 彩毫記; ca. 1594, right after *Tanhua ji*) by Tu Long
Xiangshan ji (*The Fragrant Hills* 香山記; before 1598) preface of the woodblock edition by Luo Maodeng 羅懋登 (fl. 1590s) dated to 1598
Tihong ji (*Inscribing the Red Leaf* 題紅記; 1593–98) by Wang Jide 王驥德 (ca. 1542–1623)

Huanhun ji (*The Soul's Return* 還魂記; 1598), also known as *Mudan ting* (*The Peony Pavilion* 牡丹亭), by Tang Xianzu
Nanke ji (*The Dream of Nanke* 南柯記; 1600) by Tang Xianzu

New *Chuanqi* Plays Possibly Produced in the Era

Yuwan ji (*The Jade Ball* 玉丸記) by Zhu Qi 朱期
Chunwu ji (*The Spring Weeds* 春蕪記) by Wang Ling 王錂
Cailou ji (*The Decorated Pavilion* 綵樓記) by Wang Ling
Mengjing ji (*The Dreamland* 夢境記) by Su Yuanjun 蘇元俊 (?–1576)

Bibliography

Abbreviations

CMCS *Siku quanshu cunmu congshu* 四庫全書存目叢書 (Jinan: Qilu shushe, 1997).

XXSKQS *Xuxiu siku quanshu* 續修四庫全書 (Shanghai: Shanghai guji chubanshe, 2002).

Works

A Ying 阿英, ed. *Ye Tianliao sizhong* 葉天寥四種. Shanghai: Shanghai beiye shanfang, 1936.

Abbate, Carolyn. "Opera; or, the Envoicing of Women." In *Musicology and Difference: Gender and Sexuality in Music Scholarship*, edited by Ruth A. Solie. Berkeley: University of California Press, 1993.

Abbate, Carolyn. *Unsung Voices: Opera and Musical Narrative in the Nineteenth Century*. Princeton: Princeton University Press, 1991.

Anderson, Emily Hodgson. *Eighteenth-Century Authorship and the Play of Fiction: Novels and the Theater, Haywood to Austen*. New York: Routledge, 2009.

Aoki Masaru. *Shina kinsei gikyokushi* 支那近世戲曲史. Tokyo: Kobundo shoten, 1930. *Chūgoku kinsei kigyokushi*, translated by Wang Gulu 王古魯. *Zhongguo jinshi xiqushi* 中國近世戲曲史. Shanghai: Shangwu yinshuguan, 1936. Reprint, Zhonghua shuju, 2010.

Banes, Sally. *Dancing Women: Female Bodies on Stage*. London: Routledge, 1998.

Barthes, Roland. *S/Z: An Essay*. Translated by Richard Miller. New York: Hill and Wang, 1970.

Beck, Jay, and Tony Grajeda, eds. *Lowering the Boom: Critical Studies in Film Sound*. Urbana: University of Illinois Press, 2008.

Beijing tushuguan shanben shumu 北京圖書館善本書目. Beijing: Zhonghua shuju, 1959.

Birch, Cyril, trans. *The Peony Pavilion: Mudan ting*. 2nd ed. Bloomington: Indiana University Press, 2002.

Birch, Cyril. *Scenes for Mandarins: The Elite Theater of the Ming*. New York: Columbia University Press, 1995.

Brokaw, Cynthia J., and Kai-wing Chow, eds. *Printing and Book Culture in Late Imperial China*. Berkeley: University of California Press, 2005.

Bu Jian 卜健, ed. *Li Kaixian quanji* 李開先全集. Shanghai: Shanghai guji chubanshe, 2014.

Butler, Michael, and Wang Qingzheng, eds. *Shanghai bowuguan yu Yingguo Batele jiazu suo cang shiqi shiji Jingdezhen ciqi* 上海博物館與英國巴特勒家族所藏十七世紀景德鎮瓷器. Shanghai: Shanghai Museum, 2005.

Butler, Michael, Julia B. Curtis, and Stephen Little. *Shunzhi Porcelain, 1644–1661: Treasures from an Unknown Reign*. Alexandria, VA: Art Services International, 2002.

Butler, Michael, Margaret Medley, and Stephen Little, eds., *Seventeenth-Century Chinese Porcelain from the Butler Family Collection*. Alexandria, VA: Art Services International, 1990.

Cahill, James. *Parting at the Shore: Chinese Painting of the Early and Middle Ming Dynasty*. New York: Weatherhill, 1978.

Cai Xinquan 蔡鑫泉. "Ming Huizhou zhuming huajia Wu Tingyu Zuoqian shilue" 明徽州著名画家吴廷羽左千事略. *Huizhou shehui kexue* 徽州社会科学 5 (2011): 44–48.

Cao Yunyuan 曹允源 and Li Genyuan 李根源, comps. *Minguo Wuxian zhi* 民國吳縣志. *Zhongguo defangzhi jicheng: Jiangsu fuxianzhi ji* 中國地方誌集成·江蘇府縣志輯. Nanjing: Jiangsu guji chubanshe, 1991. Vol. 12.

Carruthers, Mary. *The Book of Memory: A Study of Memory in Medieval Culture*. Cambridge: Cambridge University Press, 1990.

Chao, Yuenren. "Tone, Intonation, Singsong, Chanting, Recitative, Tonal Composition, and Atonal Composition in Chinese." In *For Roman Jakobson: Essays on the Occasion of His Sixtieth Birthday*, compiled by Morris Halle, 52–59. The Hague: Mouton, 1956.

Chen Jiru 陳繼儒 (1558–1639), ed. *Pan'e ji* 槃阿集. Original edition in Naikaku bunko. Photo-reprint in the *Hishi* collection of the Gest Library, Princeton University.

Chen, Shih-Hsiang, and Harold Acton, trans. *The Peach Blossom Fan, by K'ung Shang-jen*. Berkeley: University of California Press, 1976.

Cheng Huaping 程華平. *Ming Qing chuanqi biannian shigao* 明清傳奇編年史稿. Jinan: Qi Lu shushe, 2008.

Cheng, Weikun. "The Challenge of the Actresses: Female Performers and Cultural Alternatives in Early Twentieth Century Beijing and Tianjin." *Modern China* 22, no. 2 (1996): 197–233.

Cheng Yun 程芸. *Tang Xianzu yu wan Ming xiqu de shanbian* 湯顯祖與晚明戲曲的嬗變. Beijing: Zhonghua shuju, 2006.

Cheng Yun and Li Yanhua 李豔華. "Mingren 'fan beiqu' xianxiang chutan" 明人翻北曲現象初探. *Nanjing shifan daxue wenxueyuan xuebao* 南京師範大學文學院學報 3 (2015): 66–71.

Chonghe jushi 冲和居士. *Yi chun jin* 怡春錦. *Shanben xiqu congkan*. Vol. 19.

Cong Jingwen 叢靜文. *Nan Bei Xixiang ji bijiao* 南北西廂記比較. Taipei: Taiwan Shangwu yinshuguan, 1976.

Da Qing wuchao huidian Kangxi huidian 大清五朝會典康熙會典. Facsimile, Beijing: Xianzhuang shuju, 2006.

De Certeau, Michel. *The Practice of Everyday Life*. Translated by Steven Rendall. Berkeley: University of California Press, 1984.

Deng Changfeng 鄧長風. *Ming Qing xiqu jia kaolue* 明清戲曲家考略. Shanghai: Shanghai guji chubanshe, 1994.

Dingdiao kunchi xindiao yuefu baneng zoujin 鼎雕崑池新調樂府八能奏錦. Original Airitang 愛日堂 edition in Naikaku bunko. Photo-reprint in *Shanben xiqu congkan* 善本戲曲叢刊, edited by Wang Qiugui 王秋桂. Taipei: Taiwan xuesheng shuju, 1984–1987.

Dolby, William. *Eight Chinese Plays: From the Thirteenth Century to the Present*. New York: Columbia University Press, 1978.

Dolby, William. *A History of Chinese Drama*. New York: Barnes and Noble, 1976.

Dolby, William. "Yuan Drama." In *Chinese Theater: From Its Origins to the Present Day*, edited by Colin Mackerras. Honolulu: University of Hawaii Press, 1983.

Engel, Laura. *Fashioning Celebrity: Eighteenth-Century British Actresses and Strategies for Image Making*. Columbus: Ohio State University Press, 2011.

Fan Jingwen 范景文 (1587–1644). *Wenzhong ji* 文忠集. In *Siku quanshu* 四庫全書, *juan* 9. Digital access: https://zh.m.wikisource.org/wiki/文忠集_(范景文,_四庫全書本)/卷09#題米家童

Fan Yunlin 范允臨 (1558–1641). *Shuliaoguan ji* 輸寥館集. Facsimile reprint in *Siku jinhui shu congkan* 四庫禁毀書叢刊. Beijing: Beijing chubanshe, 2000. Vol. 101.

Fei, Si-yen. *Negotiating Urban Space: Urbanization and Late Ming Nanjing*. Cambridge, MA: Harvard University Asia Center, 2009.

Feldman, Martha, and Bonnie Gordon, eds. *The Courtesan's Arts: Cross-Cultural Perspectives*. New York: Oxford University Press, 2006.

Feng Mengzhen馮夢禎 (1548–1606). *Kuaixuetang ji* 快雪堂集. *Siku quanshu cunmu congshu* 四庫全書存目叢書. Jinan: Qi Lu shushe, 2001. *Jibu*. Vols. 164–65.

Feng Mengzhen. *Kuaixuetang riji* 快雪堂日記. Modern typeset edition edited by Ding Xiaoming 丁小明. Nanjing: Fenghuang chubanshe, 2010.

Feng Yuanjun 馮沅君. *Guju shuohui* 古劇說匯. Beijing: Zuojia chubanshe, 1956.

Foster, Susan Leigh. "Improvising History." In *Theorizing Practice: Redefining Theatre History*, edited by W. B. Worthen and Peter Holland. New York: Palgrave Macmillan, 2003.

Fu Xihua 傅惜華. *Mingdai chuanqi quanmu* 明代傳奇全目. Beijing: Renmin wenxue chubanshe, 1959.

Fu Xihua 傅惜華. *Mingdai zaju quanmu* 明代雜劇全目. Beijing: Zuojia chubanshe, 1958.

Gao Ru 高儒, comp. *Baichuan shizhi* 百川書志. Digital version, *Zhongguo zhexueshu dianzihua jihua* 中國哲學書電子化計劃. https://ctext.org/wiki.pl?if=gb&res=182640

Gao Shiyi 高士鸃, Yang Zhenzao 楊振藻, Qian Lucan 錢陸燦, comp. *Changshu Xianzhi* 常熟縣誌. *Zhongguo difangzhi Jiangsu fuxianzhi ji* 中國地方誌集成江蘇府縣誌輯. Nanjing: Jiangsu guji chubanshe, 1991.

Gautam, K. Sanjay. *Foucault and the Kamasutra: The Courtesan, the Dandy, and the Birth of* Ars Erotica *as Theater in India*. Chicago: University of Chicago Press, 2016.

Goldman, Andrea S. *Opera and the City: The Politics of Culture in Beijing, 1770–1900*. Stanford: Stanford University Press, 2012.

Goldstein, Joshua. *Drama Kings: Players and Public in the Recreation of Peking Opera, 1870–1937*. Berkeley: University of California Press, 2007.

Grant, Beata. "Through the Empty Gate: The Poetry of Buddhist Nuns in Late Imperial China." In *Cultural Intersections in Later Chinese Buddhism*, edited by Marsha Weidner, 73–86. University of Hawai'i, 2001.

Greenblatt, Stephen. *Shakespearean Negotiations*. Berkeley: University of California Press, 1988.

Gu Qiyuan 顧起元 (1565–1628). *Kezuo zhuiyu* 客座贅語. Colophon 1618. Beijing: Zhonghua shuju, 1987.

Gu Zhengyi 顧正誼 (fl. 1575–1600). *Baiyong tupu* 百詠圖譜. Original woodblock edition in the National Library in Beijing.

Guben xiqu congkan 古本戲曲叢刊. Beijing: Wenxue guji kanxingshe, 1957.

— 2nd series: *Yuxiazhai chuanqi shizhong* 玉夏齋傳奇十種, particularly, Chen Yuchan's 陳玉蟾 *Feng qiu huang* 鳳求凰.

— 3rd series: Wang Long 王鑨. *Qiu Huqiu* 秋虎丘, no. 92.

— 4th series: Meng Chengshun 孟稱舜 (1594–1684), comp. *Leijiang ji* 酹江集, no. 4. Xijizi 息機子, compiled by *Zaju xuan* 雜劇選.

Guo Yingde 郭英德. *Ming Qing chuanqi shi* 明清傳奇史. Nanjing: Fenghuang chubanshe, 2001.

Guo Yingde 郭英德. *Ming Qing chuanqi xiqu wenti yanjiu* 明清傳奇戲曲文體研究. Beijing: Shangwu yinshuguan, 2004.

Guo Yingde 郭英德. *Ming Qing chuanqi zonglu* 明清傳奇綜錄. Shijiazhuang: Hebei jiaoyu chubanshe, 1997.

Guo Yingde 郭英德. *Ming Qing wenren chuanqi yanjiu* 明清文人傳奇研究. Taipei: Wenxin chubanshe, 1991.

Hajime Yagisawa 八木澤元. *Mindai gekisakka kenkyu* 明代劇作家研究. Tokyo: Kodansha, 1959.

Han Shanggui 韓上桂 (1572–1644). *Duoyun shanfang yigao* 朵雲山房遺稿. Early nineteenth-century edition. Facsimile Google Books.

Han Shanggui 韓上桂. "Pan Jingsheng xiansheng *Luanxiao xiaopin* xu" 潘景升先生鸞嘯小品序. In Pan Zhiheng, *Luanxiao xiaopin* 鸞嘯小品. Preface dated to 1628.

Hanan, Patrick. "Sources of the *Chin P'ing Mei*." *Asia Major* 10, no. 2 (1963): 23–67.

He Liangjun 何良俊 (1506–1573). *Siyouzhai congshuo* 四友齋叢說. Beijing: Zhonghua shuju, 1983.

He Yuming. "Difficulties of Performance: The Musical Career of Xu Wei's *The Mad Drummer*." *Harvard Journal of Asiatic Studies* 68, no. 2 (2008): 77–114.

Hilmes, Michele. "Is There a Field Called Sound Culture Studies? And Does It Matter?" *American Quarterly* 57, no. 1 (2005): 249–59.

Hou Rongchuan 侯榮川 and Lu Lin 陸林, eds. *Mei Dingzuo xiquji* 梅鼎祚戲曲集. Hefei: Huangshan shushe, 2016.

Hsia, C. T. *C. T. Hsia on Chinese Literature*. New York: Columbia University Press, 2004.

Hsia, C. T. *The Classical Chinese Novel: A Critical Introduction*. New York: Columbia University Press, 1968.

Hu Wenhuan 胡文煥 (fl. 1596). Comp. *Qunyin leixuan* 群音類選. Photo-prints of woodblock edition in the National Library in Beijing. Beijing: Zhonghua shuju, 1980. *Qunyin leixuan jiaojian* 群音類選校箋, edited by Li Zhiyuan 李志遠. Beijing: Zhonghua shuju, 2018.

Hu Wenkai 胡文楷. *Lidai funü zhuzuo kao* 歷代婦女著作考. Shanghai: Shanghai guji chubanshe, (1957, 1985) 2008.

Hua Wei 華瑋. "Ma Xianglan yu Mingdai houqi de qutan" 馬湘蘭與明代後期的曲壇. *Xiqu xuebao* 戲曲學報 2 (2007): 55–82; also in *Zhonghua xiqu* 中華戲曲 37 (2008): 151–77.

Hua Wei 華瑋, ed. *Ming Qing funü xiqu ji* 明清婦女戲曲集. Taipei: Academia Sinica, 2003, rpt. 2005.

Hua Wei 華瑋. *Ming Qing xiqu zhong de nüxing shengyin yu lishi jiyi* 明清戲曲中的女性聲音與歷史記憶. Taipei: Guojia chubanshe, 2013.

Hua Wei 華瑋 and Wang Ailing 王瑷玲, eds. *Ming Qing xiqu guoji yantaohui lunwenji* 明清戲曲國際研討會論文集. Taipei: Academia Sinica, 1998.

Huang Binhong 黃賓虹. "Gugong shenhua lu" 故宮審畫錄. In *Huang Binhong wenji* 黃賓虹文集. Shanghai: Shanghai shuhua chubanshe, 1999.

Huang Shizhong 黃仕忠. "Taihe zhengyinpu yandu jihua jiqi shishi qingkuang" 太和正音譜研讀計劃及其實施情況. *Xiqu yu suwenxue* 戲曲與俗文學 1 (2019): 1–15.

Huang Wenyang 黃文暘 (b. 1736), ed. *Quhai zongmu tiyao* 曲海總目提要. Hong Kong: Dadong shuju 大東書局, 1930.

Huang Zongxi 黃宗羲 (1616–1695). *Sijiu lu* 思舊錄. In *Huang Zongxi quanji* 黃宗羲全集. Hangzhou: Zhejiang guji chubanshe, 1985.

Idema, Wilt. "Female Talent and Female Virtue: Xu Wei's *Nü zhuangyuan* and Meng Chengshun's *Zhenwenji*." In *Ming Qing xiqu guoji yantaohui lunwen ji*, edited by Hua Wei and Wang Ailing, vol. 2, 549–71. Taipei: Academia Sinica, 1998.

Idema, Wilt. "From Stage Scripts to Closet Drama: Editions of Early Chinese Drama and the Translations of Yuan *Zaju*." *Journal of Chinese Literature and Culture* 3, no. 1 (2016): 175–202.

Idema, Wilt, and Beata Grant, eds. *The Red Brush: Writing Women of Imperial China*. Cambridge, MA: Harvard University Asia Center, 2004.

Idema, Wilt, and Stephen H. West. *Chinese Theater 1100–1450: A Source Book*. Wiesbaden: Steiner, 1982.

Jiao Xun 焦循 (1763–1820). *Jushuo* 劇說. *Zhongguo gudian xiqu lunzhu jicheng* 中國古典戲曲論著集成. Vol. 8. Beijing: Zhongguo xiju chubanshe, 1959, rpt. 1980.

Jin Ping Mei cihua 金瓶梅詞話. Photo-reprint of Wanli (1573–1620) edition. Hong Kong: Taiping shuju, 1993.

Komatsu Ken 小松謙. *Chūgoku koten engeki kenkyū* 中國古典演劇研究. Tokyo: Kyuko shoin, 2001.

Komatsu Ken 小松謙. "Naifuhon-kei shohon kō" 內府本系諸本考. In *Tanaka Kenji hakase sōshū kinen Chūgoku koten gikyoku ronshū* 田中謙二博士頌壽記念中國古典戲曲論集. Tokyo: Kyuko shoin, 1991.

Kong Shangren 孔尚任 (1648–1718). *Taohua shan chuanqi* 桃花扇傳奇. Lanxue tang 蘭雪堂 edition (1895), edited by Wang Jisi 王季思 et al. Beijing: Renmin wenxue chubanshe, 1997.

Lam, Joseph S. C. "Reading Music and Eroticism in Late Ming Texts." *Nan Nü* 12 (2010): 215–54.

Lam, Ling Hon. "The Matriarch's Private Ear: Performance, Reading, Censorship and the Fabrication of Interiority in 'The Story of the Stone.'" *Harvard Journal of Asiatic Studies* 65, no. 2 (2005): 357–415.

Lam, Ling Hon. *The Spatiality of Emotion in Early Modern China*. New York: Columbia University Press, 2018.

Lei, Daphne. *Uncrossing the Borders: Performing Chinese in Gendered (Trans)Nationalism*. Ann Arbor: University of Michigan Press, 2019.

Li Guotao 黎國韜 and Zhou Peiwen 周佩文. *Liang Chenyu yanjiu* 梁辰魚研究. Guangzhou: Zhongshan daxue chubanshe, 2007.

Li Jialian 李佳蓮. *Li Yu* Beici guangzhengpu *yanjiu* 李玉《北詞廣正譜》研究. Taipei: Guojia chubanshe, 2012.

Li Jian 李健. "*Taihe zhengyin pu* xiancun banben xulu" 太和正音譜現存版本敘錄. *Xiqu yu suwenxue yanjiu* 戲曲與俗文學研究 9 (2020): 136–73. Beijing: Shehui kexue wenxian chubanshe.

Li Kaixian 李開先 (1502–1568). *Gaiding Yuanxian chuanqi* 改定元賢傳奇. Facsimile reprint in XXSKQS. Vol. 1760.

Li Rihua 李日華 (fl. sixteenth century). *Nan Xixiang ji* 李日華南西廂記. *Huizhen liu huan* 會真六幻. Compiled by Min Yuwu 閩寓五. 1640.

Li, Wai-Yee. "The Representation of History in the *Peach Blossom Fan*." *Journal of the American Oriental Society* 115, no. 3 (1995): 421–33.

Li Yu 李玉 (ca. 1610–after 1670). *Beici guangzheng pu* 北詞廣正譜, ca. 1645–ca. 1660. Facsimile reprint, 1911–1949, reprint of a Kangxi-reign (1661–1722) edition from the Blue Waterlily Book Studio 青蓮書屋. Fudan University Library.

Li Yu 李漁 (1611–ca. 1680). *Xianqing ouji* 閒情偶寄. *Lidai quhua huibian: Qingdai bian*, edited by Yu and Sun. Vol. 5.

Li, Yuhang. *Becoming Guanyin: Artistic Devotion of Buddhist Women in Late Imperial China*. New York: Columbia University Press, 2020.

Liang Chenyu 梁辰魚 (1519–1591). *Jiangdong baizhu* 江東白紵. XXSKQS. Vol. 1739. Modern typeset edition edited by Peng Fei 彭非, *Jiangdong baizhu* 江東白紵. Shanghai: Shanghai guji chubanshe, 1989.

Ling Mengchu 凌濛初 (1580–1644). *Bei Hongfu* 北紅拂. Chongzhen edition, published by Ling Mengchu, original in Shanghai Library.

Ling Mengchu 凌濛初. *Nanyin sanlai* 南音三籟. Facsimile reprint, Shanghai: Shanghai guji chubanshe, 1963.

Lingxu zi 凌虛子. *Yuelu yin* 月露音 (preface 1616). Facsimile reprint in *Shanben xiqu congkan*.

Liu Chongde 劉崇德. *Yanyue xinshuo: Tang Song gongting yanyue yu ciqu yinyue yanjiu* 燕樂新說: 唐宋宮廷燕樂與詞曲音樂研究. Hefei: Huangshan shushe, 2011.

Liu Chongde 劉崇德. *Yuan zaju yuepu yanjiu yizhu* 元雜劇樂譜研究譯注. Shijiazhuang: Hebei jiaoyu chubanshe, 2003.

Liu Chongde 劉崇德, ed. *Zhongguo gudai qupu daquan* 中國古代曲譜大全. Shenyang: Liuning renmin chubanshe, 2009.

Liu Junhua 劉軍華. *Ming Qing nüxing zuojia xiqu chuangzuo yanjiu* 明清女性作家戲曲創作研究. Beijing: Kexue chubanshe, 2015.

Liu Shuiyun 劉水雲. *Ming Qing jiayue yanjiu* 明清家樂研究. Shanghai: Shanghai guji chubanshe, 2005.

Liu, Siyuan. *Performing Hybridity in Colonial-Modern China.* New York: Palgrave Macmillan, 2013.

Liu Tong 劉侗 and Yu I-zheng 于奕正, comps. *Dijing jingwulue* 帝京景物略. Pref. 1635. Beijing: Beijing Guji chubanshe, 1980.

Liu Yingbei 劉英貝. "Wu Wei renwuhua fengge yanjiu" 吳偉人物畫風格研究. Master's thesis. Taipei: Guoli Zhongyang daxue, 2008.

Liu Zhizhong 劉致中. *Ming Qing xiqu kaolun* 明清戲曲考論. Taipei: Guojia chubanshe, 2009.

Lo Chin-T'ang 羅錦堂, trans. *Mingdai juzuojia yanjiu* 明代劇作家研究. Hong Kong: Longen shudian, 1966.

Lo Chin-T'ang 羅錦堂. *Zhongguo xiqu zongmu huibian* 中國戲曲總目彙編. Xi'an: Shanxi shifan daxue chubanshe, 2021.

Lu Eting 陸萼庭. *Kunju yanchu shigao* 昆劇演出史稿. Taipei: Guojia chubanshe, 2004.

Lu Eting 陸萼庭. *Qingdai xiqu jia congkao* 清代戲劇家叢攷. Shanghai: Xuelin chubanshe, 1996.

Lu Qian 盧前. *Ming Qing xiqushi* 明清戲曲史. Shanghai: Shangwu yinshuguan, 1935.

Lu Qian 盧前, ed. *Yuefu qunzhu* 樂府群珠. Modern type-set edition. Shanghai: Shangwu yinshuguan, 1957.

Luo Kanglie 羅忼烈. *Ming guben chuanqi* Lingyun ji 明孤本傳奇凌雲記. Hongkong: Shuye gongsi, 1975.

Luo Zhufeng 羅竹風, et al. *Hanyu dacidian* 漢語大詞典. 2nd ed. Shanghai cishu chubanshe, 2008.

Ma Xianglan 馬湘蘭 (1548–1604, a.k.a. Ma Yuejiao 馬月嬌). "Hongxian chuanqi xiaoyin" 紅線傳奇小引. In Zhao Shijie 趙世杰, *Gujin nüshi* 古今女史, *juan* 9, 11a–b. Digital library, "Ming Qing Women's Writings." Digital access: https://digital.library.mcgill.ca/mingqing/search/results-work.php

Mackerras, Colin, ed. *Chinese Theater: From Its Origins to the Present Day*. Honolulu: University of Hawaii Press, 1983.

Mann, Susan, ed. *Under Confucian Eyes: Writings on Gender in Chinese History.* Berkeley: University of California Press, 2001.

Mao Jin 毛晉 (1599–1659). *Liushi zhong qu* 六十種曲 (*Sixty Plays*). Reprint, Shanghai: Kaiming shudian, 1935.

Mao Xiang 冒襄 (1611–1693). *Yingmei'an yiyu* 影梅庵憶語. Rugao maoshi congshu 如皋冒氏叢書, 1902.

Mayer-Fong, Tobie. "The Printed World: Books, Publishing Culture, and Society in Late Imperial China." *Journal of Asian Studies* 66 (2007): 787–817.

McMahon, Keith. *Saying All That Can Be Said: The Art of Describing Sex in the "Jin Ping Mei."* Cambridge, MA: Harvard University Asia Center, 2023.

Mei Dingzuo 梅鼎祚 (1549–1615). *Luqiu shishi ji* 鹿裘石室集. Original edition in Naikaku bunko. Photo-reprint in the *Hishi* collection of the Gest Library, Princeton University.

Mei Dingzuo 梅鼎祚. *Qingni lianhua ji* 青泥蓮花記. Preface 1600. Modern typeset edition, Hefei: Huangshan shushe, 1996.

Mei Dingzuo 梅鼎祚. *Yuhe ji* 玉合記. Original edition in the library of Kyoto University.

Meng Sen 孟森. *Xinshi congkan* 心史叢刊. Hong Kong: Chinese Ancient Books Service, 1963.

Milburn, Olivia. "The Silent Beauty: Changing Portrayals of Xi Shi, from *Zhiguai* and Poetry to Ming Fiction and Drama." *Asia Major* 26, no. 1 (2013): 23–53.

Mo Boji 莫伯驥 (1878–1958). "Liushu gu" 六書故. In *Wushiwan juan lou qunshu bawen* 五十萬卷樓群書跋文. Beijing: Zhonghua shuju, 2019. Unpaginated, manuscript completed in 1947.

Monishi Miyaki 海西宮奇. Postscript to *Weishi yuepu* 魏氏樂譜. Digitized version, original in Peking University Library. https://ia600306.us.archive.org/13/items/02095092.cn/02095092.cn.pdf

Nachumi, Nora. *Acting Like a Lady: British Women Novelists and the Late Eighteenth Century Stage*. New York: AMS Press, 2008.

Nagasaki-shi shi: Kinsei 新長崎市史·近世編. Tokyo: Kyosei, 2012.

Nan Xixiang ji 南西廂記. Late Ming edition, 34 scenes. Original in the National Library in Beijing.

Ōki Yasushi 大木康. *Chūgoku yūri kūkan: Min Shin shinwai gijo no sekai* 中國游里空間: 明清秦淮妓女の世界. Tokyo: Seidosha, 2002.

Ōki Yasushi 大木康. *Mao Xiang he Yingmei'an yiyu* 冒襄和影梅庵憶語. Taipei: Liren shuju, 2013.

Ōki Yasushi 大木康 and Paolo Santangelo. *Shan'ge, the 'Mountain Songs': Love Songs in Ming China*. Leiden: Brill, 2011.

Owen, Stephen. *Anthology of Chinese Literature: Beginnings to 1911*. New York: W. W. Norton, 1996.

Pan Zhiheng 潘之恆 (1556–1622). *Genshi* 亙史. Facsimile reprint of 1626 edition in *Siku quanshu cunmu congshu, zibu*. No. 193.

Pan Zhiheng 潘之恆. *Genshi waiji* 亙史外紀. Facsimile reprint in *Siku quanshu cunmu congshu, zibu*. No. 193.

Pan Zhiheng 潘之恆. *Luanxiao xiaopin* 鸞嘯小品. 1628 edition in the Shanghai Library.

Pan Zhiheng 潘之恆. *Shejiang shi* 涉江詩. Original edition in Naikaku bunko. Photoreprint in the *Hishi* collection of the Gest Library, Princeton University.

Panke shuoren 盤薖碩人. *Bojie dingben: Citan qingwan Pipa ji* 伯皆定本詞壇清玩琵琶記. Transcript of Wanli woodblock edition. University of Tokyo.

Pascoe, Judith. *Romantic Theatricality: Gender, Poetry, and Spectatorship*. Ithaca: Cornell University Press, 1997.

Paterson, M. *The Senses of Touch: Haptics, Affects, and Technologies*. Oxford: Berg, 2007.

Peng Fei 彭非, ed. *Jiangdong baizhu* 江東白紵. Shanghai: Shanghai guji chubanshe, 1989.

Pian, Rulan Chao. "Tone and Tone: Applying Musical Elements to Chinese Words." *Journal of Chinese Linguistics* 28, no. 2 (2000): 181–85.

Plaks, Andrew. *The Four Masterworks of the Ming Novel*. Princeton: Princeton University Press, 1987.

Pu Jiangqing 浦江清. *Zhongguo wenxue shigao: Ming Qing* 中國文學史稿:明清. Beijing: Beijing chubanshe, 2018.

Qi Biaojia 祁彪佳 (1603–1645). *Yuanshantang jupin* 遠山堂劇品. *Zhongguo gudian xiqu lunzhu jicheng*. Vol. 6, 135–200.

Qi Biaojia 祁彪佳. *Yuanshantang qupin*. Digital version, Chinese Text Project, http://ctext.org/wiki.pl?if=en&chapter=716601. Also in *Zhongguo gudian xiqu lunzhu jicheng*. Vol. 6, 1–134.

Qi Mingjing 漆明鏡. *Weishi yuepu lingyunge liujuanben zongpu quanyi*《魏氏樂譜》凌雲閣六卷本總譜全譯. Guilin: Guangxi shifan daxue chubanshe, 2017.

Qi Senhua 齊森華, Chen Duo 陳多, and Ye Changhai 葉長海, eds. *Zhongguo quxue da cidian* 中國曲學大辭典. Hangzhou: Zhejiang jiaoyu chubanshe, 1997.

Qian Bocheng 錢伯城, ed. *Yuan Hongdao ji jianjiao* 袁宏道集箋校. Shanghai: Shanghai guji chubanshe, 1981.

Qian Nanyang 錢南揚. *Han shang huan wencun: Liang Zhu xiju jicun* 漢上宧文存: 梁祝戲劇輯存. Beijing: Zhonghua shuju, 2009.

Qian Nanyang 錢南揚. "*Nanci yinzheng* jiaozhu" 南詞引正校註. *Xiju bao* 戲劇報 7, no. 8 (1961).

Qian Nanyang 錢南揚. *Yongle dadian xiwen sanzhong jiaozhu* 永樂大典戲文三種校注. Beijing: Zhonghua shuju, 2009.

Qian Qianyi 錢謙益 (1582–1664). *Liechao shiji xiaozhuan* 列朝詩集小傳. Rare book in the library of the University of Chicago. Beijing: Zhonghua shuju, 1959.

Qian Yiping 錢亦平, ed. *Qian Renkang yinyue wenxuan* 錢仁康音樂文選. Shanghai: Shanghai yinyue chubanshe, 2013.

Qinhuai Moke 秦淮墨客. *Yuefu hongshan* 樂府紅珊. Imprint of 1800. *Shanben xiqu congkan*. Vol. 10.

Qiuchi dongtian Li Xixiang cangben 仇池洞天李西廂藏本. Preface attributed to Liang Chenyu. Original in Nanjing Library.

Roach, Joseph. *Cities of the Dead: Circum-Atlantic Performance*. New York: Columbia University Press, 1996.

Rolston, David. "Research Note: Introducing a Resource on Music and Oral Performing Literature in the Ming Novel *Jin Ping Mei cihua* Made Available in Celebration of the Completion of David Tod Roy's Translation." *CHINOPERL Papers* 33, no. 1 (2014).

Roy, David. "The Case for T'ang Hsien-tsu's Authorship of the *Jin P'ing Mei*." *Chinese Literature: Essays, Articles, Reviews* 8 (1986): 31–62.

Roy, David, trans. *The Plum in the Golden Vase*. Princeton: Princeton University Press, 2001.

Roy, David. "The Use of Songs as a Means of Self-Expression and Self-Characterization in the *Chin P'ing Mei*." *Chinese Literature: Essays, Articles, Reviews* 20 (1998): 101–26.

Schafer, R. Murray. *The Soundscape: Our Sonic Environment and the Tuning of the World*. Rochester, VT: Destiny Books, 1992.

Screech, Timon. "Going to the Courtesans: Transit to the Pleasure District of Edo Japan." In *The Courtesan's Arts: Cross-Cultural Perspectives*, edited by Martha Feldman and Bonnie Gordon, 255–79. New York: Oxford University Press, 2006.

Shang, Wei. "The Making of the Everyday World: *Jin Ping Mei cihua* and Encyclopedias for Daily Use." In *Dynastic Crisis and Cultural Innovation: From the Late Ming *to the Late Qing and Beyond*, edited by David Der-wei Wang and Shang Wei, 63–92. Cambridge, MA: Harvard University Press, 2005.

Shanshan ji 珊珊集 [full title: *Xinke chuxiang dianban zengding yuefu shanshan ji* 新刻出像點板增訂樂府珊珊集]. *Shanben xiqu congkan*. Vol. 14.

Shen Chongsui's 沈寵綏 (?–1645) *Duqu xuzhi* 度曲須知. *Zhongguo gudian xiqu lunzhu jicheng*. Vol. 5, 183–317.

Shen Defu 沈德符 (1578–1642). *Guqu zayan* 顧曲雜言. *Juan* 25 of his *Wanli yehuobian* 萬曆野獲編. Vol. 2, 639–52. Beijing: Zhonghua shuju, 1959.

Shen Defu 沈德符. *Qingquantang ji* 清權堂集. Original edition in Naikaku bunko. Photo-reprint in the *Hishi* collection of the Gest Library, Princeton University. XXSKQS. Vol. 1377.

Shen, Guangren Grant. *Elite Theatre in Ming China, 1368–1644*. London: Routledge, 2005.

Shen Jing 沈璟 (1553–1610). *Nan jiugong shisandiao qupu* 南九宮十三調曲譜. Photo-reprint. Beijing: Beijing daxue chubanbu, 1921.

Shen Tai 沈泰, comp. *Sheng Ming zaju* 盛明雜劇. Facsimile reprint. Hefei: Huangshan shushe, 1993.

Shengshi xinsheng 盛世新聲. Facsimile reprint. Beijing: Wenxueguji kanxingshe, 1955.

Shenyin jiangu lu 審音鑒古錄. *Shanben xiqu congkan*. Vols. 73–74.

Sieber, Patricia. *Theaters of Desire: Authors, Readers, and the Reproduction of Early Chinese Song-Drama, 1300–2000*. Hampshire: Palgrave Macmillan, 2003.

Stainer, J., and W. A. Barrett. *Stainer and Barrett's Dictionary of Musical Terms*. Rev. ed. London, 1898.

Stark, James. *Bel Canto: A History of Vocal Pedagogy*. Toronto: University of Toronto Press, 1999.

Sun Kaidi 孫楷第. *Yeshiyuan gujin zaju kao* 也是園古今雜劇考. Shanghai: Shanghai zazhi gongsi chubanshe, 1953.

Sun You 孫柚 (1540–ca. 1613). The *Jigu ge* 汲古阁 edition of *Qinxin ji*. *Guben xiqu congkan* 古本戲曲叢刊, 2nd series.

Sun You 孫柚. *Tengxi shi* 籐谿詩. Photo-reprint of a Qing manuscript in *Siku weishou shu jikan* 四庫未收書輯刊. Vol. 21. Beijing: Beijing chubanshe, 2007.

Sun You 孫柚. *Xinke chuxiang yinzhu Sima Xiangru Qinxin ji* 新刻出像音注司馬相如琴心記. *Budengdaya wenku zhenben xiqu congkan* 不登大雅文庫珍本戲曲叢刊. Vol. 9, 77–295. Beijing: Beijing daxue tushuguan, 2003.

Swatek, Catherine C. *Peony Pavilion Onstage: Four Centuries in the Career of a Chinese Drama*. Ann Arbor: University of Michigan Center for Chinese Studies, 2002, 2012.

Tan Xiong 譚雄. "Dui *Taigu chuanzong* yu *Nashuying qupu* zhong *Xixiangji qupu* de bijiao yanjiu" 對太古傳宗與納書楹曲譜中西廂記曲譜的比較研究. *Tianjin yinyue xueyuan xuebao* 天津音樂學院學報 2 (2006): 37–44.

Tanaka Kenji hakase sōshū kinen Chūgoku koten gikyoku ronshū 田中謙二博士頌壽記念中國古典戲曲論集. Tokyo: Kyuko shoin, 1991.

Tao Ting 陶珽 (fl. 1610). *Shuofu xu* 說郛續. Reprint, XXSKQS. No. 1753.

Taylor, Diana. *The Archive and the Repertoire: Performing Cultural Memory in the Americas*. Durham: Duke University Press, 2003.

Thompson, Emily. *The Soundscape of Modernity: Architectural Acoustics and the Culture of Listening in America, 1900–1933*. Cambridge, MA: MIT Press, 2002.

Tu Youxiang 屠友祥, ed. *Weishuixuan riji* 味水軒日記. Shanghai: Shanghai yuandong chubanshe, 1996.

Verma, Neil. *Theater of the Mind: Imagination, Aesthetics, and American Radio Drama*. Chicago: University of Chicago Press, 2012.

Wang Anqi 王安祈. *Ming xiqu wulun* 明戲曲五論. Taipei: Da'an chubanshe, 1990.

Wang Anqi 王安祈. *Mingdai chuanqi zhi juchang jiqi yishu* 明代傳奇之劇場及其藝術. Taipei: Xuesheng shuju, 1986.

Wang Duanshu 王端淑 (1621–ca. 1706), comp. *Mingyuan shiwei chubian* 名媛詩緯初編. Qingyintang edition, 1667. Digitalized facsimile copy available at https://digital.library.mcgill.ca/mingqing/search/details-poem.php?poemID=40069&language=ch

Wang Gang 王鋼. "Ji Xu Qingqing de *Beici pu*" 記徐慶卿的北詞譜. In *Wen Shi* 文史. Beijing: Zhonghua shuju, 1988. Vol. 31, 303–10.

Wang Guowei 王國維. *Song Yuan xiqu shi* 宋元戲曲史. Nanjing: Fenghuang chubanshe, 2010.

Wang Jianyin 王劍引 et al. *Gu hanyu dacidian* 古漢語大詞典. Shanghai cishu chubanshe, 2001.

Wang Jilie 王季烈, comp. *Guben Yuan Ming zaju* 孤本元明雜劇. Changsha: Shangwu yinshuguan, 1941.

Wang Jilie 王季烈. *Yinlu qutan* 螾廬曲談. Shanghai: Shangwu yinshuguan, 1934.

Wang Liqi 王利器, ed. *Yuan Ming Qing sandai jinhui xiaoshuo xiqu shiliao* 元明清三代禁燬小說戲曲史料. Shanghai: Shanghai guji chubanshe, 1981.

Wang Ning 王寧 and Ren Xiaowen 任孝溫. *Kunqu yu Ming Qing yueji* 崑曲與明清樂妓. Shenyang: Chunfeng wenyi chubanshe, 2005.

Wang Shizhen 王世貞 (1526–1590). *Quzao* 曲藻. *Zhongguo gudian xiqu lunzhu jicheng*. Vol. 4.

Wang Xiaoyi 汪效漪, ed. *Pan Zhiheng quhua* 潘之恆曲話. Beijing: Zhongguo xiju chubanshe, 1988.

Wanhe qingyin 萬壑清音. Original manuscript in the University of Kyoto. Facsimile print in *Shanben xiqu congkan*. Vols. 48–49.

Wanko, Cheryl. *Roles of Authority: Thespian Biography and Celebrity in Eighteenth-Century Britain*. Lubbock: Texas Tech University Press, 2003.

Wanyuzi 宛瑜子 [Zhou Zhibiao 周之標 (fl. 1610–1647)]. *Wuji baimei* 吳姬百媚. Beijing: Beijing tushuguan chubanshe, rpt. 2002.

Weilinzi 為霖子 [Feng Menglong 馮夢龍 (1574–1646)]. *Jinling baimei* 金陵百媚. Original in the Naikaku Bunko.

Weishi yuepu. Digitized version, original in Peking University Library. https://ia600306.us.archive.org/13/items/02095092.cn/02095092.cn.pdf

West, Stephen. "A Study in Appropriation: Zang Maoxun's Injustice to Dou E." *Journal of the American Oriental Society* 111, no. 2 (1991): 283–302.

West, Stephen, and Wilt Idema, trans. *The Story of the Western Wing*. Berkeley: University of California Press, 1995.

Worthen, W. B., and Peter Holland, eds. *Theorizing Practice: Redefining Theatre History*. New York: Palgrave Macmillan, 2003.

Wu Dan 毋丹. “Nanqu xiansuo hua: Ming Qing xiqu shouzhong de qingxiang ji nanbeiqu shenglü zhi bianqian, yi *Bei Xixiang* gongche pu weili” 南曲弦索化: 明清戲曲受眾的傾向及南北曲聲律之變遷——以《北西廂》工尺譜為例. *Wenhua yichan* 文化遺產 4 (2018): 70–78.

Wu Mei 吳梅. *Guqu zhutan* 顧曲塵談. Taipei: Taiwan shangwu yinshuguan, 1973.

Wu Shuyin 吳書蔭, ed. *Liang Chenyu ji* 梁辰魚集. Shanghai: Shanghai guji chubanshe, 1998.

Wu Shuyin 吳書蔭, ed. *Qupin jiaozhu* 曲品校注. Beijing: Zhonghua shuju, 1990.

Wu Shuyin 吳書蔭. *Zhongguo xiqu shilun* 中國戲曲史論. Nanjing: Nanjing daxue chubanshe, 1997.

Wu Shuyin 吳書蔭. “*Zhulin xiaoji* zuozhe kao” 竹林小記作者考. *Wenxian* 文獻 1 (1992): 262–65.

Wu Shuyin 吳書蔭. “‘Yumingtang simeng’ zuizao de hekeben tansuo”《玉茗堂四夢》最早的合刻本探索. Xiqu yanjiu 戲曲研究 1 (2007): 1–11.

Wu Xinlei 吳新雷. “Guanyu mingdai Wei Liangfu de qülun ‘Nanci yinzhen’” 關於明代魏良輔的曲論《南詞引正》, *Hebei shiyuan xuebao* 河北師院學報 1 (1993): 68–72.

Wu Xinlei 吳新雷. “Ming keben *Yuefu hongshan* he *Yuefu mingci* zhong de Wei Liangfu qulun” 明刻本《樂府紅珊》和《樂府名詞》中的魏良輔曲論, *Nanjing shifan daxue wenxueyuan xuebao* 南京師範大學文學院學報 1 (2005): 128–34.

Xia Tingzhi 夏庭芝 (ca. 1300–ca. 1375). *Qinglou ji* 青樓集. *Zhongguo gudian xiqu lunzhu jicheng*. Vol. 2, 3–84.

Xiaochizi 笑癡子. *Xuanxue pu* 玄雪譜. *Shanben xiqu congkan*. Vol. 50.

Xie Boyang 謝伯陽. *Quan Ming sanqu* 全明散曲. Jinan: Qilu shushe, 2016.

Xijizi 息機子, comp. *Gujin zaju xuan* 古今雜劇選. Preface 1568. Original in the National library in Beijing. Fifteen plays in facsimile reprints in *Guben xiqu congkan*.

Xinkan hebing Li Rihua Xixiang ji 新刊合併李日華西廂記, edited by Zhou Juyi 周居易, Wanli reign. Original in the library of the Chinese Academy of Arts 中國藝術研究院.

Xinke chuxiang yinzhu hualan Nandiao Xixiang ji 新刻出像音注花欄南調西廂記. Fuchun Hall 富春堂 edition, Wanli reign. *Guben xiqu congkan*, 1st series.

Xinke xiuxiang piping Jing Ping Mei 新刻繡像批評金瓶梅. Chongzhen reign. Original in Peking University. Facsimile reprint, Beijing daxue chubanshe, 1988.

Xu Fuming 徐扶明. *Tang Xianzu yu* Mudan ting 湯顯祖與牡丹亭. Shanghai: Shanghai guji chubanshe, 1993.

Xu Fuzuo 徐復祚 (1560–after 1629). *Sanjia cunlao qutan* 三家村老曲談. In *Lidai quhua huibian: Mingdai bian*, edited by Yu and Sun. Vol. 3, 251–74.

Xu Huiying 徐會瀛 (fl. sixteenth century), comp. *Xinjuan Yantai jiaozheng tianxia tongxing wenlin yaobao wanjuan xingluo* 新鐫燕臺校正天下通行文林要寶萬卷星羅. 1580 edition. Facsimile reprint in *Beijing tushuguan guji zhenben congkan* 北京圖書館古籍珍本叢刊. Vol. 75. Beijing: Shumu wenxian chubanshe, 1988.

Xu, Peng. “The Courtesan’s ‘Role Portrait’: Brothel Performances and the Qiu Ying Models in Late Ming Suzhou,” *Ars Orientalis* 55 (2025), forthcoming.

Xu, Peng. “Courtesan versus Literatus: Gendered Soundscapes and Aesthetics in Late Ming Singing Culture.” *T’oung Pao* 100 (2014): 399–450.

Xu, Peng. "Editing *Pipa ji* for the Late Ming Popular Theater: The Identity of the 'Singing Hermit' and His Editorial Work." *Late Imperial China* 41, no. 1 (2020): 159–201.

Xu, Peng. "The Music Teacher: The Professionalization of Singing and the Development of Erotic Vocal Style During Late Ming China." *Harvard Journal of Asiatic Studies* 75, no. 2 (2015): 259–97.

Xu, Peng. "*Tanhua ji* chuanqi xiezuo shijian kao" 《曇花記》傳奇寫作時間考 [When Was the *Chuanqi* Play *Udumbara Blossoms* (*Tanhua ji*) Written?]. *Xiqu yu suwenxue yanjiu* 戲曲與俗文學研究 (Beijing: Social Science Academic Press, 2018), vol. 6, 77–91.

Xu Shuofang 徐朔方. "*Jin Ping Mei* chengshu xintan" 金瓶梅成書新探. *Zhonghua wenshi congshu* 中華文史論叢, no. 3 (1984): 159–98.

Xu Shuofang 徐朔方, ed. *Tang Xianzu quanji* 湯顯祖全集. Beijing: Beijing guji chubanshe, 1999.

Xu Shuofang 徐朔方. *Wan Ming qujia nianpu* 晚明曲家年譜. Hangzhou: Zhejiang guji chubanshe, 1993.

Xu Shuofang 徐朔方. *Xu Shuofang ji* 徐朔方集. Hangzhou: Zhejiang guji chubanshe, 1993.

Xu Yu 许宇, comp. *Cilin yixiang* 詞林逸響. Preface 1623. Facsimile reprint in *Shanben xiqu congkan*. Vol. 17.

Yang Hsien-yi and Gladys Yang, trans. *The Scholars*. New York: Columbia University Press, 1992.

Yannan Zhi'an 燕南芝庵 (fl. 1330s). *Changlun* 唱論. *Zhongguo gudian xiqu lunzhu jicheng*. Vol. 1, 159–66.

Yao Hua 姚華. *Luyishi quhua* 菉漪室曲話. In *Xin quyuan* 新曲苑, edited by Ren Zhongmin 任中敏. Taipei: Zhonghua shuju, 1970, rpt. of 1913.

Ye Mengzhu 葉夢珠 (ca. 1623–ca. 1690s). *Yueshi bian* 閱世編. *Biji xiaoshuo daguan* 筆記小說大觀. Taipei: Xinxing shuju, 1974.

Ye Shaoyuan 葉紹袁 (1589–1648). *Ye Tianliao nian pu* 葉天寥年譜. Shanghai: Beiye shanfang 貝葉山房, 1936.

Ye Tang 葉堂 (ca. 1724–ca. 1799). *Nashuying simeng quanpu* 納書楹四夢全譜. Photoreprint in XXSKQS, Vols. 1756–1757.

Ye Tang 葉堂. *Nashuying Xixiang ji quanpu* 納書楹西廂記全譜. 1795. Shanghai Library.

Ye Yikui 葉一夔. "Editorial Principles" (*fanli* 凡例) to Weilinzi 為霖子 [Feng Menglong]. *Jinling baimei* 金陵百媚. Original in the Naikaku Bunko.

Yongxi yuefu 雍熙樂府. XXSKQS. Vol. 1740.

Yu Huai 余懷 (1616–1696). *Banqiao zaji* 板橋雜記. Modern typeset edition, *Banqiao zaji jiaozhu wai yizhong* 板橋雜記校註外一種, edited by Li Jintang 李金堂. Shanghai: Shanghai guji chubanshe, 1988.

Yu Weimin 俞為民. *Quti yanjiu* 曲體研究. Beijing: Zhonghua shuju, 2021.

Yu Weimin 俞為民 and Sun Rongrong 孫蓉蓉, eds. *Lidai quhua huibian: Mingdai bian* 歷代曲話彙編明代編. Hefei: Huangshan chubanshe, 2009.

Zang Maoxun 臧懋循 (1550–1616). *Fubaotang wenxuan* 負苞堂文選. *Siku quanshu cunmu congshu, jibu*. Vol. 168. Digital version, Chinese Text Project, https://ctext.org/library.pl?if=gb&res=3762

Zeitlin, Judith. "'Notes of Flesh' and the Courtesan's Song in Seventeenth-Century China." In *The Courtesan's Arts: Cross-Cultural Perspectives*, edited by Martha Feldman and Bonnie Gordon. Chicago: University of Chicago Press, 2006.

Zeng Xianfei 曾獻飛, ed. *Yuefu zalu shuzheng* 樂府雜錄疏證. Nanchang: Jiangxi jiaoyu chubanshe, 2015.

Zhang Chenshi 張忱石 et al., eds. *Huansha ji jiaozhu* 浣紗記校註. Beijing: Zhonghua shuju, 1994.

Zhang Dai 張岱 (1597–1679). *Tao'an mengyi* 陶庵夢憶. Taipei: Kaiming shudian, 1978.

Zhang Faying 張發穎. *Zhongguo jiayue xiban* 中國家樂戲班. Beijing: Xueyuan chubanshe, 2002.

Zhang Faying 張發穎. *Zhongguo xibanshi* 中國戲班史. Beijing: Xueyuan chubanshe, 2003.

Zhang Fengyi 張鳳翼 (1527–1613). *Chushitang ji xuan* 處實堂集選. Original edition in Naikaku bunko. Photo-reprint in the *Hishi* collection of the Gest Library, Princeton University.

Zhang Lu 張祿, comp. *Cilin zhaiyan* 詞林摘艷. XXSKQS. Vol. 1740.

Zhang Qi 張琦 (fl. seventeenth century). *Hengqu zhutan* 衡曲塵談. *Zhongguo gudian xiqu lunzhu jicheng*. Vol. 4, 265–76.

Zhang Qi 張琦. *Wusao hebian* 吳騷合編. 1637. *Sibu congkan guangbian* 四部叢刊廣編. Taipei: Taiwan shangwu yinshuguan, 1981. Vol. 49.

Zhang Shibin 張世彬. *Shen Yuan Bei Xixiang xiansuopu jianpu* 沈遠北西廂弦索譜簡譜. Hongkong: Zhongwen daxue chubanshe, 1981.

Zhang Shuying 張樹英, ed. *Mingzhu ji* 明珠記; *Nan Xixiang ji* 南西廂記. Beijing: Zhonghua shuju, 2000.

Zhang Xuan 張萱 (1558–1641). *Beiya* 北雅. The original in the National Library, Beijing; Naikaku Bunko, Tokyo.

Zhang Xuan 張萱. *Xiyuan cungao* 西園存稿. Original in Naikaku Bunko. Photo reprints in the Gest Library in Princeton University, *Hishi* Collection. Digitized version in the Hathitrust Digital Library. Facsimile reprint, *Mingdai Shiwenji zhenben congkan* 明代詩文集珍本叢刊. Beijing: Guojia tushuguan chubanshe, 2019. Vols. 120–25.

Zhao Shijie 趙世杰 (fl. seventeenth century), comp. *Gujin nüshi* 古今女史. Digital library, "Ming Qing Women's Writings." Digital access: https://digital.library.mcgill.ca/mingqing/search/results-work.php

Zhou Deqing 周德清 (fl. 1330s). *Zhongyuan yinyun* 中原音韻. *Zhongguo gudian xiqu lunzhu jicheng*. Vol. 1, 169–285.

Zhou Weipei 周維培. *Qupu yanjiu* 曲譜研究. Nanjing: Jiangsu guji chubanshe, 1999.

Zhou Yibai 周貽白. *Mingren zaju xuan* 明人雜劇選. Beijing: Renmin wenxue chubanshe, 1958.

Zhou Yibai 周貽白. *Zhongguo xijushi changbian* 中國戲劇史長編. Beijing: Renmin wenxue chubanshe, 1960. Reprint, Shanghai: Shanghai shudian, 2004.

Zhou Yibai 周貽白. *Zhongguo xiqu fazhanshi gangyao* 中國戲曲發展史綱要. Shanghai: Shanghai guji chubanshe, 1979.

Zhou Zhibiao 周之標 (fl. 1610–1647), comp. *Wuyu cuiya* 吳歈萃雅. Facsimile reprint in *Shanben xiqu congkan*. Vols. 12–13.

Zhu Jipeng 朱繼彭. *Tong Zhiling* 童芷苓. Shanghai: Huadong shifan daxue chubanshe, 1995.

Zhu Quan 朱權 (1378–1448). *Taihe zhengyin pu* 太和正音譜. In Yu and Sun. Vol. 1, 27–190.

Zhuang Yifu 莊一拂. *Gudian xiqu cunmu huikao* 古典戲曲存目彙考. Shanghai: Shanghai guji chubanshe, 1982.

Zou Diguang 鄒迪光 (1550–1626). *Shiyuzhai ji* 石語齋集. Facsimile reprint in *Xuxiu siku cunmu congshu, jibu*. Vol. 159.

Zou Diguang 鄒迪光. *Yuyilou ji* 鬱儀樓集. Original edition in Naikaku bunko. Photo-reprint in the *Hishi* collection of the Gest Library, Princeton University.

Index

Note: Page numbers in *italics* denote images, tables, and associated captions.